Advance Praise for Transparent IT

"An Enterprise's IT Architecture has never been more critical to its competitive position in a global economy. 'Transparent IT' presents a lucid explanation of Service Oriented Architecture, the benefits to be reaped from this approach and a roadmap for implementation."

Graham Glass
Author of Web Services: Building Blocks for Distributed Systems

"Technical Infrastructure has been the focus of my career, and it is refreshing to find a book that explains the importance of a strong foundation, and how that can be leveraged by a Service Orientated Architecture to realize the vision laid out in Transparent IT."

John Savill
Author of Windows Server 2003 Active Directory Design And Implementation: Creating, Migrating, And Merging Networks

"Service-oriented architecture (SOA) is an important new paradigm for flexible application of information technologies (IT) to business challenges. Enterprise IT professionals need crisp, clear, comprehensive roadmaps to SOA, and that's just what Chip Wilson has delivered in Transparent IT: Building Blocks for an Agile Enterprise.' Wilson's book clearly spells out the full competitive, organizational, and technological context of SOA in his very readable book."

James Kobielus

Author of BizTalk: Implementi   *ies
Commerce (PrenticeHall PTR*
(IDG Books, 1997), Columnis*   *twork
World, Contributor, Business Communic....*   *ior
Technical Systems Analyst, Exostar LLC*

D1114363

Transparent IT

Building Blocks for an Agile Enterprise

Chip Wilson

Geniant, LLC has merged with EMC Corporation. The author is now an Enterprise Architect with EMC Global Services.

He can be reached via email at wilson_chip@emc.com

where information lives

Many of the designations used by manufacturers and sellers to distinguish their products are claimed as trademarks. Where those designations appear in this book, and the author was aware of a trademark claim, the designations have been printed with initial capital letters or in all capitals and are accompanied by the ™ trademark symbol.

The author and publisher have taken great care in the preparation of this book but make no expressed or implied warranty of any kind and assume no responsibility for errors or omissions. No liability is assumed for incidental or consequential damages in conjunction with or arising out of the use of the information or programs contained herein.

The publisher offers discounts on this book when ordered in quantity for bulk purchases and special sales. For more information, please contact:

> Geniant, LLC
> 14001 N. Dallas Pkwy, Suite 960
> Dallas, TX 75240
> (972) 383-2600
> www.geniant.com

Except as noted below, this book copyright © 2005-2006 Geniant, LLC. All rights reserved. No part of this publication may be reproduced, stored in a retrieval system, or transmitted in any form, or by any means, electronic, mechanical, photocopying, recording, or otherwise, without the prior consent of the publisher. For information on obtaining permission for use of material from this work, please submit a written request to Geniant at the address above. Printed and bound in the United States of America.

“Web Services Infrastructure: The global utility for real-time business” copyright © 2002 Phil Wainewright. Used with permission from Phil Wainewright.

“Real Time Enterprises: A Continuous Migration Approach” copyright © 2002 Vinod Khosla and Murugan Pal. Used with permission from Vinod Khosla.

“Situated Software” copyright © 2004 Clay Shirky. Used with permission from Clay Shirky.

“Metropolis” copyright © 2004 Microsoft Corporation. Used with permission from Microsoft Corporation.

“Portals: Business on the Network Edge” copyright © 2001 Barry Morris. Used with permission from Barry Morris, President and CEO of StreamBase Systems (www.streambase.com), formerly CEO of IONA Technologies (www.iona.com). This article first appeared in Business Integration Journal (formerly EAI Journal).

Library of Congress Control Number: 2005924638

ISBN 0-9768017-0-1

First printing September 2005.

Second printing March 2006.

About the Author

Chip Wilson is the Chief Technology Officer of Geniant, a leading IT consulting company based in Dallas, Texas. Geniant has been a thought leader in the area of Service Oriented Architecture, and was utilizing Web Service technology before the first SOAP specification was finalized. Chip has been instrumental in carving out a leadership position for Geniant in the market, defining service offerings that enable clients to leverage the power and flexibility of a Service Oriented Architecture and recognize the promised benefits.

Chip was recognized by Microsoft as one of the first board-certified Solution Architects in the new Microsoft Certified Architect program. He was also one of the first recipients of the Sun Certified Architect for the J2EE platform designation when that program was first created. He has more than fifteen years experience helping enterprises in many industries gain real business value from technology solutions.

Chip grew up in the Midwest and took his time getting to Texas. He currently resides in Dallas with his two dogs. He can be reached via email through his permanent forwarding address of chipwilson@bigfoot.com.

Contents

Part II: Integration

Part III: Service Oriented Architecture Roadmap

Part IV: Supplemental Material

Foreword by David Lancashire

In the old saying "It's not what you know, it's who you know," the emphasis was on your 'connections' with people. To be successful in today's world, a businessperson must also embrace an additional set of 'connections,' those that tie information technology systems together. Just as well connected people are often more likely to succeed, businesses that are well connected will be more likely to generate revenue and deliver goods and services more cost effectively.

The technology revolution of the 1990s spawned by the launch of the Internet browser was highly visible because it impacted our world in very obvious ways. It allowed us to access information, buy products and services, and to interact with people and companies regardless of where we logged on to the Internet. The browser afforded us a personal relationship with the Web. It became your job as a business executive or CIO to find new and more productive ways of using this for business advantage – broadening distribution channels, providing customer self-service, connecting with suppliers, and so on. And many of you have gone on to do this very successfully.

In fact, your innovative work has had a profound effect on the economy as a whole. Since 2001 US labor productivity has grown at an average of 4%, compared with a rate of 1.4% from the 1970s through the 1990s. Living standards double in 50 years if productivity grows at 1.4% per year, and they double in only 18 years if the rate is 4%.

So what's next? The latest revolution is a quieter affair, with even more potential to change our business world at an incredibly high speed. This revolution involves simplifying the way that software systems of different flavors are able to access information and data from other software systems without active human intervention.

This new standards-based approach to integration is now viable because it has evolved from approaches that have been around for decades[1], and importantly, it is much less costly than prior attempts to achieve this. It presents a new business opportunity because it facilitates the automation of business processes on a much broader scale. Automation and information access without limits.

Over 70% of current Information Technology budgets are spent on dealing with this 'complexity' – fixing, maintaining, and connecting the existing environment. IDC, a leading market research firm, estimates that this will cost companies worldwide $750 billion in one year. I am privileged to lead a company called Geniant, a company where a team of talented people have tackled this problem of 'complexity' by developing a framework for helping to simplify IT environments. In this book, Chip Wilson focuses on how this infrastructure can become the agile asset your business needs. He provides a detailed look at this framework and describes a systematic and incremental way of approaching the simplification of your IT environment. If you take your organization on this journey, you will ultimately encourage innovative ways of doing business, safe in the knowledge that your IT environment has the agility to support those initiatives.

Bon Voyage!

David A. Lancashire
CEO
Geniant

---

[1] The industry has been striving to achieve this since the early 1970s, when R&D groups started drawing boundaries around software and providing access to that software only through well-defined interfaces. The business implications are revolutionary, the technology approaches are clearly evolutionary and pragmatic.

Preface

This preface defines the intended audience for this book and presents a potential track through the book for each audience. The overall organization of the book is described along with brief summaries of each chapter.

Lastly, all of the people who contributed to this book are acknowledged.

Organization

This book is organized into four parts, each part containing several chapters. The first two chapters contain introductory material for the entire book and as such are outside of the scope of the four parts. Below is a brief overview of the parts and their chapters.

Prologue

This book presents a set of goals for a modern IT organization and a roadmap for achieving those goals. Before delving into the details of this vision for the future of Information Technology, a scenario of how the achievement of this vision might transform the way a fictional company operates and competes in the marketplace will hopefully serve to whet the reader's appetite.

Chapter 1: New Perspectives

This book presents a framework for understanding the place of Information Technology in a modern enterprise. The concepts are not necessarily new, but the perspectives are.

This chapter begins by presenting an overview of these new perspectives and laying the groundwork for the rest of the book, which will dive into each in more detail.

Part I: Technology Infrastructure

The first part of the book is dedicated to examining the technologies that make up the IT infrastructure. They are examined within the context of a common framework.

Chapter 2: The Layers of IT Infrastructure

When any type of infrastructure is examined closely, it can always be broken down into component parts and layers of abstraction. A building, for example, can be seen as having a finished exterior and interior, but beneath the façade is a complex mesh of systems including ventilation, electrical, plumbing, elevators, and fire suppression. These systems are layered on top of a structural skeleton, which is built on a solid foundation appropriate to the geology of the site.

Information Technology has layers as well. There are three fundamental layers to a service oriented IT infrastructure that is agile, efficient and transparent to the enterprise, its customers and business partners.

Chapter 3: What is an Enterprise Gateway?

The highest return on investment is found at the top layer of the IT stack. This "enterprise gateway" layer is where knowledge workers utilize business services, where services are orchestrated into business processes, where real-time information about the organization is aggregated and provided to decision makers, and where all external entities interact with the entire IT infrastructure.

The enterprise gateway provides a common interface to the entire IT infrastructure of the organization.

Chapter 4: What is Application Infrastructure?

The application infrastructure layer provides the business services that run the enterprise. This is traditionally where the IT stack has provided real business value to the organization.

The applications depend upon core technology services provided by the technical infrastructure. The applications, in turn, provide business services to employees, customers and partners via the enterprise gateway and to select groups of application users via custom interfaces.

The migration to a Service Oriented Architecture breaks monolithic applications down into discrete business services and provides new levels of flexibility to the organization, enabling agile business processes that can rapidly adapt to a changing business environment.

Chapter 5: What is Technical Infrastructure?

The technical infrastructure layer is the foundation of the IT stack. The layers above depend on basic services provided by the technical infrastructure.

Technical infrastructure provides no business value to the enterprise by itself; it consists of enabling technologies that form a fundamental foundation for business applications.

Part II: Integration

This section of the book looks at integration within the application infrastructure layer, between the application infrastructure layer and the technical infrastructure layer, and between the enterprise gateway layer and the application infrastructure layer.

Chapter 6: Leveraging the Application Infrastructure

The business services implemented by the application infrastructure enable the creation of agile business processes, high-value composite applications, business partner integration hubs, management dashboards and complex application integration scenarios.

 Leveraging these services in appropriate ways can yield market-changing efficiency and agility.

Chapter 7: Application Integration Strategy

Creating an agile IT environment requires vision, planning, and execution. Without a clear strategy for integrating the organization's application infrastructure, the benefits of adopting a Service Oriented Architecture will not be realized.

An application integration strategy must take into account all of the existing application assets and provide a common approach and associated mechanisms for including them in the service fabric.

Chapter 8: Leveraging the Technical Infrastructure

Applications depend on the technical infrastructure, and there are several strategies for leveraging the technical infrastructure from applications.

Applications must be built on a solid, flexible, and centrally managed technical infrastructure and integrated into a service-oriented architecture.

The presence of technical infrastructure is a given; the ability to leverage it from the application infrastructure is not and must be designed into the application infrastructure.

A technical infrastructure must provide the means for IT operations to provide a secure, connected, managed, and monitored environment.

Part III: Service Oriented Architecture Roadmap

This part of the book presents a roadmap for adopting a Service Oriented Architecture, including the techniques for adoption, the execution of the adoption program, the business case for the program, and the organizational impact.

Chapter 9: Building a Service Oriented Architecture

The decision to adopt a Service Oriented Architecture is the beginning of a journey for the entire organization. The approach taken may vary for each company, but the goal of building an agile, loosely coupled suite of business services and leveraging this application infrastructure from the enterprise gateway remains constant. Executing an SOA strategy is a process of adopting practices and tools that implement this vision.

The various strategic and tactical decisions and processes a company can implement to arrive at an SOA can be divided at the highest level into two categories, "bottom-up" and "top-down."

Chapter 10: The Business Case

Understanding the business case for the new IT infrastructure will enable the champions to sell the program to management and investors. The costs and benefits come from several sources, and understanding each will help convince the various stakeholders of the business value to be recognized by adopting an SOA.

Chapter 11: Execution

A clear vision, a good business case, and adequate funding are necessary prerequisites for becoming an agile enterprise.

Turning the vision into reality takes analysis, planning, and hard work, with many tradeoffs to be made along the way. The agile enterprise is a journey with no final destination – it is a strategy that will continually impact IT decisions and projects.

Chapter 12: Organizational Impact

This chapter examines the impact on the organization of the adoption of an SOA and the migration to an agile enterprise based on a transparent IT infrastructure. Ways that the organizational change can be managed are explained.

Epilogue

The epilogue continues the fictional scenario begun in the prologue and takes a look at the potential benefits of implementing the program described in Transparent IT.

Part IV: Supplemental Material

A number of essays, articles, and whitepapers were referenced throughout this book and were important to the formulation of the ideas presented here. Several of the most important pieces are reprinted in this section for ease of reference.

Web Services Infrastructure: The global utility for real-time business **by Phil Wainewright**

This brief whitepaper was seminal in crystallizing the idea of IT as infrastructure, enabled by a Service Oriented Architecture.

Real Time Enterprises: A Continuous Migration Approach **by Vinod Khosla and Murugan Pal**

Achieving the Real Time Enterprise is a primary objective of adopting an SOA. This whitepaper presents the idea in great detail along with abundant justification for the adoption program.

Situated Software by Clay Shirky

The idea that software can and sometimes should be developed for small groups of users in a cost-effective manner is elegantly presented and defined in this essay. Although the examples given are in the academic world, the same concepts can be applied to business applications.

Metropolis by Pat Helland

Pat Helland proposes a metaphor, consisting of eight analogies, that the evolution of Information Technology currently underway is similar to the changes that took place in manufacturing during the industrial revolution.

Portals: Business on the Network Edge by Barry Morris

Barry Morris presents the view that the Enterprise Portal will become increasingly important as the single point of contact between the enterprise's IT infrastructure and the employees, customers, and business partners.

Audience

This book was written with a number of different audiences in mind of varying roles and responsibilities. Since it attempts to cover a lot of new concepts and material for a diverse audience, it is foreseeable that some of the material might not be applicable to the interests of all readers.

The key audiences are identified below, along with a suggested track through the book for each.

Executive Management

All C-level and VP-level executives are the primary audience for this book. This is the level of the organization where the concepts of transparent IT and the agile enterprise must first be presented, sold, and bought into.

This book defines the future of Information Technology. Understanding what the goals of transparent IT are, why they are important and what an enterprise needs to do to accomplish them are the key objectives for this audience.

This reader should begin with chapters 1, 2, and 3, but he or she may wish to skip to Part III after that if the material is deemed too technical.

Management

The directors and managers of the enterprise will ultimately be the ones implementing the roadmap identified here, at the direction of their senior management.

Defining the steps and techniques, both technical and organizational, that must be undertaken to adopt a Service Oriented Architecture and facilitate the agile enterprise is a large part of the content of this book.

In addition to the content identified as important for executive management, management should also read chapters 4 and 5 at a minimum.

Architects and Technical Staff

Plenty of technical information is presented here, though the focus is intentionally high level. Although there are many strategies for addressing technical challenges, there are neither code snippets nor XML.

For the technical audience, the main goal of this book is to bring their thinking up to a business level and to align their daily activities with broader business objectives.

At a minimum, technical readers should start at the beginning and read the first two parts of the book. They would also benefit from reading the chapters in Part III and the supplemental material.

Acknowledgements

This book would not have been possible without the tremendous support from all of the people at Geniant.

I want to start by thanking David Lancashire, the CEO of Geniant. In addition to being my boss, I also consider him a friend and mentor. When I brought the idea of this book to him, he became its biggest champion, and I don't think I would have completed it without his support and encouragement. I certainly would not have completed it as quickly!

Geniant has a tremendous collection of talented individuals, and I am consistently awed by what we accomplish as individuals and teams. Many people contributed to the successful completion of this book, including, in alphabetical order by first name:

- Alan Josephson
- Bob Jansen

- Cameron Fuller
- Cory Councilman
- David Lancashire
- Drew Naukam
- Edward Perez
- Eric Hunter
- Floyd Hamandi
- Glen Cudmore
- Joel Geyer
- John Arnott
- John Savill
- John Shute
- Kelly Hughes
- Kristian Rickard
- Nick Tovell
- Stephen Andrews
- Tommy Bradford

I particularly want to thank Eric Hunter for his insightful feedback on the first draft of this book, which contributed greatly to the overall quality of the end result.

I also want to thank the following people for their valuable feedback and editing of the second draft:

- Graham Glass
- Jason Bloomberg
- Phil Wainewright

The cover design was created by Bob Shema of Design Block Zero. The diagrams inside the book were created by Tommy Bradford, Bob Shema, and Kelly Hughes with suggestions and insights from many of the people listed above.

Prologue

This book presents a set of goals for a modern IT organization and a roadmap for achieving those goals. Before delving into the details of this vision for the future of Information Technology, a scenario of how the achievement of this vision might transform the way a fictional company operates and competes in the marketplace will hopefully serve to whet the reader's appetite.

The Missing Customer

Amy smoothly rolled out of bed and muted the television as her cell phone cheerily bleeped the chorus to Britney Spears' "Toxic." She dug around among the personal effects on her nightstand until she felt the vibration of the phone's ring and flipped it open while bringing it up to her ear in a practiced motion. She glanced at the screen almost unconsciously in the process, recognizing the photo of Sue she had snapped in a bar almost two years ago.

"Hey, what's up?"

"Are you getting excited?"

"About what?"

"The ski trip – Whistler! It's less than a month away, you know."

"Oh that – I haven't really thought about it much yet."

"Do you have all your gear?"

"Uhhh…I guess. I was just going to take the same gear I took when we went to Tahoe last year."

"What? You almost froze to death in that cheap cotton base layer!"

"Base layer?"

"Yeah, you know – long underwear."

1

"Oh. Yeah it was kind of cold."

"'Kind of cold?' You hardly stopped complaining the whole time you were on the slopes! You need to get a couple pair of ColPoly's."

"What's that?"

"It's the latest in base layer tech. It's made from a synthetic fabric that repels moisture from the outside and pulls moisture away from your body. It's super-warm and lightweight."

"Oh. Okay, where do I get those?" Amy grabbed a pen from her nightstand and groped around for a scrap of paper to write on. Her fingers landed on this month's cable bill, and she placed it on her knee and scratched "call Polly – long underwear" on the envelope.

"The fabric is patented, and OG has an exclusive contract with the manufacturer."

"OG?"

"Outdoor Gear – as in og.com. You really are out of it – did I wake you up or something?"

"Uh, yeah, sort of. So I can only get these things from og.com? How much are they?" Amy wrote "og.com" on the envelope as she tried to keep it from sliding off her knee with the same hand that she wrote with.

"Who cares how much they are, but you better get off your butt and order them because they are *the* piece of equipment to have this year, and I heard that John had to wait three weeks to get his."

"Okay, I'll order them now." She suddenly remembered that John was going on the trip this year and started to worry about the rest of her skiing wardrobe. Maybe she should upgrade a few more pieces as well….

"Call me back after you order them." Sue was already hanging up as she finished the sentence.

"Okay," Amy said to the dead line and closed the phone, tossing it on her nightstand. She tried to remember what gear she had taken to Tahoe, and what had worked, both style-wise and functionally. She remembered looking at the photos of herself in the powder-blue wool cap and thinking that it made her look way too feminine next to Sue's ultra-fashionable grunge skull cap. She held the envelope on the nightstand with one hand and wrote "hat" next to the other notes.

Amy pulled her laptop out of her backpack and flipped the cover up, smiling as she logged on with her password of "t0x1c"; her own cleverness never failed to amaze her. The screen lit up with the photo of Britney she had snapped with her cell phone camera the last time her tour had come to town. The colors were over-saturated and the resolution was poor, but it was her personal keepsake from the show and she liked it for the memories it brought.

She opened her web browser and checked the notes she had made on the cable bill, and then typed "og.com" into her browser. The website for Outdoor Gear rapidly materialized in front of her, and she was drawn to the closeout gear sale which promised savings of 40 percent to 60 percent off of regular prices. She browsed through the sale items for several minutes before remembering that there was a specific item that she had come to buy; a quick check of the envelope reminded her.

Amy typed "call Polly" into the search field of Outdoor Gear and was rewarded with an unattractive error message that stated bluntly: "No items found". She cursed under her breath and typed "long underwear" into the search field. This time she got a results page displaying "1 to 10 of 52 matches". She scrolled down the page, impressed by the array of tops and bottoms in various styles and colors, and tried to make sense of all of the technical jargon describing the various fabrics.

She reached the bottom of the page and didn't recognize anything that looked like "call Polly", so she found the "Next" button at the bottom of the page and clicked that. She scrolled through the next two pages of results with the same outcome, and then on the fourth page she spotted the "ColPoly" items. She muttered a self-deprecating "Duh" as she realized her spelling error and clicked on the first item, a stylish turtleneck pictured in a rich burgundy with thin black stripes.

The product page extolled the virtues of the new fabric and bragged about the exclusive contract that OG had with the Chinese patent holder and manufacturer. Amy didn't really care about all of the hype – if Sue said she should buy it then that was all she needed to know. She clicked on the "Add to cart" button.

Amy read the screen that was displayed: "The item that you have selected is out of stock. Please return later and re-order your merchandise."

She cursed under her breath again and grabbed her cell phone off of the nightstand without looking. She flipped it open and dialed *23 for Sue.

    "Did you get them?"
    "They're out."
    "You're going to be cold again…"

The Competitor

The conference room was quiet despite being full of OG's upper management. The mutters of a few hushed conversations could be picked out above the hum of the air conditioning, but most kept their heads down and pretended to review their papers or day planners. The meeting had been called by Jack, the CEO of OG, to discuss the fulfillment issues OG was having with the unexpected popularity of the new ColPoly base layer garments. The meeting request had not been polite, and the CEO was late.

The conference room door opened suddenly and the CEO walked in carrying his briefcase, which he set down at the head of the conference table and popped open. He pulled out a sheaf of papers and looked around the room.

"Good morning. Thanks for coming. As most of you know we negotiated an exclusive distribution contract with the patent holder and manufacturer of the ColPoly garments. The success of the product has exceeded all of our expectations, with very little investment into the marketing and sales effort. I can only conclude that the product truly is revolutionary or at least an order of magnitude better than the closest competitor. Our research indicates that 87 percent of the sales are driven by word of mouth and that 64 percent of the customers who purchase one of these products have never visited OG's site before."

"All this is, of course, great news, except for the fact that for the last week we have been unable to sell the ColPoly products because we don't have any left, and I can't seem to get a straight answer on what the problem is. So, what is going on? Barbara, how many times in the past week has someone tried to purchase a ColPoly item and been turned down?"

"The site statistics indicate that we're losing on average 2600 sales per day, but since most of the customers are new and don't have an account, we have no way to determine whether they are truly unique customers or whether they are returning to check the status."

Jack grimaced and shook his head. "Assuming they are new and given the average purchase of $47 for ColPoly customers, you're telling me that we're losing over a hundred thousand dollars a day in revenue? There's only a month left in the season!"

There was a tense silence in the room as everyone avoided Jack's gaze and focused on the papers in front of them. Several people pretended to jot down notes on legal pads. The silence hung in the air for what seemed like minutes.

"We had no idea when we signed the contract last summer that the demand would be so high," Fred, the VP of fulfillment, started hesitantly to explain. "We ordered an initial shipment of what sales predicted would be enough product to last through the season. This vendor is not integrated into our supply chain system yet – IT is working on an interface between our system and theirs, but the project is behind schedule and will not be ready for several months. We can manually place another order with the supplier, but we need a good understanding of how many we can sell during the rest of the season. It will take at least two weeks before we can get product into the delivery channel."

"Two weeks! Why is it so hard to integrate new suppliers with our systems?

4

The products we sell change every season; if we can't learn how to integrate new suppliers in short order, we are going to continue to have these kinds of problems. How do we fix this?"

The silence descended.

The Information Worker

Frank settled into his business class seat and pulled his laptop out of his carry-on, lowering the tray table and opening the laptop onto it. It was a long flight to Shanghai, and he needed the time to prepare for his meeting with the manufacturer of ColPoly.

He started by going to the workspace that had initially been set up to analyze the impact of the new material on eXtreme Sports Gear's (XSG) sales of base layer items for this year's skiing and boarding season. Once the problems in OG's fulfillment channel had come to light, the purpose of the workspace had morphed into account pursuit activities. As head purchaser for XSG, Frank was charged with traveling to China to meet the manufacturer of ColPoly and attempting to purchase any excess inventory that may be on hand. Although OG had an exclusive distribution contract, the rumor was that the patent holder could break that agreement if OG couldn't satisfy market demand, which they clearly were failing to do.

Although Frank didn't realize it, the workspace had been copied to his laptop's internal storage the last time he was connected to the corporate intranet. It's a good thing, too, because the airline still didn't offer any sort of Internet access, even when the plane was at the gate. The next time he connected his workspace would be seamlessly synchronized with the corporate repository, downloading any changes to his laptop and uploading Frank's changes for everyone else to access. No one had ever explained to Frank how this worked, and he was happy to be ignorant. Synchronizing information was not Frank's job.

Frank's job was to figure out how to counteract the precipitous drop in XSG's sales resulting from the unexpected popularity of the new fabric. Pointing fingers and laying blame was irrelevant – OG had simply gotten lucky. No one could have predicted that the new products would completely eclipse the prior year's.

Frank's cell phone buzzed in his inside jacket pocket – he had missed a call from Andy on the marketing team and there was a message waiting. Hopefully this would be the latest sales figures from XSG's retail stores that he had requested as soon as they were available. He dialed his voice mail and listened. The numbers weren't good, but they were good to know. After the message ended, he pressed buttons on his cell phone, using the menus to save the voice mail into the collaboration space for the pursuit team. It might be a couple of days before the figures were available through the official channels, and he wanted to be sure everyone had access to them in the meantime.

Frank dug into the marketing and sales figures in the workspace again, trying to think through all of the alternative ways of working with ColPoly's manufacturer and the parameters that would control the profitability of each scenario.

The Factory

ColPoly was the first high-tech fabric manufactured at the Shanghai plant owned by the Chinese conglomerate known to Americans as TBG. Most of the plant floor was dedicated to the traditional fabrics and knock-offs of Western designer clothing.

In the north-east quarter of the building, though, were obviously new machines of a completely different nature from the rest of the factory. These machines made up the ultra-modern manufacturing line for the new base layer garments that had become so popular with the winter sports enthusiasts in America and Europe this year.

TBG had not invented the fabric now sold as ColPoly; they had been somewhat lucky to have stumbled across the patent holder, a small New England company that was struggling to stay afloat. TBG had bought the patent and hired the original company to serve as consultants, setting up the manufacturing line in Shanghai and helping TBG market the new products to the West.

When OG had approached TBG with the proposal to buy all of the ColPoly they could produce for the season, the management at TBG had jumped at the opportunity to recoup the investment they had made in the new equipment and patent.

Now the ColPoly products were stacking up in TBG's warehouses because OG couldn't take delivery, and the communication channels between the companies were rapidly breaking down. OG's failure to buy the latest production was clearly a violation of the exclusive contract, and TBG was ready to find alternative distribution channels.

The Meeting

Frank waited outside of Mr. Chang's office for the meeting he had been trying to get ever since XSG's business analysts had determined what the impact of ColPoly and OG's exclusive distribution contract would have on this season's sales. He had all of the data he needed and knew what he wanted, and what he could afford to pay for it.

Mr. Chang's secretary walked in and, with only a light accent, said "Mr. Chang is ready for you. Please follow me."

"Thanks." Frank got up and picked up his briefcase, then followed her down the hallway and into Mr. Chang's office.

"Welcome to TBG, please call me Mr. Chang," Mr. Chang said as he walked from behind his desk to shake Frank's hand.

"Frank Williams, nice to meet you. I'm the Vice President of purchasing for eXtreme Sports Gear."

"It's very nice to meet you, too."

Frank launched into his spiel on XSG – describing the company, the product line, the target markets, and the company's two sales channels: the online presence, and the chain of retail stores they had acquired two years prior. As always, he emphasized the tight channel integration they had achieved post acquisition and the benefits that integration provided, like increased customer satisfaction, improved loyalty, and increased sales.

When Frank finished, Mr. Chang asked a couple of polite questions about XSG and then offered to take Frank on a tour of TBG's factory.

Most of the tour was uninteresting and uneventful for Frank. He politely nodded and smiled as the various parts of the manufacturing process were explained. He recognized the ColPoly products coming off of the new line, and watched them being loaded onto pallets and taken to the warehouse next door on forklifts.

When they got to the warehouse, Frank's heart skipped a beat. There were rows and rows of pallet shelves, with three levels. A large percentage, maybe even a majority of the pallets contained ColPoly product. Frank tried to hide his eagerness, and nonchalantly asked Mr. Chang whether they had any excess inventory of ColPoly.

"Excess? All of this is excess. Our distributor is having problems integrating their supply chain system with our systems, and they are not taking delivery of our ColPoly product. Soon we will have to shut down the manufacturing line because our warehouse will be full."

"XSG would like to help you out by taking some of this excess inventory off of your hands. Do you think that would be possible?" Frank's voice was very measured – he did not want his excitement to show.

"How quickly can we get a contract in place and begin shipments?"

Frank paused for a moment, going over in his head the steps he would need to execute to make the deal happen. "I can have a contract in front of you tomorrow, and we can begin taking shipments next week."

"So fast? You know you must use our shipper – only one shipping company in Shanghai that TBG works with. We deliver to your final destination – that is the contract we have with our shipper. You must send our systems separate orders for each destination. Can you do that?"

"You mean separate orders for each retail store and for each of our web fulfillment centers?" Frank thought for a minute, and then decided to go out on a limb. "Yes, we can do that. That won't be a problem."

"I look forward to seeing your contract. I will have my secretary connect you with our legal and AR people, and they can fill you in on our standard terms. That way your contract will not receive too much resistance, understand?"

"Yes, I understand. Thank you very much."

The Hotel

As soon as Frank made it back to his Shanghai hotel he connected his laptop to the hotel's Internet access and opened up the collaborative workspace for the ColPoly pursuit team. As the local copy of his workspace was automatically synchronized with the current version located on XSG's corporate servers, Frank saw the updates and new items from the other team members appear in the workspace.

The cell phone message from Andy had developed into a discussion, and Frank quickly read through the messages, trying to get the general idea of what was being said. It appeared that one of the business analysts was questioning why XSG's sales of base layer items had ticked up significantly in the past week, and the consensus seemed to be that OG's fulfillment problems were causing some customers to fall back on competing products, probably because their purchases were time-sensitive.

Frank opened the worksheet where the team was keeping track of the lost sales that were being attributed to the ColPoly products, and noticed that the figures from the cell phone message and the subsequent discussion were already in the calculations. His messenger client popped up with a message from Chad on the BA team. He hit the button to record the text conversation into the collaborative workspace and then answered.

"I had a good meeting today with TBG. They are ready to sign the right contract, and I got all of their preferred terms and conditions. I'm going to work something up and present it to them tomorrow. We could have product in the stores in two weeks."

"That's great! I'll work up some sales projections based on that timeline."

Frank left the conversation open and watched the projection worksheet update as Chad began working on it. After making a quick mental calculation of his commission, Frank went to the sales section of XSG's enterprise portal and opened the latest supplier purchase contract template, creating a new contract in the ColPoly pursuit workspace. TBG had given him a document with sample boilerplate terms. He opened this document beside XSG's standard contract and then sent a message to the manager of the legal team.

"I need to work up a contract quickly. Anybody got any bandwidth to help?" Frank paused to see if he would get an immediate response.

"Joe is working a low priority purchasing contract for summer. What have you got?"

"ColPoly."

"Really? That's great! I'll ping him and get him to help you right away."

"Thanks."

Next Frank sent an e-mail to the catalog manager, explaining the situation and asking her to kick-start the content creation for the website, the e-mail newsletter and the print catalog. He also suggested a print mailer to announce the availability of the new products, and perhaps a display for the retail stores. Frank hoped that they could start taking pre-orders as soon as the contract was signed.

Frank was about to turn his attention to the business process when his messenger popped up again. This time it was Joe in legal.

"I hear congratulations are in order?"

"Not quite yet – we need to put a contract in front of TBG tomorrow, but I think they are ready to sign."

"What have you got?"

"Just a second," Frank switched to the two contract documents and selected the option to collaborate on them, then selected Joe's name from the list of workspace members currently online. "The first doc is our standard supplier purchasing contract. The second contains some terms and conditions that TBG wants to see in the contract I present tomorrow. We need to create a contract that will satisfy you guys in legal as well as TBG."

"No problem. I'll get right on it."

"Thanks."

As Joe started working on the contract, Frank returned his attention to the business process changes that would be necessary to satisfy TBG's unique shipping requirements. Although he wasn't a business process analyst, he knew that XSG normally aggregated orders for suppliers, and then used its own distribution network to move the products to the retail stores and to web customers. The new requirement would mean that XSG would need to incorporate sales projections and inventory data for the individual retail stores and web distribution centers into the ordering process, and then transmit the actual destination data to the supplier. He thought it would be tricky, but doable.

Frank noted that Sherry on the business process team was online, and opened another messenger conversation, this time with her.

"You busy?" he asked.

"Never too busy to talk to my favorite road warrior. What's up?"

"I think I've landed the ColPoly deal."

"Whoa – that should get you a nice bonus!"

"Yeah, but I have a challenge that I need your help with."

"Split the bonus with me? ;-)"

"How about sixty-forty? ;-)~" Frank explained the shipping requirements to Sherry, adding her to the contract collaboration session as a reader so she could see the specific clauses related to the arrangement. She asked a few questions and then confirmed that the change was possible and that she would get to work on it right away. Sherry closed the conversation and the transcript appeared in the workspace, associated with the contract that Joe was still working on.

The conversation with Chad lit up again. "OK, I've got the sales projections updated in the forecasting system. Your worksheet should reflect the new data now."

Frank switched to the projection worksheet and quickly glanced at the graphs, which now showed the projected sales of the new product. "Why is there an initial jump?"

"Pent-up demand. We're assuming that OG won't fix their problems before we hit the market."

"Sounds good. Thanks for your help."

"Just doing my job. Good luck tomorrow. Let me know if you need anything else."

Frank closed the conversation and saved it in the workspace associated with the latest version of the projection worksheet. He added a row that calculated the commissions based on the projected sales, and smiled when he saw the result.

An incoming e-mail caught Frank's attention; it was from April, the manager in charge of customer communication, the euphemism for the catalog division. She had the items ready to post to the web for pre-order as soon as the contract was signed, and had an e-mail announcement ready as well. Frank took a quick look at both in the workspace before replying to her e-mail. He promised to let her know as soon as he had a signature. All was going well so far.

Next Frank heard back from Sherry on the business process team. The changes to the ordering process for the ColPoly items were complete and implemented. As soon as orders for TBG products started coming in they would be routed through the new process and sent to the TBG systems as individual shipments to XSG's retail stores and web distribution centers. Frank replied with appropriate amounts of kudos and enthusiasm for Sherry's quick turnaround. He would likely have been even more impressed had he watched over her shoulder as she developed the new business process by dragging icons around on her screen and connecting them with lines, creating a graphical depiction of the new flow and writing the associated business rules in what was essentially abbreviated English, then deploying everything to the production environment with a few mouse clicks.

The conversation with Joe now flashed on Frank's screen, and he opened it to see what was happening. "OK, I've merged the two contracts and eliminated the conflicting sections. I kept all of the terms that TBG suggested. I've submitted the contract for approval by management. Once it's approved, you're good to go."

"Great. When do you think your manager will get to it?"

"He's already looking at it. You should hear within the hour."

"Thanks!" Frank saved this transcript as well, associating it with the contract. He pulled the document up and read through the draft version, noting that it looked more like TBG's contract than XSG's standard template. That should help with the final discussions tomorrow. As he was reading, the status changed from draft to approved, indicating that Joe's manager had signed off.

Frank closed the workspace and headed for the restaurant. There was plenty of time for a nice dinner before hitting the sack for the night.

Back at the Factory

Frank's appointment with Mr. Chang was just before noon local time – and he showed up early. When the secretary came out to escort him back to Mr. Chang's office, it was still 15 minutes before the scheduled start time. Apparently he wasn't the only one who was eager.

After the normal pleasantries, Frank pulled out a printed copy of the contract the team had put together the night before. He wasn't exactly sure what the process would be like, having never worked with TBG before and having limited exposure to Chinese business customs.

Mr. Chang sat down at his desk and immediately started reading through the contract. His reading was punctuated by smiles and nods of his head. When he reached the end, he stood up and offered his hand to Frank, who took it.

"So we have a deal?" Frank said with a smile.

"We have a deal. I will send this to my legal counsel for final approval, but you can rest assured that the contract is satisfactory and we have an agreement."

"Excellent. May I take you out for lunch?"

"Why, yes, that would be nice. Do you like Chinese food?"

Not knowing exactly what kind of Chinese food Mr. Chang was referring to, he felt it prudent to say, "Yes, of course."

"We will go to my favorite restaurant and celebrate our new arrangement."

On the way to the restaurant Frank discretely sent a text message to April, telling her that he had a verbal confirmation and the signature should come soon. She replied that she would pull the trigger on the customer communication.

Frank and Mr. Chang enjoyed a lengthy, leisurely lunch at a posh restaurant in downtown Shanghai. Although most of the dishes were unfamiliar to Frank, he expressed an enthusiastic liking for them, even the ones he found distasteful. Afterward, they returned to Mr. Chang's office, where he called his secretary and asked her whether the contract had been signed. She brought it in, and Frank added his own signature below Mr. Chang's and someone's Frank didn't recognize.

Mr. Chang then stood and offered his hand again. "I have something to show you," he said with a toothy smile.

"OK, what's that?"

"Look at my screen." Mr. Chang spun his display around so that Frank could see it from across the desk. There was a video window open showing a live feed from a black and white video camera. Frank recognized the loading dock of the warehouse he had been in yesterday. A forklift was loading pallets of ColPoly onto a truck. "That is your first shipment. We received an electronic order while we were at lunch. Your stores should have our product very soon.

Frank tried not to show his own surprise that everything had come together so quickly. Instead he smiled and said, "XSG looks forward to doing a lot of business with TBG."

The New Customer

Amy looked up from the latest issue of "Self" as the familiar strains of "Toxic" emanated from her cell phone. The dated picture of Sue was on the screen.

"Hi Sue."

"Hey. I just got an e-mail from eXtreme Sports Gear. Somehow they have started selling ColPoly and they are taking pre-orders now."

"Don't they have a store on Main?"

"Yeah. Go to their website and get your order in. Call me back."

"Okay."

Amy grabbed her laptop off the table and logged onto xsg.com. The front page was splashed with the announcement of the availability of the ColPoly products. She clicked through to the details and selected a couple of colorful turtlenecks and two pairs of black bottoms. During checkout, she indicated that she wanted in-store pickup. The final confirmation screen indicated that she should be able to pick up her order in a week. She called Sue back.

"I ordered them."

"Good. When are they supposed to be in?

"Next week."

"Cool – you still have plenty of time before we leave for Vancouver. Are you excited yet?"

"Very – I know I won't be cold this time!"

"Nope. Gotta go – talk to you later."

...to be continued...

Chapter 1:   New Perspectives

*This book presents a framework for understanding the place of
Information Technology in a modern enterprise. The concepts
are not necessarily new, but the perspectives are.*

*This chapter begins by presenting an overview of these new
perspectives and laying the groundwork for the rest of the book,
which will dive into each in more detail.*

The Progression to SOA

The central theme of this book is that the adoption of a Service Oriented
Architecture (SOA) as the basis for an organization's Information Technology
will enable the organization to achieve sustained growth and adapt to a changing
economic and competitive environment.

The key tenets of this argument are introduced here at a high level:

- All Technology is Infrastructure

- Infrastructure Supports the Enterprise

- Infrastructure is Outsourced

- Information Technology Drives Visibility

- Information Technology is Infrastructure

All Technology is Infrastructure

The main premise of this book is that technology, in all of its forms, is "just" infrastructure:

> in·fra·struc·ture: n. An underlying base or foundation especially for an organization or system.[1]

There are many kinds of infrastructure that, for the most part, are ignored by the vast majority of people as they go about their day to day business. Shoppers at Wal-Mart purchase inexpensive food storage containers in a convenient environment with no thought to the factories in Asia that produced the goods, the petroleum industry that created the raw materials for the plastic used by the factories, the electrical, plumbing and sewer systems that provide basic infrastructure services to the factories and the store, and the transportation industry that brought the finished product to the store. The shopper drives on public roads with street lights and road signs to a clean, well-lit store with shelves of products in convenient packages and combinations. It is the nature of infrastructure to be transparent, and the degree to which infrastructure can and is ignored by its users is a primary measure of its utility.

Infrastructure Supports Enterprise

The purpose of infrastructure is to support the operation of the enterprise. Infrastructure should never be created for its own sake – there should be a clear business case for any infrastructure project. For example, a city would never begin to lay new sewer and water lines in an undeveloped area without a clear understanding of why the utilities were needed, what kinds of development (factories, office buildings, residential units) were planned, what the likelihood of each potential development coming to fruition was, and what the resulting revenue and economic benefits would be for the city and its residents. In most cases, the infrastructure will only begin to pay for itself over time, but if a realistic Return on Investment (ROI) model cannot be constructed that clearly shows a positive return in a reasonable period of time, a rational city or enterprise would not embark on the project.

Information Technology decisions should be handled the same way as other infrastructure decisions. First, there should be a clearly articulated business need. Once this need is understood, various options for meeting the need should be researched and analyzed, and an ROI model should be created. If a viable solution can be found with a positive ROI in a reasonable period of time, only then should the project be attempted. Tying projects to business goals and needs is a key step along the road to a rational IT environment.

Infrastructure Should Be Outsourced

At the dawn of the industrial revolution, manufacturers were transitioning from a model where component parts were not interchangeable and each assembled product was unique, to one in which the components manufactured by a factory were interchangeable, allowing the factory to gain the benefits of scale associated with mass production. As component standards began to cross factory, company, and even industry boundaries, manufacturers began to specialize on the areas where they added the most value to the production process, effectively outsourcing those parts that were less strategic to other specialized companies.

For sustained growth, healthy organizations outsource nonstrategic infrastructure projects to specialists. The reasons for this are obvious – why would a company whose primary business is insurance ask employees to construct a new building for the company? Not only would this impact the company's revenue by diverting resources away from the primary business goals, but the resulting office space would probably be of questionable integrity.

The construction of infrastructure consists of many highly specialized fields. In the context of an auto manufacturer, there are companies that specialize in vehicle design, companies that manufacture standard nuts and bolts, companies that produce sheet metal, companies that make general-purpose manufacturing machines like welding robots and paint booths, and companies that design sales and marketing campaigns. When a customer buys a customized car from a dealer, that dealer is acting as an agent, coordinating the activities of the auto-manufacturer, the lend/lease company, and the aftermarket companies, and providing overall project management. The participants focus on their core business, while outsourcing the other functions to companies for whom they are core. This specialization leads to greater efficiency within each organization.

Once a piece of infrastructure is in place, the ongoing monitoring and maintenance of it is outsourced as well, while the users of the infrastructure go about their particular businesses, leveraging the common infrastructure to generate profit by adding value to some higher business process. Once a general contractor is finished with the construction of a new office building, for example, the ongoing maintenance and upkeep of the building and all of its associated systems is outsourced to various specialized companies, usually coordinated under the umbrella of a management company, which adds value to the business process of running the office building by doing all of the associated legwork, freeing up the tenants of the building to go about their respective businesses, trusting that the lights will stay on and the bathrooms will be cleaned.

Information Technology should operate in the same manner. In today's world, however, this is very rarely the case, and the reasons are mostly related to the immaturity of the IT industry. The way most IT shops operate today is equivalent to the time when each city needed a full complement of trades and had to be self-sufficient, before the railroad created a common transportation infrastructure allowing the movement of goods from city to city, driving standardization and creating opportunities for specialization and greater levels of efficiency.[2]

Information Technology is undergoing a fundamental shift comparable in scope to the changes in manufacturing that occurred during the industrial revolution. IT is as important to modern business as building construction, but companies are beginning to realize that their infrastructure does not have to be created from scratch.

Information Technology Drives Visibility

Information is the lifeblood of business today. Not only is change a constant, the rate of change is continually accelerating. Data that are out of date can be worse than useless – they can lead to decisions that harm the interests of the organization. Today's companies must compete on the world stage, and they must react rapidly to changes in their market, the rise and fall of competitors, merger and acquisition activity, and the potential that revolutionary new ways of doing business could change the competitive landscape overnight.

The flow of information with suppliers and channel partners is critical to the efficient operation of the company. A manufacturing company, for example, needs to minimize inventory while simultaneously minimizing customers' wait time. Accurate and timely information flow between an organization's business processes is essential to maximizing efficiency.

Management increasingly needs access to real-time, or near real-time, information about all facets of the business in order to react to a changing environment. Processes that don't provide visibility into their business activity are corporate blind spots that are potentially disastrous.

Customers today require information as well. Buyers want to know whether an item is in stock, how long it will take to deliver and whether or not it has been shipped. Consumers want to know how much money is in their accounts and what the performance of their investments has been over any period of time.

Just as information is the lifeblood of a company, Information Technology provides the arteries through which that blood flows.

Information Technology is Infrastructure

Information Technology supports the execution of business processes and makes them more flexible and efficient. Granted, there are some companies for which Information Technology is their core business; some of the largest companies in the world are in this category. However the products and services these companies sell are designed to facilitate other business processes, and to that extent these technology driven companies can be thought of as utilities or suppliers of infrastructure to other businesses.

The evolution of Information Technology currently underway is similar to the changes that took place in manufacturing during the industrial revolution. This metaphor draws heavily on the work of Pat Helland in his "Metropolis" whitepaper, which is included in the supplemental section of this book for reference.[3] In order to better understand how this metaphor can be useful to understanding IT as infrastructure, Helland provides eight analogies, summarized and paraphrased below:

1) **IT organizations today are like cities before the railroads:**

   - they have evolved over time

   - they are isolated from each other and self-sufficient

   - they each have their own culture

   - opportunities are driving them to become more modern, to provide a common infrastructure and to become more integrated both internally and externally

2) **Applications today are like factories before transportation created an opportunity for standardization of parts and raw materials:**

   - they serve a limited market

   - they operate independently of each other

   - they are vertically integrated and all of their parts and subassemblies are created from scratch

   - they are being driven by competitive pressures to focus on their core business

3) **The spread of computer networks, particularly the Internet, is like the spread of transportation, particularly the railroads:**

- they allow customers a broader range of choices

- they enable aggregation of vendor offerings

- they increase the expectations of interoperability, interchangeability, and integration

4) **Services based on standardized messages are like manufactured goods based on standardized parts:**

- intra-organizational standards lead to inter-organizational standards

- centralized control of a specification enables mass utilization

- the ability to adhere to the standard becomes increasingly important to the survival of the company

- the existence of standards increases the demand for conformance

- failure to incorporate the standards will eventually destroy a company

5) **Business processes composed of services are like finished goods assembled from components:**

- they deliver value by combining the output of multiple companies

- clearly defined interfaces enable composition and assembly, the same components can be used in different assemblies

- each business can focus on their core competencies

6) **Business processes are becoming drivers of service design the way retailers became drivers of product design:**

- standardization of features creates commoditization

- wider availability enables packaging

- usage is decoupled from production

7) **Technical infrastructure is like urban infrastructure:**

- common utility services are retrofitted into preexisting resources
- connecting to the common utility services requires a combination of communal resources and private resources
- the existence of common utility services leads to a mandate for their usage
- inefficiencies associated with a failure to centralize common utility services can be catastrophic

8) **IT governance is like city government:**

- each environment has different objectives and goals
- planning is required to reach these objectives and goals
- infrastructure needs depend on the particular set of objectives and goals
- cooperation between the central authority and the subjects is required for success
- resource allocation must be balanced based on various priorities

Certainly these analogies provide a strong basis and framework for viewing IT as infrastructure. Companies that maintain a strong focus on their core business will rely on standards-based, outsourced components, much the way cities rely on a standards-based electrical grid, outsourced to independent utility companies.

Services Enable Sustained Success

The key to successfully outsourcing services is to define the interfaces to the services in a clean manner. Companies that successfully make this transition to a service-based business model have the advantage of selecting outside providers to fulfill some of these services when it can be shown to be more cost effective. A clean service interface facilitates outsourcing of the service provisioning and creates a competitive market of service providers.

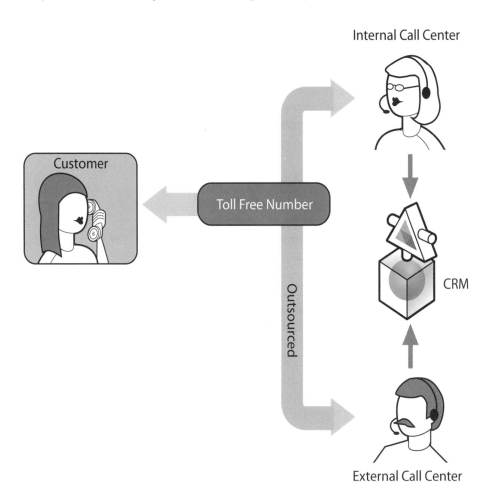

One example might be a customer support call center. The interface with the customers might be designed as a toll-free telephone number. The call center depends on other services to successfully fulfill its promise of timely resolution of customer problems. To do this it needs access to the history of the customer's interactions with the business, the particular product and service packages that the customer has purchased, and any relevant support information. The interfaces between the customer support call center and these other services must be defined in a clean way as well. Assuming that all these interfaces are well designed, the company should be able to completely outsource the call center service to another company, while continuing to maintain the same functions in the CRM and product support areas. The customers continue to call the same toll-free number and don't perceive any difference in the quality of service when the underlying service provider is completely swapped out.

Another way that services facilitate business is through flexibility in pricing and billing models. For example, well-defined service interfaces facilitate billing models that are based upon usage. In the call center example, it becomes almost trivial to charge based on the number of calls or the aggregate length of support calls. This facilitates outsourcing by providing an easy way for the company providing the service to bill the company buying the service, as well as a mechanism to track the cost of the service provision and feed that cost back into the pricing model.

Services are modular and independent in nature, and can therefore be developed, purchased, or outsourced incrementally. This adds tremendous flexibility by transitioning from an IT environment focused on multi-million dollar monolithic projects to one in which investments are orders of magnitude smaller. Smaller investments mean lower risk and potentially greater ROI because of the law of averages. Even if some projects fail, the lower investment will mean that the overall ROI of all IT projects is higher.

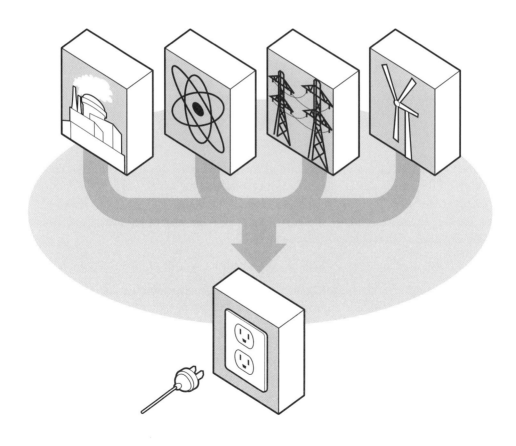

Well-designed service interfaces facilitate changes in the underlying implementation by providing a generic interface. Once business processes are modified to depend on the generic interface rather than any specific service provider, then the provider can be changed without affecting the business process. This applies equally well to outsourcing the service or keeping the service internal while changing the underlying technology mechanism. Once internal service implementations are competing with services from other specialized providers that provide the same interface, each company becomes more flexible and can focus on those business processes that are core to its value proposition. The modularity of services allows them to be easily outsourced on an incremental basis, allowing for more flexibility in choosing the best implementation for each.

Just as general purpose, interchangeable components and an efficient means of transportation allowed manufacturers to combine parts and subassemblies from specialized companies into higher value products, generic services can be combined into larger packages that can then be offered as services of their own. Their modularity allows them to be combined in multiple ways to target specific markets, without requiring a custom service offering for each.

Companies that want to continue to grow will require a Service Oriented Architecture in order to allow them the flexibility to choose how each service is best provided based on a constantly changing business environment.

What is SOA?

Service Oriented Architecture is defined by a set of practices and technologies for building IT systems out of parts. Building systems out of parts is a more general concept than SOA, and can be applied to many industries. It is easy to make an analogy to the automobile industry, where cars are assembled out of many different parts with well-defined interfaces.

The two key prerequisites that enable the construction of systems from parts are:

- A catalog of parts that defines what parts are available for use and their characteristics and interfaces
- Tools that can be used to assemble parts into systems

Both of these prerequisite technologies for SOA adoption will be discussed in greater detail in later chapters.

ZapThink defines SOA this way:

> Service-Oriented Architecture (SOA) is an approach to distributed computing that abstracts complex, heterogeneous IT systems into composite, business-oriented Services. However, SOA goes beyond this limited, technical definition to embody a broader form of enterprise architecture. SOA, or more broadly, Service Orientation (SO), is an approach to organizing and managing all of the resources within and external to the enterprise, including people, process, and technology, by representing IT functionality as Services that business users can compose into processes defined by business, rather than technical, users in a flexible, agile manner. In other words, the vision of SO is a vision of IT responding to the needs of the business as any other enterprise resource ought, as opposed to the rigid, complex IT environments that limit business agility today.[4]

A Service Oriented Architecture breaks apart the monolithic application environments present in today's IT organizations into independent parts that provide a standardized set of services to all consumers. Rather than providing application- and technology-specific interfaces for each integration point, the services provided are generic and are decoupled from both the underlying implementation of the service and the technology on which it is implemented, allowing them to be utilized in a heterogeneous environment and decoupling the implementation of the service from the specification of its interface.

Decoupling services from their implementation allows the implementation to be swapped out for another provider with minimal or no disruption to the business processes that the service supports. This has been the 'holy grail' of IT for decades, but only with the advent of modern service oriented industry standards supported by the majority of technology vendors has this become achievable.

The traditional way IT integration projects are addressed is similar to the way goods were manufactured before the industrial revolution. Every part was created by hand and no two parts were alike. When goods were assembled from multiple parts, the craftsman had to select parts that would work together and then customize them to create a finished product. Parts from one would not necessarily work in another of the same kind, even if they were made by the same person.

Implementing a Service Oriented Architecture is similar to creating uniform parts that are interchangeable. Each one is the same within certain defined tolerances, and they can be swapped out between different assemblies. Mass production becomes possible along with the associated economies of scale. Once parts are standardized, one provider can be swapped for another with little or no impact on the assembly process. A Service Oriented Architecture allows individual service implementations to be changed with little or no impact on the business process.

Why Now

The migration from traditional integration to an SOA is neither quick nor inexpensive, but it pays for itself through greater agility and efficiency. Similar to the infrastructure projects undertaken by governments, the processes for implementing an SOA, described in the rest of this book, have up-front costs that are only recouped when a significant portion of the SOA is deployed. In order to justify the implementation of an SOA, it is important to understand what benefits will be gained when it is deployed.

Agility

There is one overriding reason for adopting an SOA strategy: implementation of an SOA makes a company more flexible and more efficient.

Modern companies compete on a global stage in an environment of continually accelerating change and rapidly morphing markets. To survive, a company must be able to react to the changing environment. To excel, a company must drive change, forcing competitors to follow suit. As technology increasingly becomes central to the business processes of corporations, the flexibility of IT systems, or the lack of it, can increasingly enable or hamper the company's ability to evolve. The flexibility inherent in an SOA allows an enterprise to respond quickly to a changing business environment.

Avis, for example, uses customer service as a differentiator in an industry where customer loyalty has historically been low. In order to roll out new customer service offerings quickly to compete with competitive offerings from other companies or, better yet, to introduce service offerings that the competition had not even thought of, Avis needed to reduce the IT effort associated with implementing new customer services. Avis implemented a Service Oriented Architecture and provided the basic building blocks for the universe of possible customer service offerings, allowing the business to quickly assemble the services into new and unique offerings.[5]

Integration and automation between enterprise systems and those belonging to the company's suppliers, customers, and business partners have been shown to increase the efficiency of the supply chain, decrease the inventory necessary to meet customer demand, increase customer satisfaction, and increase the value derived from business partnerships. In the past, these integration points have generally been brittle and costly to maintain. Utilizing service oriented interfaces that are based on interoperable standards and that hide the underlying complexities of implementation for linking internal systems to external partner, customer, and supplier systems decreases development and maintenance costs over time and establishes the enterprise as a thought leader. Once interfaces are established in a generic, industry standard manner, further efficiencies are gained by utilizing the same services for multiple external entities.

The Great Exhibition of 1851, held in London, was notable for the introduction of a couple of technology innovations that are relevant to the discussion here. The first was the introduction to the British arms industry of the "American Method" of gun manufacture. Prior to this method, guns were manufactured by craftsmen, with each individual part being created within the context of a single weapon and designed to work with the other parts crafted for that weapon. Since each part was unique, they were not interchangeable between guns. When a part broke and needed to be replaced, a new part had to be crafted specifically to work with that gun.

The American Method, in contrast, focused on creating identical parts that all met the same, standardized specifications. This allowed a gun to be constructed from any set of parts, and for parts to be interchangeable between weapons, greatly simplifying the maintenance of weapons in the field. This standardization of parts is a direct parallel to the idea of standardized service interfaces.

The second relevant innovation was the exhibit hall itself, which came to be known as the Crystal Palace, and for which the exhibition is known. The architect, Sir Joseph Paxton, designed the building so that it could be assembled from a set of modular parts that were built to identical specifications. Prior to this innovation, buildings were constructed rather than assembled, again in a craftsman-like manner. The parallel here is to the idea that applications can be assembled from services provided by other applications, as opposed to being constructed from scratch.

Much of the typical enterprise's core business logic is locked inside of monolithic, so-called "legacy" applications. Leveraging this business logic from enterprise portals, other applications, and workflow applications is tedious, expensive, and often results in brittle, tightly coupled interfaces. Many companies choose the route of recreating business logic in new applications rather than attempt to leverage existing applications.

Service oriented interfaces expose the business functionality of applications to the enterprise and enable the aggregation of these functions into composite applications. By exposing these core processes through standard business interfaces, companies can finally reach the nirvana of component reuse that has been advocated for decades. Although the benefits of component reuse have been discussed at great length, it is worth summarizing some of them again:

- Increased reliability due to the use of services already in production systems

- Increased consistency, repeatability and manageability of the software development process

- Ability to leverage the work of highly specialized developers across multiple projects

- Increased standards compliance through reuse governance body

- Reduced development lifecycle

The role of enterprise software applications is to enable the efficient and flexible execution of business processes. Automation of business processes is the primary objective of every IT department.

Increasingly, business processes are instantiated via software applications. As the business environment becomes more competitive, the business processes implemented in software must be able to change rapidly. Business software must be constructed in a manner that encourages adaptability in business processes. The adoption of a comprehensive SOA will provide the applications that provide business processes the flexibility to adapt at the ever increasing rate of market evolution.

As companies grow through mergers and acquisitions, systems are acquired that are different from and incompatible with existing systems. Rather than undergo a huge migration effort to transform the acquired IT infrastructure into the acquiring companies existing environment, implementing an SOA can allow both systems to coexist in a heterogeneous environment.

A modern enterprise requires timely information on the operation of the business in order to make adjustments in business processes to keep pace with a changing market. Customers, partners, and employees all require real-time information. An SOA enables real-time business by exposing back-end systems to everyone who needs access via a single point of contact.

Efficient IT

Legacy application integration approaches suffer from high complexity and brittleness. Both of these attributes lead to high maintenance costs, which amount to millions of dollars of unnecessary expense in most organizations. Because the applications are tightly coupled to each other, they are dependent upon specific implementations; changes in one application have a ripple effect, causing every application integrated to it to require changes as well. This has implications for release and deployment schedules, as the applications must be released and deployed in lock step with each other. For applications that are maintained by different teams or different companies, this can be a project management nightmare.

When applications are integrated using proprietary interfaces, the integration team must include individuals with experience in each of the application interfaces involved. Assembling such a team is often difficult, since resources from different organizations need to be freed from their existing responsibilities at the same time in order to implement the integration project. Often this is so difficult that the project is never initiated.

This style of integration also suffers from a long development cycle, the result of the underlying complexity and tight coupling. Changes in the competitive landscape can be difficult to react to in a timely fashion, because the application development teams cannot change the software quickly enough. This slow responsiveness creates opportunity cost, as market opportunities are missed.

Besides missed opportunities, long development cycles also cause unnecessary, and sometimes useless, development to occur as application changes are implemented that become irrelevant before they are ever deployed and utilized.

Differentiators

An SOA can enable a company to differentiate itself from its competitors in several ways. Faster service is an easily identifiable benefit, as customers, employees, and business partners are given appropriate levels of access to back-end systems. Rather than making a request for information that might take hours or even days to fulfill, customers and partners get information in real time. This level of service differentiator can lead to increased market share.

A single point of contact with the IT infrastructure based on industry standard, cross-platform technologies, and interfaces allows business partners to interface directly with the enterprise in an efficient, cost-effective manner. Making a company easy to work with, or a company's information, applications and business processes easy to interface with, will attract partners who recognize the cost savings of services versus traditional integration technologies like Electronic Data Interchange (EDI).

Achieving loose coupling shortens the product development lifecycle by making the IT infrastructure agile and able to adapt to new products and channels. A shorter development lifecycle leads to a shorter time to market and the potential for increased market share.

An agile IT infrastructure can allow a company to perform more customization of offerings, to address diverse customer needs with targeted offerings efficiently. By providing a service or product that is specific to a target market, market share can be taken from more generalized offerings that cannot be customized as quickly or efficiently because of rigid systems.

Many industries are already forming consortiums and organizations to define standard service interface definitions. Companies that are in front of or leading these standards initiatives become thought leaders in their industry, raising their profile relative to their competitors. Being first has other benefits as well; companies that define the industry standards can define them in a way that works well for their IT infrastructure.

Risk Mitigation

Adopting an SOA can be a strategy for mitigating risk. There are multiple types of risk faced by an IT organization that an SOA can help mitigate.

Most IT shops have a number of systems that have outlived the desirability of the platform they are implemented on, but they continue to run some part of the business and have been fully depreciated, making it difficult to replace them, and thereby locking the enterprise into supporting obsolete platforms.

The approach to these situations in the context of an SOA is to service-enable these legacy systems using service interfaces that hide the underlying complexities of the applications while exposing a set of generic business services. Instead of a "rip-and-replace" strategy, where legacy systems are re-implemented in newer technologies and then replaced with the flip of a switch, SOA promotes a "leave-and-layer" approach.

By layering service interfaces over legacy systems, they can be re-implemented in an incremental fashion by providing new services that fulfill the same interface contracts. This helps mitigate risk by making the migration incremental instead of all at once, and by allowing the enterprise to switch back to the older service interface should the newer implementation run into problems once in production. The two services can even be run in parallel if they are designed correctly.

Another way an SOA helps mitigate risk is by isolating systems provided by outside vendors from the overall IT environment. If a vendor goes out of business or raises licensing fees to a point where they are no longer competitive, a clean service interface to the vendor's system will enable the enterprise to replace the application with another implementation while minimizing the impact on the rest of the IT infrastructure.

Services and Services

Throughout this chapter the word "service" has been used in two related but different contexts, and it is important to understand the different usages. The word "service" in the business world refers to a revenue generating offering, something that the company performs for a customer who sees value in it and is therefore willing to pay for it.

A "service" in the IT world refers to some functionality of a reusable software component that can be performed when called upon by another software component. This is generally the sense meant when the term "Service Oriented Architecture" is used; though SOA could certainly be generalized to the entire business environment as well.

Both types of services are best designed from the outside in. In other words, you should design your services based on what the customer wants and will perceive as valuable. For business services, this means thinking about what the customer will pay for and how they would like to receive the service. In the case of a software service, this means thinking about the software components that will be clients of the service, what operation they would like the service to perform and the way they would prefer to communicate with it.

Wrap-Up

This chapter summarized the key tenets of the framework presented in this book, which provides a holistic view of IT environments and organizations. Key among these is the idea that IT is infrastructure, and that infrastructure should be transparent.

Supporting the enterprise by making it more flexible and efficient is accomplished by means of a Service Oriented Architecture. A SOA enables application integration and exposes the IT infrastructure to employees, partners, and customers.

The idea that infrastructure is usually outsourced so that companies can focus on their core competencies follows from observations of other types of infrastructure, and the premise that IT is infrastructure leads to the conclusion that IT should be outsourced. The implementation of a SOA enables this outsourcing where it is cost effective.

In the next chapter, a framework for understanding the IT infrastructure in a holistic fashion will be presented, which will facilitate later discussions on how to achieve the goals presented here.

Part I: Technology Infrastructure

Chapter 2:   The Layers of IT Infrastructure

When any type of infrastructure is examined closely, it can always be broken down into component parts and layers of abstraction. A building, for example, can be seen as having a finished exterior and interior, but beneath the façade is a complex mesh of systems including ventilation, electrical, plumbing, elevators, and fire suppression. These systems are layered on top of a structural skeleton, which is built on a solid foundation appropriate to the geology of the site.

Information Technology has layers as well. There are three fundamental layers to a service oriented IT infrastructure that is agile, efficient and transparent to the enterprise, its customers and business partners.

Three Macro Layers

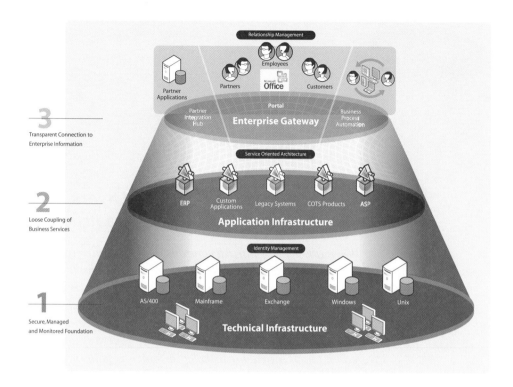

Enterprise Gateway

The top layer of IT infrastructure consists of the interfaces into the applications utilized by employees, customers, and business partners. The goal of this layer is to provide a single consolidated view of the enterprise that is both consistent and appropriate to the individual users.

The term "gateway" within the conceptual framework presented here has a slightly different meaning from the technical one often found in the IT industry. Products are sold as "gateways" when they either provide or restrict access to some part of the IT infrastructure to or from outside systems. In the sense meant here, the enterprise gateway layer is providing a single point of entry to all people and systems that need services from the IT infrastructure. Although the difference is subtle, it is important to keep in mind that the enterprise gateway is not referring to a single product or machine, but rather to a conceptual layer of the IT infrastructure.

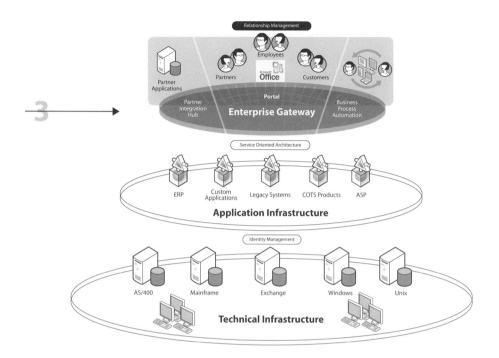

One component of the enterprise gateway is the Enterprise Portal. The portal provides a view into the applications that make up the application infrastructure layer, while simultaneously blurring the lines between the applications to provide a unified user experience. Instead of switching between different applications with different user interfaces to accomplish a task, users work with composite applications that utilize the underlying business services provided by multiple applications. The portal presents a customized view into the IT infrastructure that is tailored to each individual user's needs.

Partner integration is another important function of the enterprise gateway. Though some functionality will be designed for human consumption, more and more will be implemented as services that are utilized by business partners' IT infrastructures to enable a high level of inter-organizational business process automation.

The key to understanding the services provided by the enterprise gateway is to think of self-service – providing a way for employees, customers, and partners to access the services they need in a way that is convenient and transparent to them.

Application Infrastructure

The middle layer consists of all of the applications that facilitate the business. These applications are based on multiple technologies and may be developed internally, while others are packaged. In any enterprise of significant size, these applications will be at various stages of development, maintenance, or retirement.

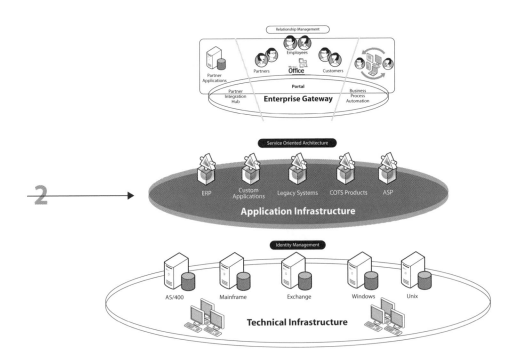

Applications may consist of a few users in a single department or they may include massive collections of functionality and service a broad range of different users, such as ERP systems. They may be hosted on a departmental server, in a data center under the control of the organization's IT department, or at an application service provider (ASP) where they provide services to many different organizations.

Applications provide the business services on which the agile enterprise is built. This is where a Service Oriented Architecture is implemented and utilized for all application integration requirements. The business services in the application infrastructure layer provide the basis upon which the enterprise gateway is built.

Anytime a system will be assembled from parts, there must be a catalog of the available parts that allows the assemblers and their tools to select the appropriate parts. The assembly of composite applications in the enterprise gateway from services provided by the application infrastructure requires a catalog of available services. This concept is sometimes referred to by the technical term "metadata," which will be discussed in greater detail in later chapters.

Technical Infrastructure

The foundational layer of an enterprise IT infrastructure consists of the hardware and software that enables the development and deployment of applications. Machines and the wires that connect them together in networks are the most fundamental parts of the technical infrastructure. These include routers, hubs, data networks, power networks, personal computers, and server computers.

Operating systems are another major component of this foundational layer. Modern operating systems provide many more services than basic process, memory, and file management and are more accurately referred to as platforms. Most platforms include higher level services like security, identity management, basic collaboration, messaging services, and libraries of runtime services for applications to leverage.

The term platform has become somewhat overloaded in the IT industry. In the context of this book, platform refers to the hardware and software that define how a computer is operated and determine what other kinds of software can be deployed on the system. Any foundational services that can be leveraged by applications deployed on the system are included in the definition of platform. The automobile industry has a similar meaning for platform, and the analogy is useful in understanding platform in this context. An auto manufacturer will design a chassis and frame, which can accommodate one or more powertrains and will use this "platform" as the underlying foundation for multiple models within their product lines. It is in this same sense that the word is used here.

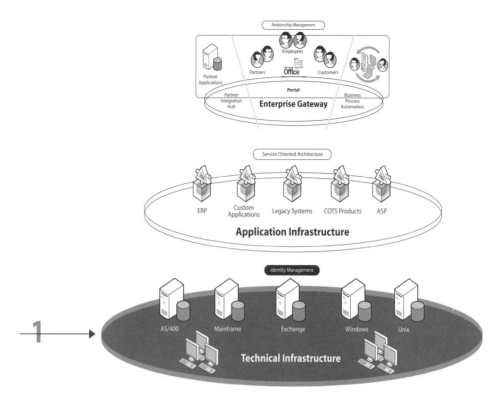

A number of other software components are considered part of the technical infrastructure layer as well. These include directories, databases, e-mail, application server software, and thin client software (e.g., browsers and smart client software such as office suites).

The technical infrastructure layer also includes all of the tools necessary to monitor and manage the various components of this and higher layers, including network monitoring, identity provisioning and management, software deployment and monitoring, clustering and fail-over.

Wrap-Up

This chapter described the three-layer framework for understanding the IT infrastructure that will be referenced throughout this book. This framework takes a holistic view of IT infrastructure and creates a vocabulary for understanding and discussing the components of the IT infrastructure, as well as their relationships and interdependencies.

This chapter also introduced a graphical element that will be used throughout Part I and Part II. On the first page of this chapter, the graphic that appears above the chapter heading represents the three layers of IT infrastructure as detailed in this chapter and the diagrams within it. A similar graphic will appear at the beginning of each subsequent chapter in Parts I and II, indicating which layer or layers the chapter addresses.

Chapters that primarily address the technologies and issues related to the enterprise gateway layer will start with this graphic. This layer provides a single point of contact to the entire IT infrastructure for employees, customers, and business partners. This top layer leverages the business services provided by the application infrastructure layer to achieve the goals of transparent IT.

When the application infrastructure layer is the primary focus of a chapter, it will start with this icon. This layer consists of the applications that facilitate the business and their integration points and interdependencies. This is where a Service Oriented Architecture is implemented by exposing the basic functions provided by the applications as business services.

This icon indicates that the chapter is related to the technical infrastructure layer of the IT stack. This foundational layer consists of the computers, networks, and platform software that applications are deployed to and depend on.

Chapters that are concerned with the vertical integration between two layers will begin with a graphic depicting the two layers they address. This one indicates that the chapter addresses the vertical integration between the enterprise gateway layer and the application infrastructure layer.

This graphic is used when a chapter contains information related to the vertical integration between the application infrastructure layer and the technical infrastructure layer.

The next three chapters will examine each of these layers in more depth, beginning with the enterprise gateway layer and proceeding down through the IT infrastructure stack.

Chapter 3: What is an Enterprise Gateway?

The highest return on investment is found at the top layer of the IT stack. This "enterprise gateway" layer is where knowledge workers utilize business services, where services are orchestrated into business processes, where real-time information about the organization is aggregated and provided to decision makers, and where all external entities interact with the entire IT infrastructure.

The enterprise gateway provides a common interface to the entire IT infrastructure of the organization.

Goals

The goals of the enterprise gateway layer are business oriented rather than technology oriented. These goals, if achieved, typically yield the highest ROI because they are closely aligned with business objectives, but are only possible when the layers beneath provide a robust set of business services upon which to build. Often the needs of the enterprise gateway will drive the adoption of an SOA. "Chapter 6: Leveraging the Application Infrastructure" goes into greater detail on how the components of the enterprise gateway leverage the services provided by the application infrastructure.

Most enterprises already have many components of the technical infrastructure and application infrastructure layers in place, though these must be migrated to a Service Oriented Architecture. The enterprise gateway, however, is still in a conceptual phase for most organizations, and many haven't yet conceived it.

Easy to do Business With

As more companies become service oriented, customers come to expect ever-higher levels of service. The ease with which a customer interacts with an organization may determine whether the customer comes back or takes future business to a competitor. Organizations that are easy to do business with have a fundamental advantage over less customer-friendly organizations, and can leverage this competitive advantage to take market share away from their competitors. Once an industry begins to trend in this direction, organizations that lag in this respect will have to embark on more customer-friendly business service implementations just to maintain their existing customer base.

Customers view the organization from the outside and don't care how business processes are implemented internally, so long as they are confident that their transactions are securely received and processed. They expect all of the channels to be seamlessly integrated, and integrated in real time, with feedback that the integration has occurred. Interactions between the customer and the organization via multiple channels, even simultaneously, should provide a consistent level of service and a consistent view of the information relevant to the customer. The experience of interacting with the organization should be transparent for the customer.

Customers expect integration between the organization's online channel, physical presence, call center, mobile device, and kiosk interfaces. Being able to check the inventory of a particular store via a corporate website is just the beginning. Once the customer has found an item in stock at a local store, they might want to purchase it online and then pick it up at the store. If they can't find it locally, they may want to order it over the phone and have it shipped, but may later return it to a local store if the product is defective or doesn't meet their needs. A customer of an airline might want to order a ticket online but receive gate information on his or her cell phone or PDA. Any limitations that exist between the organization's channels become a liability as customers demand and competitors race to achieve ever higher levels of channel integration.

As companies join forces with business partners to provide more integrated services to customers, customers view the ultimate provider of the integrated services as the single point of contact for the package. This requires not only tight integration between the organization's internal processes and channels, but with the business partners as well. After all, why would a customer purchase a package of services from a single provider if they must contact individual business partners for customer service on the various components of the package? The enterprise gateway is not only the interface between the organization and the customer, but between the organization and the business partners as well.

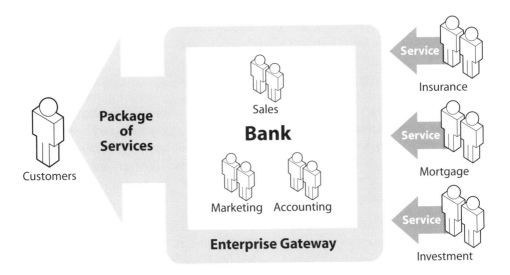

In order to provide the kinds of services customers expect from the enterprise gateway, business processes must be integrated not only across channels, but also across departments and business units. This requires application silos and organizations to provide standard service interfaces to the entire enterprise, so that all business processes may leverage these services. Much of this integration will begin at the enterprise gateway layer of the IT infrastructure, but will move down into the application infrastructure layer as the need for application integration spreads across the user base.

Designing services at the enterprise gateway layer that have appropriate interfaces and granularity requires knowledge of what the customer really wants and needs, rather than what management thinks the customer should have. These interfaces should provide a standardized view of the entire organization, while the underlying implementation remains specific to the IT environment and leverages the organization's differentiators and prior investments. This interface design philosophy can be thought of as an outside-in approach; it takes a holistic view of the services provided by the organization and its business partners and specifies an interface that is appropriate to the customer's view, looking in from the outside.

Although many organizations have customer-facing services already in place, few are providing a single view of the organization. An essential part of the enterprise gateway is this combined, holistic view. Where multiple customer-facing services exist and overlap, they should be merged into a single logical interface. Channel integration will both enable and demand this migration to a single interface, but the efforts are independent of each other.

Integration with Back-End Systems

In order to provide a single, seamless interface to the entire organization, the enterprise gateway must be integrated with the back-end systems. This is a primary goal of Service Oriented Architecture. The enterprise gateway utilizes business services provided by the application infrastructure layer, just as the application infrastructure layer utilizes foundation services provided by the technical infrastructure layer.

Another important integration function of the enterprise gateway is to adapt the various and overlapping application domains responsible for the various channels within the organization into a single, logical interface that crosses channel boundaries. Connecting the CRM, inventory, order tracking, and manufacturing systems so that the customer can easily navigate between these application domains without being aware of the boundary is often a necessary part of providing that single face to the customer and being easy to do business with.

Customized User Experience

The customer's interface into the enterprise must not only be a seamless view of the entire organization, but must also take into account everything that is known about the customer, as well as the customer's individual preferences. The ability for each customer to create his or her own composite portal application by aggregating information of personal interest is becoming more prevalent. The companies that are able to accomplish this personalized aggregation provide a valuable service to their customers and are differentiated from their competition. As the enterprise gateway becomes a commodity technology, companies that fail to implement this level of customization might ultimately fail as companies.

In order to provide this level of customization, all information related to a customer, such as who the customer is and what they do must be available to the enterprise gateway. This means that the applications in each channel must expose accurate, real-time information via business services, so that the enterprise gateway can leverage these services to provide a highly targeted user experience. This level of agility also provides important opportunities for up, down and cross-selling services to a customer based on their buying habits and needs.

Personalizing the experience for employees based on their roles and responsibilities within an organization allows them to be more productive for the organization, since relevant information is targeted toward that employee based on who he is and what he does.

This level of service need not be free, especially for companies that are "first to market" with these innovations. Services provided by the enterprise gateway and utilized by a customer may be billed to the customer on a per transaction or subscription basis. Corporate customers may be charged licensing fees to gain access to the services of the enterprise gateway. Online retailers may take the approach of becoming a reseller, by providing a better online shopping experience than other retailers can provide themselves. Amazon is a great example of this strategy. Amazon is able to leverage their highly customizable and personalized online shopping platform to generate new revenue streams by exposing the back-end functionality to business partners as services.

The ultimate goal is to allow customers to create their own specific business processes out of the services provided by the enterprise gateway. This ability turns the entire enterprise into a highly customizable set of services, while automation eliminates the cost normally associated with this level of customization. By giving customers access to the basic services provided by the organization and allowing them to create their own aggregate business processes, the organization is allowing the customer demand to drive the business, which ultimately means the customer gets exactly what he or she wants and will have no need to look anywhere else.

Self-Service

The ability for customers, employees, and business partners to access the business services provided by the enterprise gateway whenever and however they want is an important part of the value proposition for the enterprise gateway. Not only are the customers, employees, and business partners empowered to access these services, but the inherent automation provided by the enterprise gateway and the underlying Service Oriented Architecture mean that the services are provided at much lower cost to the organization, allowing resources to be reallocated to higher ROI activities and turning clerical positions into knowledge workers.

The need for the enterprise gateway services to be available 24 by 7 by 52 means that the underlying Service Oriented Architecture must be redundant and fault tolerant, and the technical infrastructure it is built upon must be highly available and self healing. The days when users could be given a message that the services they were requesting were temporarily unavailable due to scheduled system maintenance are quickly vanishing. A company that can't provide services nearly 100% of the time will be eclipsed by ones that can.

A consistent user experience is even more important in the context of self service. No matter whether he or she is accessing their information via the Web, a call center, or at a retail location, the user should get the same information at any given time. The identifying attributes of the customer are also important – if the website allows the user to set up a login ID and password, then the call center should ask for that information, rather than a cumbersome account number. This common user experience applies to services that are part of different business processes as well as those that cross channels.

As mentioned before, it is important that the design and definition of the service interfaces be appropriate to the needs of the service consumers. For the enterprise gateway, this means coarse-grained, industry standard interfaces to complete business processes that cross channels, departments, business units, and even organizations.

Real-Time Business

There are significant benefits to be gained from moving business processes from a manual data collection and reporting model that provides feedback on a monthly or quarterly basis to one that operates in real time. These benefits include increased agility and responsiveness to changing market conditions. The paper "Real Time Enterprises: A Continuous Migration Approach" by Vinod Khosla and Murugan Pal explores these benefits and also details an approach for achieving a real-time enterprise. This paper is included in the supplemental material of this book.

Integrating applications using real-time interfaces is preferable in a Service Oriented Architecture to those that are not real time, though there are still situations when the latter is a better choice. The emphasis is on total access to the entire state of the organization at any time and from any interface. Traditional batch-oriented processing systems are inherently limited in their ability to provide real-time access to information. Over time, more responsive information processing models will replace, or in some cases already have replaced, batch processing.

Agile Business

Business process agility is *the* primary goal of the modern IT organization. To meet this goal, the enterprise gateway should provide access to a foundation of business services that can be easily reconfigured to support the ever-changing business processes. This reconfiguration of business services must be completed in real time without modifying the underlying services or interrupting the supported business processes. Initially, this reconfiguration will be the domain of business analysts and managers, but as the business achieves higher levels of agility through improved services, more and more stakeholders will be able to create their own customized business processes, including business partners and even customers.

Services are the enabling technology for business agility. Because services are independent of each other and use industry standard, cross-platform protocols they can be easily plugged into new business processes and their data can be easily transformed into appropriate structures based on their usage. Without the loose-coupling that services provide, business processes become rigid and difficult to change without significant development effort.

Customers and competition are two major drivers of the change that necessitates business process agility, but they are not the only ones. Regulatory changes are drivers as well, calling for the adoption and integration of strategic applications to fulfill newly imposed requirements. Mergers and acquisitions drive change, as overlapping systems are incorporated into the existing IT environment. An SOA with well-defined interfaces can provide a mechanism for the retirement of redundant applications while minimizing impact to the rest of the IT environment.

Arguably the most important reason for creating agile business processes via an SOA is to enable business process outsourcing. By defining a clean interface to a service and decoupling it from the rest of the IT environment, that service can be easily outsourced. In an outsourcing model, a different organization provides an alternative implementation of the same service interface at a lower cost. This allows organizations to focus on those business services that are vital to their core business model while letting other companies provide the less-critical services.

Composite Applications

Although the enterprise gateway layer contains applications, they are fundamentally different from the applications that make up the application infrastructure layer. The applications in the application infrastructure layer provide the basic business services for the enterprise, while the applications in the enterprise gateway layer combine those fundamental business services into business processes.

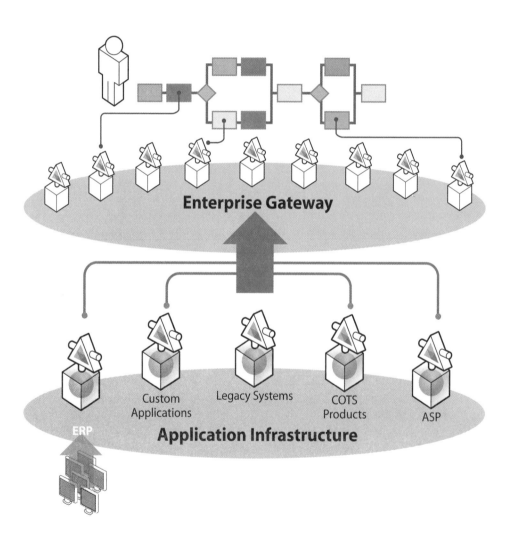

All of the applications in the enterprise gateway layer are composite applications – aggregating business services provided by applications in the application infrastructure. Application development, when applied to enterprise gateway applications, is more appropriately referred to as "Application Assembly," since composite applications are assembled from parts of other applications through service interfaces.

There are several types of composite applications that make up the enterprise gateway. We will look at each in more detail.

Business Process Management

The capability to easily assemble business services into business processes without undertaking complex development projects requires a platform for designing, deploying, managing, monitoring, and maintaining business processes.

Before the creation of the first general purpose spreadsheet program, business people who wished to analyze and summarize data in IT systems were required to request a report generation program from IT and wait for the project to be prioritized and implemented. Once it was complete, changes to the report required another iteration of IT involvement. The spreadsheet allowed business users to create *adhoc* analysis programs and generate reports without the intervention of IT, and greatly improved the effectiveness of many knowledge workers. The next big step in this evolutionary process will enable business users to create and maintain entire business processes without relying on IT.

In order to allow knowledge workers to interact with the Business Process Management (BPM) platform, a set of tools must be provided that allows the business analysts to assemble business processes from the application services, in a form that they are comfortable with. Most BPM platforms implement this business process design tool using some form of graphical editor to lay out the flow of information between services. Microsoft BizTalk™, for example, can utilize graphical models created in Visio to create and maintain its orchestrations.

Business process automation can be accomplished in a custom manner, though this approach will not allow the business process owner to define and maintain the business processes, which is far more efficient than having the development teams do it on their behalf. The highest return on investment will usually be achieved through the use of business process automation products from various vendors. These products are fairly mature and can leverage the services provided by the application infrastructure even when the applications are from a variety of disparate platforms and technologies.

Human workflow is an important part of BPM. Although the goal of process automation is to minimize the necessity for people to execute the business processes, this is only a goal and will never be fully achievable. Even highly automated business processes can have exception scenarios where a person must make a judgment call on how to proceed. The ability of the BPM platform to include elements of human workflow into business processes is necessary to allow this type of processing.

In a heterogeneous environment with many applications on various platforms and from multiple vendors, it is inevitable that the services provided by different applications will have different ways of expressing the fundamental data entities of the enterprise. In order to assemble services with different data structures into cohesive business processes, the BPM platform must provide transformation capabilities to map one data structure onto another.

In addition to the different data structures defined by applications for common entities, different communication protocols are also likely used for integration. Some applications may utilize application programming interfaces, while others might utilize EDI. Interfacing with all of the necessary communication protocols requires support for adapters. Most BPM platforms will come with a number of adapters already written, and they should always include the ability for the organization's IT department to write their own custom adapters using a framework provided by the BPM platform.

Even simple business processes often include decision points where the process can take one or more paths based on the context. Often these different paths will involve different sets of applications and services, which require the BPM platform to route messages to different parts of the application infrastructure. As business processes become more automated and their complexity increases accordingly, the need to support complex routing scenarios grows as well.

The process of approving a potential renter, for example, begins with the potential renter submitting an application to move into an apartment. The application initiates three different checks that run concurrently, a criminal background check, a credit history check, and a residence history check. The criminal check is usually a manual process, while the other two are automated. When all three processes complete, the results are evaluated.

Another aspect of business processes that should be accessible to business oriented users are the business rules. These rules are ideally specified in some natural language format, utilizing a vocabulary that is mapped to the underlying data structures by the developers. Business users can then make use of this vocabulary to create and maintain the business rules without additional development.

In order to enable the real-time enterprise, the business processes must expose status information to higher level monitoring applications such as dashboards. The BPM platform should provide robust business activity monitoring features.

Dashboards

Knowledge workers need access to information related to business activity in order to fine-tune the organization on an ongoing basis. The transformation to a real-time enterprise creates a need for real-time business activity monitoring, where data is communicated in minutes rather than weeks, months, or quarters.

Dashboards are composite applications that consume information from business activity monitoring services and communicate the information to knowledge workers and other decision makers in real time and in a format that is easily understood. This combines the attributes of customization with the ability to aggregate information from back-end systems, yielding a day-by-day or even minute-by-minute view of the information that particular managers are responsible for tracking and optimizing. The ability to change the metrics monitored and the way they are calculated and communicated is an important aspect of dashboards, as enterprises change their service offerings to remain competitive.

Enterprise Portal

The enterprise portal is the single point of entry to the organization's systems for all human users, both internal to the company and external. It is the electronic face of the company. The users of the enterprise portal can be broadly categorized into three groups: customers, partners, and employees.

Customers use the enterprise portal to interact with the organization. They expect that the enterprise portal will reflect the same information and functions available through other channels, such as through the telephone and at the organization's physical presence.

The most important function that customers should be able to perform using the enterprise portal is shopping for goods and services. After all, that is what the customer's relationship with the enterprise is based on. The ability to perform comparisons of product features and prices, service offering packages and associated pricing models, and even to compare these to products and services offered by competitors will enhance the shopping experience and build customer loyalty. Channel integration is very important to the shopping experience; the ability to determine whether or not an item is in stock in a local store before traveling there, calling the store, or requesting home delivery require high levels of integration between the enterprise portal and back-end systems.

Once the customer has decided on a product or service, they should be able to purchase it with a minimal amount of effort. If the purchasing process is inefficient or cumbersome, the customer may abandon the purchase all together. Channel integration is again important; customers increasingly want to utilize the enterprise portal to reduce the amount of time spent in a physical store shopping for an item, looking for a sales associate, and waiting in line.

In the event of an online purchase that will be shipped, the customer expects visibility into the fulfillment process via the enterprise portal. They would like to know what state their order is in, when it is expected to arrive, and what conditions may cause its delivery to be delayed. They would also like to have input into the fulfillment process, so that they can help the organization make informed decisions based on the customer's needs. All these functions require the enterprise portal to have real-time integration with the systems that comprise the fulfillment business process.

Customer service functions are a big part of the enterprise portal, and enabling the customer to access them in a self-service manner increases customer satisfaction while simultaneously decreasing costs for the enterprise. Offering support manuals and other documentation is a bare minimum; problem diagnostic tools, updates and recall information, frequently asked questions and answers, and problem reporting are becoming a necessity for a competitive enterprise. The customer support functions of the enterprise portal should offer help in this context; through integration with the customer relationship management system, the enterprise portal can both track the interactions with the customer and leverage that information to provide a customized service experience.

Customers want the ability to access and maintain the information the organization stores about them. Account maintenance functions are an important part of the enterprise portal from the customer's perspective. Contact information, products and service preferences and interests, and privacy and marketing preferences should all be maintainable by the customer in a self-service manner.

Though some of the services customers want from the enterprise portal are also appropriate for partners, there are several functions required by partners over and above what customers need. Others are provided in a different scale, since business partners will typically interact with the enterprise portal in a more strategic way than customers.

Business partners that are also customers will want a more robust interface into the order entry system. They will require the ability to create larger orders and manage more detailed configuration and logistic options. Partners will also require a higher level of visibility into the fulfillment and invoicing processes.

Suppliers will want high visibility into sales forecasts and manufacturing schedules, so that they can plan for the needs of the enterprise.

Resellers of the organization's products and services need complex portfolio management functions in the enterprise portal. They may also need to re-brand some customer-facing services offered by the enterprise portal so that they can package them into their own enterprise portal.

Allowing employees to perform self-service functions via the enterprise portal increases productivity and access to information. Human resources functions are a key part of the employee services offered by the enterprise portal, and they can lead to significant cost savings in the human resources budgets, especially in the area of benefits maintenance.

Training is another important service the enterprise portal provides to employees. Training can take the form of documentation, instructional videos and presentations, and interactive courses. An employee's progress through training programs can also be tracked via the enterprise portal, providing an important feedback loop into the performance appraisal and career development processes.

The ability of an enterprise portal to provide a unified face to the workforce of a disparate company should not be underestimated. An employee portal can be an important communication channel and unifying force, something that is especially important to large organizations that are geographically dispersed, as well as companies that have grown through mergers and acquisitions. The enterprise portal can be a unifying force that benefits the company by increasing productivity.

Portal applications are composite applications by design and are natural consumers of services. Once an SOA is adopted, enterprise portals will achieve ever higher levels of customization for specific users and communities, while requiring fewer development resources. SOAs are tremendous enablers of enterprise portal and business dashboard applications. "Chapter 6: Leveraging the Application Infrastructure" will go into greater detail on how enterprise portals can leverage the power of an SOA to achieve the goals outlined here.

Portals serve as a host environment for different types of client applications. In addition to fully integrated portal applications, portals can also host smart clients.

Smart Clients: Running your Business with Microsoft Office™

Smart client (n) *Definition:* Smart clients are easily deployed and managed client applications that provide an adaptive, responsive and rich interactive experience by leveraging local resources and intelligently connecting to distributed data sources.[6]

Smart clients are applications that solve some broad set of use cases in a generic way. Microsoft Excel™, for example, is a generic application for performing many types of calculations on numeric data in a broad range of formats and structures. These applications are heavily utilized by information workers, many of whom perform all of their job responsibilities using these applications.

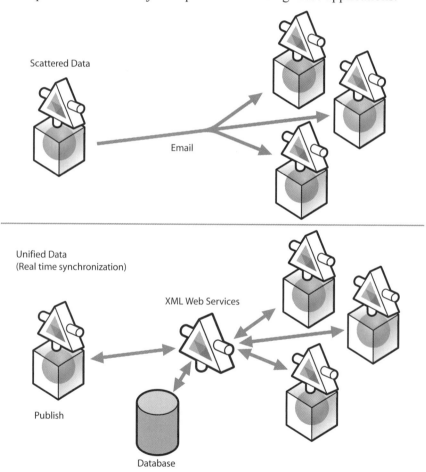

These applications provide much more than just the rendering capability of a Web browser, but they do not contain logic that is part of the business application. Instead, they contain logic that is specific to a particular class of task, such as composing a document, filling out a form, working with e-mail, or performing calculations on numbers. These smart clients are usually part of an office suite. Smart clients can be part of a workflow application implemented using collaboration tools, or they can implement the user interface of a specific business application by leveraging the services provided by the application infrastructure layer.

The biggest drawback of these types of applications in the past has been that they create islands of information by storing the results of the information worker's efforts in flat files in the file system, making it extremely difficult to access in an enterprise-wide fashion. Often the information locked in these data islands is also stored in the corporation's back-end systems, meaning that the files created by the smart clients represent a snapshot of the data and must be manually synchronized with the corporate data store by the information worker. This is clearly not the best use of time for these typically highly compensated employees.

As enterprise systems are exposed in a Service Oriented Architecture, smart clients are able to access the corporate data directly via services. This eliminates data islands by storing the results of an information worker's efforts in the corporate data stores rather than flat files on a hard drive somewhere. Furthermore, it eliminates the need for the information worker to manually synchronize the smart clients with the enterprise systems by enabling the smart client applications to do this automatically.

The generic nature of smart clients enables a tremendous amount of customization by information workers (i.e., the users themselves). There have been many efforts over the years to put the power of computer programming into the hands of business people, but arguably the only software applications to accomplish this are smart clients. By connecting these powerful applications to back-end systems, applications can be easily created for small groups of information workers, even for individuals. Traditional software development would be too costly to provide these highly specialized use cases to small user communities, but smart clients connected to a Service Oriented Architecture enable the users themselves to create the applications with a positive return on investment.

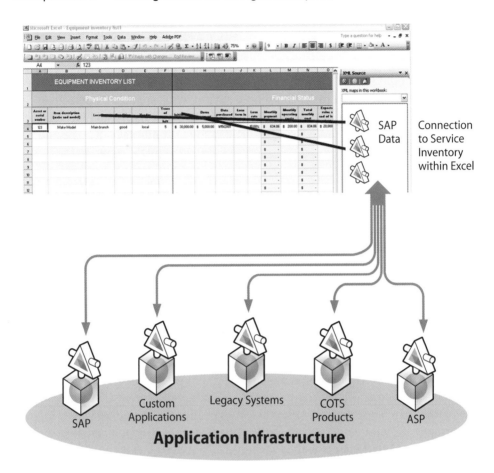

The ability for end users to customize their applications to this degree is not always desirable. In some cases it may be necessary to implement a degree of governance over the modifications that are allowed to smart client applications. In certain scenarios it may be beneficial to separate the smart client application designer role (e.g., the person who creates the spreadsheet template and connects it to the SOA) from the end user role, who can only use the application as defined by the designer.

These smart client applications are typically stored as documents that are understood and executed by their associated smart client. Managing these documents, which are essentially applications themselves, can get out of control in the same way that the data islands do. It is essential that the organization implement a document repository for these applications, and that the document repository be integrated into the enterprise portal, providing the information workers with the essential tools of version control, collaboration, and security.

Mobile Devices

Another important platform for smart clients is mobile devices. These devices continue to gain more capabilities and connectivity to public and corporate networks. Exposing back-end systems via a Service Oriented Architecture enables the use of these mobile devices to accomplish essential job functions from the field. Moving the process steps closer to the time and place of the real world events that initiate them creates greater efficiencies, improving access to information and further enabling a real-time enterprise.

Personal Digital Assistants have been around for a while now, but only recently have they gained the capabilities necessary to make them powerful clients for an IT environment built using a Service Oriented Architecture. Modern PDAs have multiple modes of connectivity, including digital cell phone networks and WiFi as well as through docking stations connected to laptops or desktops. Application development frameworks for PDAs, such as J2ME and the .NET Compact Framework are now capable of hosting moderately complex applications. These devices can provide a custom interface geared toward the limited display and input capabilities of the device but built on the same services as other clients.

Cell phones have also become important tools for mobile professionals, though their integration into the overall IT infrastructure still leaves a lot to be desired. As the cell phone and PDA continue to converge and voice over IP becomes more prevalent, higher levels of integration will be possible, and the cell phone will become a first-class citizen of the organization, accessing corporate applications in real time from anywhere on the globe.

One area where cell phones, pagers, and PDAs are already being utilized in the overall IT environment is to deliver notifications to mobile users of important events in ongoing business processes that need to be addressed. In this way these devices have become part of the overall workflow in many organizations. Further advancements, including improvements in device capabilities, voice response systems and connectivity will ensure the place of these devices in the enterprise gateway layer.

Laptops are, of course, important clients in IT environments today. Since these machines have most or all of the capabilities of desktop workstations with the added benefit of mobility, they are replacing desktops for many mobile workers. Though the sometimes-connected model presents challenges for applications developed for laptops, the use of business services to implement business logic, coupled with smart client applications and the capability to cache data for off line use, mean that some applications can be implemented in a manner that transitions seamlessly between a connected state and a disconnected state.

Tablet PCs are becoming more functional as improvements in handwriting recognition and display technology make the technology less intrusive. Form-based applications for tablet PCs can utilize the same application services as their keyboard and mouse-based cousins, saving the application development organization the added development effort of reimplementing the business logic for each device. Some data entry frameworks even allow the same form to be used on a tablet as on a regular laptop or desktop computer. Applications that require the storage and access of digital ink, such as captured signatures, should provide business services to allow tablets to store this type of data, as well as services for retrieving the images from other contexts.

An emerging type of input device couples a digital pen with micro-encoded paper, allowing the user to write on the paper, then later dock the pen and upload the captured information to back-end business services, where it can be stored in the corporate information systems. Advanced printing technologies allow forms to be generated with pre-populated information, which can then be added to using a digital pen. When the pen is docked again, the additional captured information is automatically associated with the correct printed form, based on a micro-coded serial number on the form that is read by the pen. One example of the use of this technology is HP's Forms Automation System for the healthcare industry:

"It's more easy, convenient and mobile, and is transparent for doctors using the technology," Bertrand Houyvet, the system's worldwide product marketing manager at HP told E-Health Insider. "Information is updated into the system and put into the patient file."

"You record the strokes coming from your own writing, and what you get out of it is an XML file. You can use that to build an image and create a PDF, or you can get the data and take information from the handwriting."

The pen works by reading tiny 'points' on forms printed out on standard office paper by the software, and taking these points as cues for each of the individual data fields. Rather than scanning the data, the pen remembers each stroke as well as pressure and speed; data for up to 200 forms can be stored in one pen. Software which comes in the HP digital pen & paper suite then deciphers the data, uploaded through the USB port, into a useable format.

Existing known data about a patient, such as ID numbers or names and addresses, can be pre-printed on the forms, which work on standard office paper.[7]

Even more futuristic devices are undoubtedly already in the research and development labs of technology companies. Corporations that adopt a Service Oriented Architecture are preparing for the unknown, by providing a framework for accessing their application infrastructure from a wide variety of devices and applications in a loosely coupled, easily maintainable manner.

Partner Integration Hub

The ability to link business partners to back-end systems can provide tremendous ROI through more efficient integration and automation of business processes that cross organizational boundaries. Business partners have a formalized relationship, which results in a significant volume of exchange. This kind of relationship is a natural opportunity to leverage an SOA, but at the same time it creates some unique challenges that are not part of an organization's internal integration strategy. These challenges are addressed in the IT infrastructure by the partner integration hub. A partner integration hub exposes business services to partner organizations to facilitate integration with suppliers and consumers of the enterprise offerings. These services aggregate internal services and provide an abstract, industry standard interface to the entire IT environment for external organizations that do business with the enterprise.

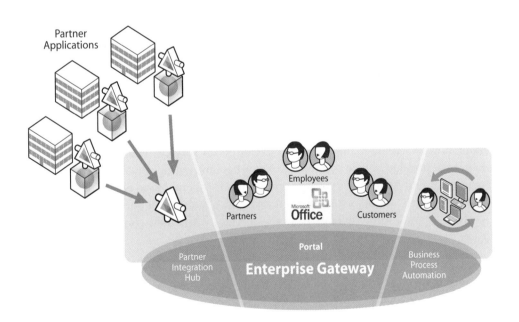

It is important that the interfaces hosted by the partner integration hub are designed in an industry standard way, if not actually implement an industry standard interface. Since these services will be utilized by multiple business partners and be part of multiple channels, they should be seen as generic in the sense that the business partners could use any number of service providers to accomplish the same thing. Although there may be some resistance to this approach because it essentially commoditizes the interfaces across an industry, it is actually the implementation of the services that have value, not the interface to them. Implementing the same service interfaces as a competitor allow business partners to easily switch between service providers, which forces organizations to compete by providing better implementations of the services. Service implementations can compete on performance, cost, reliability, flexibility, or could expose more traditional competitive advantages like inventory availability.

Some industries are already forming consortiums and alliances to define standard service interfaces across their respective industries. Most of these are still in their infancy and few are implemented yet. Companies that are out in front of this effort participating in or leading these groups are seen as thought leaders in their industry, which creates a certain amount of goodwill toward their brands. Being an early adopter of these partner integration services also means that these companies will capture market share early from their competitors, who are slower to adopt new technologies and ways of doing business. A company that is building a partner integration hub in an industry without a standards body should form one. This creates the additional competitive advantage of driving the industry toward a standard interface based on the company's implementation of a partner integration hub.

The partner integration hub can provide new revenue models for the organization in addition to the other benefits it provides. This is especially true for early adopters who will have the discretion to charge for services that competitors do not yet provide. Once service interfaces become commoditized across an industry, it will be harder to charge a premium for them due to price competition. This gives early adopters a better ROI on partner integration hubs since they will be able to garner more revenue from the services while their competitors play catch-up.

There are several ways that partner integration hubs can provide revenue. One obvious choice is by charging on a per transaction basis, essentially taxing each service invocation or each complete business process. Although this is an attractive model in many ways, it is also the most difficult to implement. Tracking service invocations is not hard, but the business processes surrounding the reconciliation of invoices for services with the associated business processes can be problematic and inefficient. An alternative to this model that is easier to implement and track but that does not directly account for usage is one based on a licensing fee or subscription. Since business partners are well known entities, they can be charged for access to the partner integration hub on a contractual basis that has little or no implementation in the gateway, other than the prerequisite authentication and authorization. The right revenue model, and even whether or not there should be any revenue, depends on the organization and the industry.

Regardless of whether or not business partners will be charged for access to the integration hub, the organization should implement a partner certification program. This program should include aspects such as training business partners in the appropriate usage of the services, verifying that the partner's systems are utilizing the services correctly, and ultimately issuing the partner credentials for the production hub. This certification program is another potential source of revenue, or at least cost recovery.

Wrap-Up

In this chapter the goals of the enterprise gateway layer were presented and examined from a business perspective. The ability of the enterprise gateway layer to meet these goals was explained.

There are various types of composite applications that make up the enterprise gateway layer, and each of these was examined in detail, including their dependencies on the layers below.

In the next chapter, the application infrastructure layer will be examined. This is where a Service Oriented Architecture and the business services that enable the existence of the enterprise gateway are implemented.

Chapter 4:   What is Application Infrastructure?

The application infrastructure layer provides the business services that run the enterprise. This is traditionally where the IT stack has provided real business value to the organization.

The applications depend upon core technology services provided by the technical infrastructure. The applications, in turn, provide business services to employees, customers and partners via the enterprise gateway and to select groups of application users via custom interfaces.

The migration to a Service Oriented Architecture breaks monolithic applications down into discrete business services and provides new levels of flexibility to the organization, enabling agile business processes that can rapidly adapt to a changing business environment.

Applications

The key components of a Service Oriented Architecture are the services themselves. Although the service interface definitions are arguably the most important part of the design of the architecture, without actual implementations of the services it remains just that, a design.

Applications are where the rubber meets the road in an SOA. They provide the business logic to fulfill the contract defined by the service interface. This role makes applications the most important components of the SOA.

Enterprises already have applications, though they may not be service-enabled. Adopting an SOA is not a rip-and-replace proposition; it is instead a leave-and-layer approach. An SOA enables an enterprise to leverage its existing investment in applications, achieving ever-greater levels of integration and customization without an associated increase in complexity and cost.

Applications are the reason that IT exists:

> ap·pli·ca·tion: n. A complete, self-contained program that performs a specific function directly for the user. This is in contrast to system software such as the operating system kernel, server processes and libraries which exist to support application programs.[8]

Modern enterprises have a mix of applications serving numerous user communities, based on various technologies, and at different stages in their lifecycle from initial inception through operation and retirement. Replacing all of these existing applications with a single new platform is neither possible nor desirable for most organizations, though the continued move to monolithic ERP systems in some industries is a notable exception to this.

The goal of an SOA is not to replace the heterogeneous computing environment already present with a homogeneous one. Rather, the goal is to service-enable the existing applications using industry standard technologies and interfaces, to weave the business services provided by all of these diverse applications and technologies into a seamless fabric that can be leveraged for application integration, and to provide new levels of agility and transparency at the enterprise gateway layer of the IT stack.

It is important to have an understanding of the landscape present in most IT shops. To do this, it is helpful to look at the different technologies and types of applications present in the application infrastructure layer from three different perspectives:

- **Application Architecture:** the internal architecture of an application determines how it fulfills its functional requirements and defines the strategy for exposing this functionality as services

- **Application Development:** whether applications are developed in-house or purchased from an outside vendor affects the strategy for migrating them to an SOA

- **Application Hosting:** where an application is deployed is an important factor in identifying the appropriate strategy for service-enablement

These discussions will not only explain the strategies for leveraging the existing investments in applications, but will also set the stage for later discussions.

Common Application Architectures

Regardless of the other attributes that categorize an application, the majority of business applications can be categorized via their internal architectural attributes into several high level architectural patterns. The architecture of an application has profound implications on how the application is deployed, utilized and maintained, and ultimately on the user experience. The application architecture also constrains the options available for exposing the application functions as services.

The common architectural patterns found in the application infrastructure layer are:

- Mainframe
- Standalone
- Client-Server
- Server-based
- Distributed Computing
- Data-centric

Each of these will be described in more detail below, along with their associated benefits and drawbacks, and strategies for service-enablement.

Mainframe

Mainframe applications, which for the purposes of this discussion include applications on midrange platforms like the IBM iSeries™, come in two basic architectural patterns, interactive and batch. Both patterns involve deploying the entire application to a single computer.

Interactive applications are those that include a user interface component, typically a character mode only interface displayed on either a dedicated terminal or on a workstation utilizing terminal emulation software. These have been around for decades and run many mission-critical systems in large organizations all over the world.

In a **batch** application, data is collected for a fixed period of time and stored in a holding area. When the collection period is complete, the application processes the batch of data and moves it through all the required phases, performing validation, updating data stores, generating reports and invoices, etc.

Interactive mainframe applications can be very effective at tasks such as data entry, where the sparse interface and centralized architecture are benefits. Because the entire application resides on the mainframe, the terminal hardware and/or software used to access the user interfaces is inexpensive.

The cost of these computers and their associated applications, although high, has already been fully depreciated in many enterprises. The applications are usually serving the business, and the business logic has been proven out over time.

The hardware supporting these applications tends to be more reliable than the more modern computing platforms, although this has changed dramatically in recent years and there is no reason to think that this will continue to be an advantage for the mainframe architecture.

Many business processes operate on a regular schedule with phases that are repeated at regular intervals. This is the kind of application at which batch processing systems excel.

There are many drawbacks to the mainframe architecture however. The development languages used on these systems are archaic by modern programming standards, and it is often difficult to identify any reusable business logic that can be leveraged by other applications. Maintenance costs are high and development cycles are long, due primarily to the low levels of code reuse, and high levels of duplication.

Although the mainframe architecture is fairly good at hosting business logic, it is poor at providing a rich user experience. The "green-screen" user interfaces require large investments in employee training and typically have a high cognitive cost associated with their use, as users struggle to remember arcane key sequences and commands.

The long development cycles typical of mainframe applications hinder progress toward the goal of an agile enterprise. Moreover, the legacy status of most mainframe applications locks the enterprise into outdated and inefficient business processes.

Mainframe applications are difficult for users to understand and utilize. They are usually designed around the way the application works, as opposed to the way the users work. These aspects impact the organization's ability to achieve the goal of transparent IT.

The ideal approach to moving a legacy environment to an agile, less costly environment will recognize the need for the user community to have enhancements developed quickly and to balance that with the need not to break the existing systems, while balancing both with the need to reduce and/or control costs.

The first step in bringing these environments into a modern SOA is to identify the business functions that they should fulfill. Defining clean service interfaces for these business functions is the next logical step in the macro process. Once these services have been identified, an approach to wrapping the legacy business logic with service interfaces must be identified. The exact wrapping approach will depend on many factors, and a series of prototypes should probably be created to evaluate several possible technology choices and select the best for the enterprise. Once the best design is determined, the core business functions of the legacy applications can be leveraged via a standard service interface.

With service interfaces in place wrapping the legacy functionality, it becomes easy and cost effective to incorporate these business services into modern applications and even in enterprise gateway applications. This will greatly increase the usability of the legacy business logic and decrease the effort associated with delivering new enhancements to the applications built on it.

In the event that the organization decides to sunset the legacy mainframe technology, the service wrappers become a key vehicle for accomplishing this in an incremental fashion with minimal impact on the rest of the IT infrastructure. As individual services are implemented by newer applications, the service interface can stay the same, making the change in the underlying implementation invisible to the applications that utilize the service. Once all of the services have been implemented on newer platforms, the mainframe can be turned off.

Stand-Alone

Though the power of networks has invaded the design of seemingly every application, there are still a few situations where stand-alone applications exist and have value for some user base.

Since these applications, by definition, are not part of the broader IT environment, their relevance to this discussion is minimal. Since they are not integrated with other applications, there is no strategy for exposing their functionality as business services. In the event that the functionality of a stand-alone application needs to be provided to a user base broader than a single user, the application should be rearchitected as a multi-user application.

Client-Server

The client-server architectural pattern utilizes two primary architectural components. A centralized server houses a database and might contain some amount of business logic. Distributed client machines contain the bulk of the application business logic, along with all of the user-interaction logic.

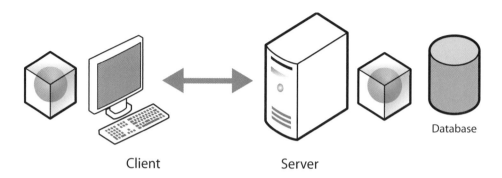

Database

Client   Server

The client-server pattern marries the rich user experience provided by the graphical user interface (GUI) found in stand-alone applications to the benefits associated with a shared data store. By utilizing a single database, users are able to work together on a business process.

This pattern suffers from a number of limitations. Because every client machine requires a software install, the deployment of the application has high cost, both initially and as new users are added and subtracted from the user base. Since most of the business logic is deployed to the client machines, it cannot be easily leveraged in services provided to other applications. The practice of including the business logic in the client with the presentation logic usually leads to a mingling of the two, which reduces maintainability and reuse of business logic.

Changes to the business process implemented by a client-server application are difficult and lengthy undertakings because the client applications contain the business logic together with the presentation logic. This has a negative impact on the agility of the enterprise.

Client-server applications typically provide a cohesive set of functions around a small number of use cases. Knowledge workers that perform multiple use cases as part of their jobs must work with several applications in an environment where the client-server application architecture pattern is prevalent. This constant context switching imposes the infrastructure on the user and violates a key tenet of transparent IT, that the technology be invisible to the users.

The challenge of service-enabling a client-server application is that the business logic, which is the primary piece of a business service, is part of the client application and usually tightly coupled to the presentation logic. In the worst case scenario, only the database of a client-server application can be utilized to service-enable the application. There are many designs that improve on this scenario though. For example, a client-server application that utilizes stored procedures with significant amounts of business logic could be service-enabled by leveraging these from a service layer. The exact approach will depend upon the design of the client-server application.

Server-Based

An alternative model to the high cost and inflexible client-server pattern is the server-based model, often referred to as the thin client model. This style of architecture is frequently seen in offerings like Salesforce.com that came along with the advent of Application Service Providers (ASPs). In this pattern, all of the business logic remains on the server and is hosted in an application server container. Presentation logic is, for the most part, deployed on a server as well, though a separate application server container is used in well-designed applications, allowing multiple service layers to leverage the same application business logic. Client machines contain a thin renderer, such as a Web browser, that is generic and can render the presentation layer of many applications.

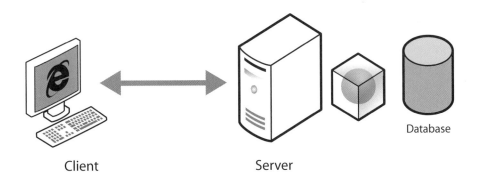

Client   Server

The server based architectural pattern solves the problem of deploying the business logic to the individual client machines. The deployment of the renderer is decoupled from the server, allowing the application to be changed more easily since only the server must be touched.

Centralizing the application logic also allows the application to scale more readily, since the server deployment can be clustered without impacting the clients.

This architectural pattern was the first to make good use of application server technology. The application teams are freed from the burden of having to implement these frameworks of services for each application by moving the responsibility for many of the application level support services out of the individual applications and into the application server and associated containers.

The biggest limitation to the server-based application architectural pattern is the renderer, although it has been addressed somewhat with recent technologies. Even the most recent versions of Web browsers cannot provide the rich user experience of a thick client, and the requirement for server-based applications to support multiple browsers means that they are often developed for the lowest common denominator.

Server-based applications contribute to the ability of the organization to become more agile. By deploying the business logic on the server, it becomes easier to make changes to the logic and deploy those changes to the production environment. Exposing the functions these applications provide as services will further this goal; they are usually the ones that are easiest to migrate to a Service Oriented Architecture.

Server-based applications are best-prepared to enable the implementation of a transparent IT infrastructure. Since all of the business logic is already implemented on centralized servers, it is relatively easy for the IT organization to monitor the application and to ensure that Service Level Agreements (SLAs) are met. Once the application functions are exposed as services, they can be easily leveraged for application integration scenarios and by the enterprise gateway layer, where they can be composed into agile business processes, accessed by smart clients, and leveraged by the partner integration hub and the enterprise portal.

Service-enabling these applications is fairly straightforward. All modern application servers support services, so the primary challenge is to identify the correct service interfaces to implement for each application. Once the service interfaces are defined, the underlying business logic already present in the applications can be re-used to implement the services.

Distributed Computing

Truly distributed applications are not common because of their high level of complexity and associated cost. These applications are deployed along functional lines to relatively large numbers of machines, often with varying capabilities and resources appropriate to the function they perform. The various functional components may be tightly coupled via communication protocols like RMI and CORBA, or they may use asynchronous messaging (which may or may not be tightly-coupled, depending on the protocols and message formats) to hand off data and requests for services.

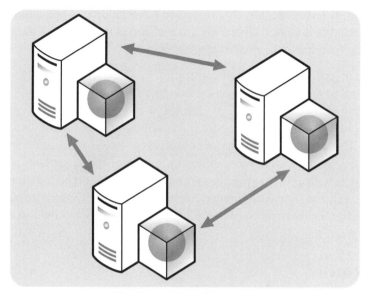

Distributed Application

This architecture is best suited for comex "systems of systems," where different computers perform different functions and have different resources available to them, appropriate to the function they perform.

Since most of the components in a typical distributed computing architecture are already servers, they have the associated benefits of server-based applications.

The communication protocols used to link together the components of a distributed computing application are brittle, costly, and proprietary. Protocols like CORBA were hailed as cross-platform, but after two decades of experience with the technology, it is clear to most that the cross-platform interoperability promised by CORBA has not and will never materialize.

These systems tend to be extremely complex. Changes to the application often ripple through the various components and outages are frequent. The tightly coupled nature of the interconnections makes the application susceptible to single points of failure and designing redundancy into the application can be extremely challenging.

The distributed computing architecture negatively impacts an organization's ability to become more agile, because the application is brittle and difficult to modify.

The brittle nature of distributed applications coupled with the prevalence of single points of failure negatively impact their availability. Applications that cannot be reliably accessed have a negative effect on the ability of the IT organization to achieve the goal of transparency.

The key to migrating a distributed application to a Service Oriented Architecture is to realize that the application can be thought of as multiple applications that are providing services to each other. The services are implemented on legacy protocols and should be ported to newer, cross-platform and interoperable standards. By treating each component as a server-based application and following the service-enablement strategies for server-based applications, an application with a distributed computing architecture can be transformed into a more reliable, Service Oriented Architecture, while simultaneously opening up the business services of the various components to the rest of the IT infrastructure.

Data-Centric

Some applications are all about the database. They typically have thin user interface layers implemented using forms technology coupled directly to the underlying database schema.

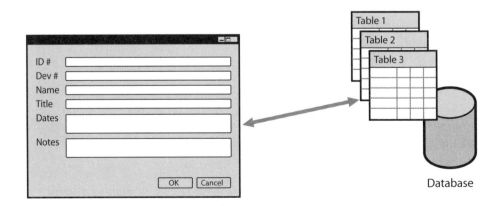

Development tools that can automatically create form-based data entry screens, search screens, and reports based on a database schema are an inexpensive way to develop such applications when there is little or no associated business logic and little need for sophistication in the user interface.

On the other hand, if the data have any real value to the enterprise, then eventually there will be a need for associated business services related to the data. When these types of applications reach this level of importance to the organization, a costly rewrite and, typically, a redesign of the database schema are necessary.

The tight coupling between the user interface and the underlying data schema makes these applications resistant to change and, therefore, impacts the organization's ability to become more agile. The lack of business logic in the application usually leads to the coupling of other applications to the data schema, which makes the entire set of applications more rigid and brittle, further restraining the organization's ability to adapt to changing business conditions.

The user interfaces generated by these types of tools reflect the design of the database rather than the needs of the users and are therefore less than transparent. It is always undesirable to try to force people to think like machines. The goals of transparent IT require that software be designed the way people want and need to use it.

The best strategy for migrating these applications to a Service Oriented Architecture is to take a step back from the data and think about what business services are involved in the various applications that access the database. Once these services are identified and service interfaces are designed, a layer of business logic should be implemented over the database, exposing the business services and hiding the underlying database schema from the rest of the IT infrastructure. The applications coupled to the database schema can then be modified to access the business services instead, preparing the entire set for the agile enterprise and transparent IT.

Application Development

Most organizations have a combination of applications developed internally and applications purchased from Independent Software Vendors (ISVs). The adoption of a Service Oriented Architecture requires different strategies for these two types of application development. It is imperative that the adoption program consider both types of applications and develop strategies for incorporating each into the overall IT infrastructure.

Custom Applications

Every organization with an IT department has some number of internally developed applications. In organizations where the industry is mature and business processes are standardized across organizational boundaries there may be very few custom applications. Other organizations may have developed everything from scratch.

Often there is a high correlation between custom application development and the ability of a company to not merely compete in its industry but to lead the industry technologically and periodically redefine the industry sector. The reason for this is obvious; if an organization is running exactly the same software as all of its competitors, IT is effectively taken out of the competitive equation. Companies then must compete in other areas of their business. This may be the best approach for some industries, where advanced technology in the area of business processes offers relatively little competitive advantage compared to other areas, such as operational scale or the availability of inexpensive resources.

The primary disadvantage of custom development is that it involves the company in activities that are not part of its core business. The fact that most enterprises have large custom development organizations reflects the immaturity of the IT industry and the degree to which IT is not yet treated as infrastructure.

The strategy for service-enabling custom applications will require the organization to either migrate the applications using internal staff, following the strategies appropriate to the application's architecture, or to engage the help of an IT consulting company. The goals of transparent IT and the importance of cleanly designed service interfaces tend to favor the use of outside resources, at least to the extent that consultants are utilized to define the architecture and to mentor the existing IT staff in the architecture and design of an agile Service Oriented Architecture.

Packaged Applications

Many organizations choose to buy commercially available "packaged" applications to run some portion of their business. These applications attempt to provide a generic core of functionality that applies to all businesses, with special add-on packages and configurations to accommodate specific industries. This level of customization is rarely sufficient to meet any company's needs, so consulting organizations offer customization services to tailor the applications to a specific business need.

For example, Enterprise Resource Planning suites are the largest of the packaged applications, encompassing such functionality as purchasing and budgeting, billing, order management, fulfillment, and revenue recognition. ERP suites provide complete soup-to-nuts systems that run the entire enterprise.

ERP suites were preceded by less ambitious packaged applications that addressed specific business areas, such as:

- Materials Requirements Planning
- Customer Relationship Management
- Supply Chain Management
- Accounting Packages
- Human Resource Management Systems

The primary benefit of packaged applications is that they are already proven out in one or more production environments, and they have been shown to work, at least to the extent that they are running existing businesses.

Rather than settle for one vendor's implementation of diverse functions that are often generalized across multiple industries, many companies take a "best-of-breed" approach to one or all of these areas. This allows an organization to achieve competitive advantage by implementing potentially more efficient business processes. The downside of this approach is, not surprisingly, the integration effort associated with marrying applications from different vendors.

One traditional argument for packaged suites is that utilizing a single vendor increases the level of integration. This high level of integration has been accomplished through tight coupling, which contributes to high development costs for the ISVs and high implementation and maintenance costs for their customers. With more and more ISVs moving to an SOA, the "tight integration" argument has much less weight, and analysts predict that a best-of-breed mix-and-match approach will become desirable and will be demanded by customers.

The use of packaged suites usually forces a company to adopt the business processes implemented by the software, rather than automating the current business processes. The business processes provided are by definition the same processes implemented at every company that purchases the suite. This has the effect of standardizing business processes across industries, nullifying any opportunity to achieve competitive advantage through business process innovation. This approach not only hinders agility, it is the opposite of an agile enterprise.

The emerging strategic solution is to not settle for a suite of applications from a single vendor but to demand that every packaged application purchased by the organization provide an open, standard service interface to most or all of the business services provided by the application. This approach allows each best-of-breed application to integrate into the organization's overall Service Oriented Architecture, where it can be integrated with the other custom and packaged applications and leveraged by the business processes and enterprise gateway.

Application Hosting

The ways that applications are hosted in a modern enterprise have an impact on how the application can be incorporated into the overall IT infrastructure and how it can be leveraged as part of a Service Oriented Architecture. There are three basic hosting strategies that are pertinent to this subject:

- Internally Hosted Applications
- Application Service Providers
- Outsourced

Each of these will be described in more detail, and strategies for integrating them into the agile enterprise will be addressed.

Internal Datacenter

Most custom applications and many packaged applications with a server component are hosted by the IT organization in one or more datacenters. These operational environments are maintained by employees of the enterprise. The hardware is in the datacenter and is either owned or leased. The networks and computers all fall under the control of the IT organization.

An obvious benefit of this arrangement is that it gives the enterprise and the IT organization ultimate control over the IT infrastructure. Changes to applications, platforms, and hardware are all options available to meet the evolving business needs of the organization.

This internal ownership is also the primary disadvantage of this approach. The core business of the enterprise is not to develop and maintain an IT infrastructure, and to the extent that these efforts and activities distract from the core business, they are a drain on the company.

Given the current state of the industry, internal hosting of custom applications can yield the highest levels of agility and transparency because it gives the enterprise's IT organization ultimate control over the evolution of the applications that facilitate the business. Many IT shops lack the ability to effectively exercise this level of control and are ineffective at executing their mission.

Application Service Providers

ASPs are companies that provide hosted software services to other companies typically accessed over the Internet. They provide the entire infrastructure surrounding the services and offer varying degrees of customization. Some are organized around vertical industry segments, while others deliver horizontal functionality across industries.

ASPs are one way to recognize the potential for transparent IT to be outsourced. By relying on a specialized infrastructure company to provide the software services required by the enterprise, resources are freed up to focus on the core business.

Selecting the right ASP can be critical. Once software services are outsourced, switching to a different ASP can be difficult unless the service interfaces are defined in a standard way and are implemented by multiple ASPs.

If ASPs have well-designed, modular service interfaces to the functionality they provide, the use of ASP-hosted services can greatly enhance the agility of an organization, allowing business services to be selected and utilized as the changing business needs of the organization dictate.

Similarly, the use of ASPs can further the goals of transparent IT. Just as more mature infrastructure industries are routinely outsourced to specialized companies, whose job it is to manage the infrastructure and ensure that it is so reliable and easy to use that it disappears, so too can ASPs make the IT infrastructure transparent to its users.

A key, if not the primary requirement, when selecting an ASP is a well-defined, industry standard service interface that can be plugged into the application infrastructure via a Service Oriented Architecture. The existence of competitive ASP offerings that implement the same service interface provides additional advantages to the organization.

Outsourced

The third option for application hosting is similar to the ASP model, except that instead of hosting services designed and implemented by the ASP, the outside entity hosts applications, whether custom or packaged, that were developed or purchased by the enterprise.

This approach combines the benefits of custom development and packaged application selection with the benefits of outsourcing the ongoing operation of the IT infrastructure. The enterprise is not limited to the services provided by an

ASP, but instead has control over the services provided without having to take responsibility for their ongoing operation and maintenance.

Although the additional control offered by this approach is a benefit, it does not relieve the IT organization from the effort necessary to design and implement the IT infrastructure.

This approach offers the potential for the highest levels of agility combined with the best opportunities for achieving high levels of transparency. It is up to the IT organization, however, to design an infrastructure capable of meeting these expectations.

Wrap-Up

This chapter has defined what makes up the application infrastructure layer and how the applications can be categorized. The benefits and drawbacks of each application style were described and strategies for leveraging each category of application were presented.

In order to achieve the levels of flexibility necessary to compete in the modern market, a Service Oriented Architecture must be adopted at the application infrastructure layer and utilized for all application integration needs. These services can then be leveraged by the enterprise gateway layer to provide even greater business value to the organization. In order to accomplish these goals, the application infrastructure must be built on a solid foundation. This foundational layer, the technical infrastructure, will be addressed in the next chapter.

Chapter 5:   What is Technical Infrastructure?

The technical infrastructure layer is the foundation of the IT stack. The layers above depend on basic services provided by the technical infrastructure.

Technical infrastructure provides no business value to the enterprise by itself; it consists of enabling technologies that form a fundamental foundation for business applications.

Foundation

The importance of a solid, well-designed and flexible technical infrastructure to the creation of an agile enterprise, the successful adoption of a Service Oriented Architecture, and to achieving the goals of a transparent IT cannot be overstated. Services are layered over and depend on a company's technical infrastructure. A weak, inflexible, brittle infrastructure will hobble an SOA before it's out of the gate. A strong infrastructure will form the foundation that a strong SOA can be built upon. More details on how the technical infrastructure services should be utilized by the application infrastructure layer are covered in "Chapter 8: Leveraging the Technical Infrastructure."

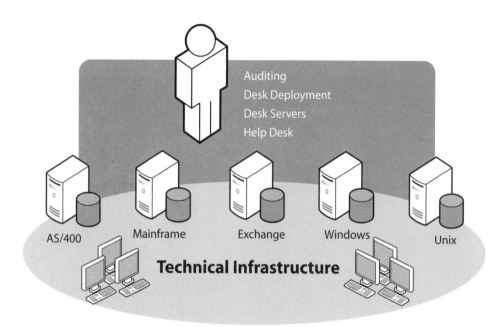

In this chapter the components of the foundational layer will be examined in more detail. These include:

- Computers

- Networks

- Identity Management

- Databases

- Application Servers

- Collaboration Tools

In addition to these foundational services that the technical infrastructure provides to the layers above, the management aspects of the technical infrastructure will also be discussed, including:

- Auditing

- Deployment

- Monitoring

- Project Management

- Help Desk

Computers

The most fundamental building blocks of the technical infrastructure layer are computers. The invention of the general purpose computing machine created the myriad possibilities in today's IT landscape.

A modern IT environment consists of many different kinds of computers from many different manufacturers, with a broad range of computational capabilities, processor architectures, connectivity options, peripheral devices, and storage options. Merely keeping track of all the computer hardware that a modern enterprise possesses is a significant and ongoing undertaking.

The various computer architectures present in the enterprise typically run different versions of various operating systems from multiple vendors. Even operating systems from the same vendor are packaged for different usage models and are typically deployed at multiple release levels within a single organization. If the IT environment is expanded to include the machines and operating systems owned and operated by the business partners and customers of the enterprise, then the overall architecture becomes even more diverse.

Clearly this creates a number of challenges for any IT organization and these challenges are constantly increasing. Although some organizations attempt to decrease the complexity by "standardizing" on a single platform, this is rarely achievable and results in great effort being expended to make the chosen platform fulfill purposes for which it was never designed. Moreover, these standardization projects often lack a compelling business case and ROI model and, therefore, should not be undertaken.

The needs of the modern enterprise and the demands placed on the technical infrastructure are such that a heterogeneous environment of specialized machines and platforms is a requirement. No single platform can meet all the needs of an enterprise of any significant size, and even if it could, the likelihood that the organization will never acquire or be acquired by a company with different platforms is so low that it is negligible. The goal of the IT organization should be to choose the right solution for each business need and to foster an environment where different platforms can interoperate easily, efficiently, and cost effectively.

Computers provide the hardware on which the applications that implement the business services execute. Without a solid computing infrastructure, the ability to build an agile enterprise that leverages a Service Oriented Architecture will be compromised.

Networks

Before there were networks, there were computers. Integration was not an issue because each computer was an island. Tight coupling was the obvious way to accomplish anything -- applications were written for a particular machine and interacted with the other applications on that machine, assuming that the hardware was dedicated, which it often was.

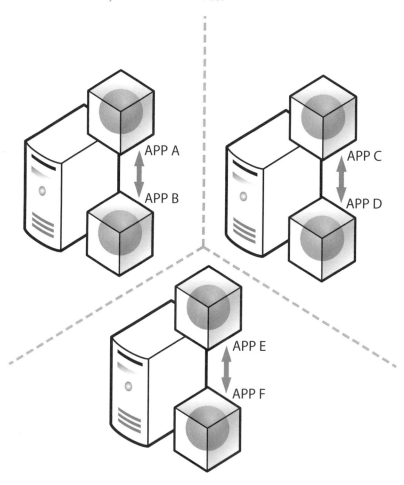

When computers were isolated in this way, life was comparatively easy for the IT architect. There was only one computer, one operating system, one architecture, no interoperability, no security (other than physical), and certainly no cross-platform integration headaches.

Connecting computers together using networks enabled many economies of scale. Data stored on one machine could be accessed by programs on another machine. The sharing of data, for a long time, was the primary usage of networks. Data sharing is a brittle interface, though, because historically structured data formats have been rigid, nonextensible, and nonportable. Changes to the underlying data format caused ripple effects among all the machines and programs accessing that data.

It can be argued relatively easily that the vast majority of machines in any organization are underutilized. Although some midrange and mainframe systems regularly handle loads greater than 60% of their capacity on an ongoing basis, many more machines are rarely if ever utilized to anywhere near their optimum capacity. The target utilization for a given machine will ultimately depend upon its role within the technical infrastructure and the quality of service agreements it is bound by, but often the hardware deployed is underutilized, and this excess capacity represents inefficiency within the IT infrastructure. Networks do not solve this problem, but they offer a mechanism for addressing it, since they enable work that can be performed in parallel to be distributed among multiple machines. This is the essence of distributed computing.

In order for a distributed application to perform its functions, the various components on different machines must communicate with each other via the network. Many communication protocols have been developed over the history of distributed computing, but until recently they all suffered from the same brittle interface attributes as data sharing. Most have the additional requirement that the platforms, for the most part, be homogeneous.

In distributed computing, the deployment of the application components across networked machines is typically static. Each machine is assigned a portion of the processing burden based on some form of functional decomposition. The number and function of the machines is stable. Although this method of achieving parallel processing can take advantage of multiple machines, it lacks the flexibility to adapt to changing processing requirements and the availability of additional processing resources.

Grid computing attempts to resolve this limitation of distributed computing by distributing the same functionality to a dynamically configured network of computers. Although it has provided an effective method to distribute the processing, grid computing is still very limited in what applications it supports and doesn't always optimally leverage computing resources. Grid computing also requires a monitoring and distribution agent whose purpose is to manage the distribution of processing across the grid, but does not contribute to the basic functionality of the application.

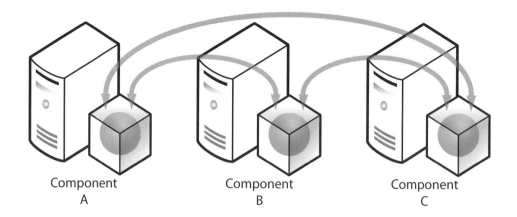

Component   Component   Component
A   B   C

All of these mechanisms have attempted to solve the same problem; how does an organization make greater use of the processing resources available to accomplish more work?

Sun's trademarked tagline is "the network is the computer."[9] This sums up the ultimate goal of an SOA; create an environment where users can treat the pool of available computing resources as a collection of business services, without regard to what machines are fulfilling each service, how they go about doing it, or what underlying resources are currently available to fulfill the services.

The network is a key enabling piece of an SOA. It is what allows applications to access services that are implemented by other applications, which is the basis for service oriented application integration. Similarly it allows the components of the enterprise gateway to access the business services implemented in the application infrastructure and, thereby, creates the opportunities for building an agile enterprise with a transparent IT infrastructure.

An organization's technical infrastructure includes many highly complex components related to the network, including:

- Basic network layout and architecture

- Network configuration

- Routing schemes between the machines on the network

- Management of the bandwidth and capacity utilization

- Network load balancing and fail-over between redundant machines

- Contingency and disaster recovery planning

For the purposes of this book, it is enough to say that all of these and more must be addressed in order to implement a robust, flexible, maintainable, and scalable network environment upon which an agile Service Oriented Architecture can be built.

Identity Management

Identity management is one piece of the technical infrastructure that is critical to the implementation of the entire IT stack, as well as the goals of an agile enterprise and a transparent IT infrastructure. The platforms and utilities of the technical infrastructure layer, the applications in the application infrastructure layer, and the composite applications in the enterprise gateway layer all require a common repository for the management of identities, credentials, and authorizations in order to ensure that people and applications are allowed to perform specific functions. Without this piece of infrastructure, securing services will be overly complex, or, worse, security will be compromised.

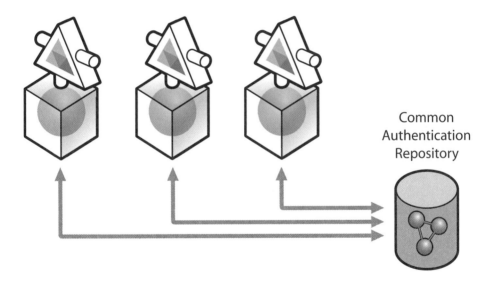

Common
Authentication
Repository

Though authentication mechanisms are necessary, they are insufficient to adequately secure an SOA by themselves. The capability to assign roles to various applications, and to secure services so that they may only be invoked by applications in the appropriate role, is also necessary. This is commonly known as authorization and is the keystone of role-based security, also necessary for the success of an SOA. It is imperative that the infrastructure underlying an

SOA include a common framework for authorization of service invocations. It is also important that the infrastructure address the scope of roles — whether a common set of roles will be used across all applications or whether there will be intermediaries and/or role transformation mechanisms.

When an SOA spans multiple enterprises, a federated identity management infrastructure is required in order to avoid the complexities of replicated repositories. Rather than relying on a single master repository and replication, federated systems allow authentication and authorization data to reside in multiple, peer-to-peer repositories in a trusted network.

Since a primary function of the authentication and authorization infrastructure that supports an SOA is to authenticate applications to one another, a Public Key Infrastructure (PKI) is usually required. The policies, tools, and software components required to implement an effective and secure PKI are far from trivial, and must be carefully thought out and planned in order to provide a secure foundation for the entire IT infrastructure stack.

Databases

Every business is an information business and information is distilled from data. Without data, applications can provide nothing more than transient utility to the business, like calculators or clocks. In order for data to be useful, they must be stored in a manner useful to applications.

Databases provide, first and foremost, a means of storing data over relatively long periods of time, even when the machines are not operating. This form of storage is often referred to as "persistent storage," because the data persist over time. The simplest forms of databases are files, which may provide only the attribute of persistence. Files are, without a doubt, the most common form of persistent data storage.

Beyond the ability to store data for long periods of time, databases also provide structure to data. Without structure, applications could not make sense of data and storing it would not have much value. Relational databases add a formal mathematical model to the way data are structured and can manage complex relationships between large datasets.

More advanced databases provide transactional access to the underlying data ensuring that:

- Two applications do not attempt to modify a datum at the same time
- Each application gets a self-consistent view of data that are in the process

of being modified

- Related modifications are treated as a single change to the database
- Application changes are stored, or "persisted"

An important attribute of relational databases is that they are easily searchable using a standard query language. Since the relationships between data are potentially complex, the query language must be sufficiently robust to express queries that span these relationships. With all of this complexity and power comes a corresponding requirement that the databases be tuned appropriately for performance.

Broadly speaking, databases are used in two ways in most enterprises today. The most common way is as an operational data store; one that is primarily responsible for managing the data related to the ongoing business processes and the operations of the organization. The second way is as a data warehouse, where historical data are stored for purposes of analyzing trends and predicting future operational needs and potential optimizations. Even though a data warehouse typically contains data that were originally operational, the structure of the data is often quite different in the two different applications and, therefore, requires different configurations and tuning parameters.

Some more complex datasets are distributed across more than one database, with relationships spanning machines, platforms, and even database vendors. These environments require extra care from the technical infrastructure team to keep them running efficiently.

Database configuration is a complex, esoteric area of technical infrastructure that requires dedicated professionals, typically with knowledge of and specialization in a particular database product. Without proper configuration, the applications that provide services to the rest of the business may perform poorly because they cannot access the data in a timely manner. This is an area where the appropriate application of specialized skills can provide large performance benefits in high level business processes.

Although databases provide long-term storage, the hardware resources they utilize can and often do fail, potentially rendering the data inaccessible. These outages can be extremely costly to an ongoing enterprise, as the business processes that depend on the data grind to a halt, and potentially must be restarted from scratch. A properly designed backup and contingency plan appropriate to the criticality of each database will ensure that the costs of any downtime are minimized.

As e-mail and other forms of electronic communication have become more critical to the information flow of modern enterprises, the importance of electronic communication to corporate legal proceedings has increased as well. Many court cases have resulted in subpoenas of electronic communication related to various subjects. The definition and implementation of a document retention policy and the ability to recover electronically stored documents within the retention window (as well as the ability to destroy all documents outside the retention window) can mean millions of dollars to a company in legal fees and jury awards.

Data are the core of an information business — and every business is an information business. Take care that the organization's databases are designed correctly and the services that depend on them will operate efficiently and consistently, so that the knowledge workers who utilize the services are free to focus on the business processes. A solid, reliable data storage foundation is a necessity for the goals of an agile enterprise and for achieving transparent IT.

Application Servers

The supporting services upon which applications are built are another important part of an organization's technical infrastructure. Often these services are provided by the platform itself; applications that depend upon the underlying platform for basic services are sometimes referred to as "native" applications. These applications are inherently coupled to the platform and it can be difficult or impossible to deploy them to a platform other than the one for which they were written. Sometimes migrating these applications to a newer version of the same platform can be difficult, depending upon which platform they were developed for and the set of services they leverage.

In the mid to late 1990s, another layer of abstraction was introduced to alleviate the problems associated with tightly coupling applications to the underlying platform. This additional layer of abstraction, dubbed an "Application Server," provides the basic services applications require in a platform neutral manner.

A basic concept of application servers is the "container." Containers provide several of the most fundamental services that applications need, such as:

- Thread Pooling
- Component Lifecycle Management
- Transaction Management
- Database Connection Pooling

- Message Queuing

- Memory Management

- Authentication and Authorization

Application servers require complex configuration that is dependent on the applications, the deployment environment, and the state of the resources upon which the applications depend. Multiple types of containers utilized by the different types of components typically host an application, with each container designed and configured for the services required by the components it hosts and manages.

One very important benefit provided by the additional layer of abstraction that application servers and, more specifically, containers provide is a means for load balancing service requests to an application. Because the basic request dispatching logic is not in the application components themselves, the application can be effectively scaled by deploying multiple instances of the same components to an array of machines. Hardware and software load balancers can work together to manage complex deployments of machines on different platforms and with diverse processing capabilities. Machines can be added and subtracted from a production environment without taking down the services provided by the applications and without disturbing the business process utilizing them.

Another key benefit provided by application servers is the ability for a server that encounters a nonrecoverable software or hardware failure to automatically divert incoming requests to a backup server that was "waiting in the wings." This level of fail-over allows mission critical applications, and even those that are less than mission critical, to maintain a level of fault tolerance that allows the business processes dependent upon their services to continue to execute unimpeded by the failure.

The first application servers and containers that achieved widespread deployment were based on the Java platform specification and came from vendors such as IBM, Sun, and BEA. These application servers achieved a certain level of platform independence by providing a standard interface between the containers and their hosted components, allowing organizations to develop applications for one application server and later migrate to another.

Microsoft understood the value that the additional layer of abstraction the application server and container combination provided and leveraged the lessons learned from the Java camp to design a more modern and flexible application

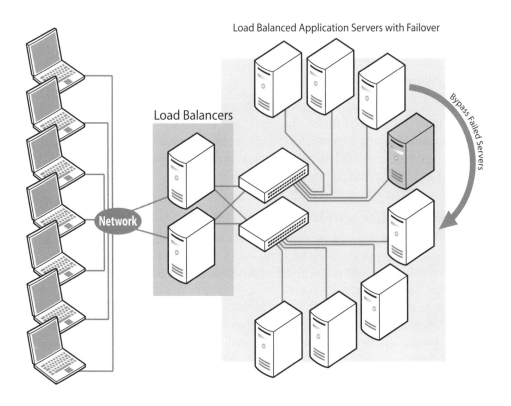

server, the .NET platform. While the .NET platform maintains all of the features and flexibility of the Java platform, it adds a couple of key features. The Java platform allows applications to be ported to multiple platforms so long as the development language is Java. Microsoft's .NET allows multiple languages to coexist within a single Windows application server and to interoperate seamlessly by providing an identical set of platform services to every language. Additionally, the .NET platform provides interoperability services with the many legacy technologies used on previous Microsoft platforms, something that is difficult or impossible to achieve on the Java platform without compromising stability and/or performance.

Services are provided by applications in the application infrastructure layer and these applications are hosted within application servers. Application servers are an essential part of the technical infrastructure for any modern IT environment. The features provided by these servers and their containers require careful and deliberate consideration by qualified specialists in order to achieve the level of reliability and flexibility needed by a robust SOA.

Collaboration Tools

Providing the fundamental and necessary tools that allow knowledge workers to collaborate is one of the most important functions of technical infrastructure. Modern organizations employ a wide array of knowledge workers in myriad capacities, with an equally diverse set of devices appropriate to their respective job requirements. All of these different types of workers need to collaborate on documents, business processes, and their associated workflows in an efficient and nonintrusive manner.

An important part of most collaboration is the ability to manage content of different media types in a way that groups logically associated information into "collaboration spaces." These electronic work areas are often *adhoc* and short lived, and they must be flexible to support the myriad types of collaboration that occur in any organization. Most of all, the content must be easy to find and easy to manage while collaborating.

It has been said that e-mail is the "killer application" for the Internet – the application that made the technology relevant. E-mail is the most common collaboration tool in use today. Most knowledge workers could not perform their basic job responsibilities without reliable access to e-mail.

The technical infrastructure components necessary to make e-mail work efficiently include the basic ability to send and receive messages and also encapsulate the long-term storage and backup of this increasingly important means of communication.

Interfaces to the identity management systems allow users to easily lookup other e-mail users and identify them as recipients of messages. This is another essential service provided by an effective electronic mail platform.

The ability to tie the e-mail system into higher level business processes by using it as a part of a human workflow process can be extremely powerful. To accomplish this successfully, the electronic mail system must be a highly available solution that the business processes can depend upon.

Meetings are a frequent occurrence in any modern organization, whether they are physical meetings in a conference room (or hallway) or virtual meetings via conference call, video conference, or Internet. Meetings provide an essential method for people to collaborate. Technical infrastructure should support this means of collaboration in several ways, including:

- Managing the use and availability of resources such as conference rooms
- Coordinating the schedules of employees so that meeting planners can

easily select times and venues when participants are available

- Supporting the use of virtual meetings by providing the necessary infrastructure components

Since meetings are a means of collaborating, the technical infrastructure should support this activity by providing a way to associate *adhoc* collaboration spaces with meetings. This allows users to access and collaborate on items such as notes, presentations, and documents associated with a meeting.

Another popular communication tool used in the workplace is instant messaging (IM). Organizations do not want sensitive conversations occurring over instant message channels hosted on the Internet by a disinterested third party. The technical infrastructure needs to support instant messaging among employees in a secure, reliable way. IM should support the ability to look up recipients in the same directory used by the other collaboration tools and should be integrated into the other collaboration tools so that instant message conversations become an inherent part of a collaboration space.

Phone calls and voice messages are another important tool used to collaborate, though they are becoming less so as other technologies become more convenient to use and better integrated into the technical infrastructure and other collaboration tools. Disruptive technologies like voice over IP have the potential to raise the relevance of telephone communication, as the technical infrastructure begins to support the integration of phone communication with the rest of the collaboration tools. Conference calls can be recorded easily and the resulting recording stored in a collaboration space for later reference. As voice mail systems become better integrated into the technical infrastructure, it should be possible to forward a voice message to a collaboration space where others can access it, as needed.

Collaboration tools are a key enabling component of the agile enterprise, allowing knowledge workers to form *adhoc* teams and respond to rapidly changing business conditions. Achieving transparency and integration between the various collaboration tools and the applications that facilitate the business will allow an organization's knowledge workers to focus on the core business processes.

Centralized Management of Technical Infrastructure

A technical infrastructure that provides the services necessary to support a modern organization in a flexible and efficient way is by definition highly complex. Managing such an environment can be challenging; managing it in a distributed manner is impossible. Without a centralized management system and organization the technical infrastructure will degrade over time. As the degradation occurs, the various pieces will break down as product versions diverge, changes are made that have unintended consequences, and finger pointing between various parts of the IT organization hamper efforts to maintain the technical infrastructure.

When any infrastructure starts to degrade, it begins to impose itself on those that depend upon it. It is difficult, if not impossible, to ignore infrastructure when it is not functioning efficiently and effectively. Most office workers, for example, can go to work in their offices every day for months without ever thinking about the heating and air conditioning system in the building. When the air conditioner stops working on a sweltering July afternoon, however, everybody in the office is suddenly thinking of nothing else but the air conditioner and very little real business is accomplished.

The technology infrastructure of the enterprise is no different. The goal of transparent IT is to make the technology disappear, so that the knowledge workers within the enterprise no longer have to think about it. In order to keep the IT infrastructure humming along smoothly, a number of mechanisms must be in place to monitor and manage it.

Auditing

In order to manage the technical infrastructure the team must know what is occurring in their environment. Everything from Personal Digital Assistants (PDAs) to servers to mainframes should be tracked within the enterprise. Not only does the status of the equipment need to be tracked, but also the current configuration and versions deployed, the licensing and ownership information, the support contracts, and the service level agreements.

Since the technical infrastructure is constantly changing, it is extremely important that the catalog of deployed components be updated as part of the purchasing, maintenance and retirement processes. Changes can and will cause problems – knowing what changed can be the difference between a problem that is easily resolved at low cost to the organization and a disaster that gets escalated to upper management.

An automatic scanning facility can provide an important backup, should the processes that maintain the technical infrastructure inventory fail. The ability to discover changes to the hardware and software deployed and report them through an exception process should be a service provided by the technical infrastructure to the support team.

Deployment

One of the most demanding challenges for the technical infrastructure team is deploying new or modified services to the technical infrastructure while minimizing the impact to the ongoing business processes and operation of the enterprise. Traditional client server systems suffer from the requirements that all of the client machines require a software install. Client software must be updated when a new version is released and usually all workstations running the application must be upgraded at the same time. Server-based, thin-client systems alleviate these requirements by deploying all of the application components to centrally managed servers, which can then be upgraded without affecting the clients. It is important to realize that most of these applications actually do have a client component, but the component is general rather than application specific and is managed on a separate release schedule from the server. This is a good example of the concept of "loose coupling."

In most technical infrastructure environments, smart clients are the most common. Managing the deployment of software to these machines, often of disparate configurations and sometimes limited connectivity, is extremely expensive to do manually. An automatic deployment system that pushes changes to the smart clients deployed can make this process manageable, efficient, and cost effective.

Application servers are often active twenty-four hours a day, seven days a week, which can make upgrading the applications deployed on them difficult. Ideally, the application server software supports hot deployment of applications, allowing new versions of components to be deployed while the application is running. Business processes already started should continue to execute on the old version while new instances of the processes should execute on the newer version. Once all of the business processes executing on the older version are complete, the older version of the application or component should be automatically removed from the server. Short of this scenario, application servers can still be upgraded in a seamless manner, though the process is more manual and time consuming for the technical infrastructure staff.

The Sarbanes-Oxley act places regulatory requirements on the deployment of applications at public companies in the United States. These requirements affect the processes, procedures, and organization of the technical infrastructure team and must be taken into account when defining these.

Another important feature of the technical infrastructure layer is the ability to deploy and maintain platform software and patches; maintain an inventory of software and hardware; and meter the use of software on all the systems in the technical infrastructure layer. Ideally this should be implemented centrally and should not require IT staff to visit every desktop and server in the enterprise. This capability is often referred to as "Zero-Touch Deployment," and is increasingly a requirement for the efficient management of the IT environment, especially in an organization of medium size or larger.

Monitoring

Knowing what is happening in the technical infrastructure at all times is crucial to managing it. All components have aspects that are valuable to monitor. Capacity utilization, for example, can tell the staff that a network segment is saturated, while application monitoring can tell them which application is using the bandwidth and authentication and authorization monitoring can tell them which users are accessing which application services. Effective network and application monitoring can provide a method to minimize downtime by proactively resolving issues before they become critical.

Trend analysis of activity can be invaluable in problem determination and resolution as well as capacity planning. The ability to correlate various types of monitor data has a multiplicative effect on the value of the data.

Components of the technical infrastructure that encounter problems or faults should report them to the centralized monitoring facility, where they enter a human workflow process for resolution. Often the ability to analyze simultaneously occurring faults in different components can point the staff to a single root cause that might not have been so obvious if each fault were analyzed in isolation.

Real-time monitoring of security attributes and performance, coupled with intrusion detection, alerting facilities and intrusion prevention can stop or limit the damage done by hackers, viruses, and disgruntled employees. The technical infrastructure should be designed in a way that provides the services for preventing intrusions and failing that for isolating compromised components, while limiting the effect on ongoing business processes.

Project Management

It requires a significant project management effort to manage the complexity necessary to provide the technical infrastructure services needed by an agile enterprise. Typically there are multiple projects in various stages of implementation with deployment and resource dependencies that cross team and even organization boundaries.

The management of changes to the technical infrastructure is an important responsibility of the project management office associated with the technical infrastructure organization. Tracking changes and their dependencies, along with their associated back-out procedures, consumes a significant portion of the project management effort.

One of the trickiest parts of project management is managing the availability of resources required for various projects and ensuring that they are available when required, while attempting to maximize the utilization of all resources. Resources from server hardware to staff with highly specialized skill sets all need to be assigned to projects at the appropriate times.

The technical infrastructure components typically come from a wide array of vendors of various sizes and types. The project management office must ensure that the licensing agreements and service level agreements are appropriate for the project, the component, the required availability, and the budget.

Help Desk

The help desk is probably the most visible and therefore most critical part of the technical infrastructure. Everyone from the CEO to the mailroom utilize the services provided by the help desk. As a result, the staff, procedures, and tools available need to reflect the criticality and high profile of this function

Problem reporting is the most obvious service provided by the help desk. It's important that the ability to report problems matches the importance of the systems that run the enterprise. A Fortune 500 company with a worldwide operational presence cannot afford to have a help desk that is only available forty hours a week.

It is important that the help desk provides multiple communication channels for reporting problems and communicating resolution status. While e-mail may be the best way for reporting some problems, it clearly will not work for reporting problems with e-mail. Likewise, a phone number is useless when the phone system is not functioning.

When problems are reported, it's important that all the relevant information is collected. It is equally important that the help desk does not waste effort and time collecting useless information. If ten people call to report that they don't have access to the Internet, how much memory is installed in their respective computers is irrelevant.

Following problem reporting, problem resolution is the next most important service provided by the help desk. A user who contacts the help desk wants his or her problem to be resolved as quickly as possible. A number of tools need to be provided to the help desk staff to enable them to provide the best service possible.

The first line of attack in problem resolution should be a database of previously reported problems and their associated resolutions. Navigating this database must be highly adaptable, so that multiple symptoms for a single problem will all refer to the same solution. It is also important that the database provide a means for determining that the problem being reported really matches an already documented solution. There are very few things in a business day more frustrating than contacting the help desk and being guided through multiple procedures, none of which resolve the problem. This hurts the credibility of the entire technical infrastructure organization.

When issues cannot be resolved by the help desk staff using the problem database, there must be a clearly defined and efficient escalation procedure. This procedure results in the appropriate resources being engaged quickly with a minimum of disruption to the organization.

In the event that a problem is associated with a purchased or licensed product, the help desk must have access to the appropriate vendor contacts in order to resolve the issue. This highlights the importance of service level agreements with vendors that are aligned with the importance of the provided component to the enterprise and its operations. For example, if the help desk is required to have a one hour response time to any critical problem reported at any time for a particular application, then any vendors providing components the application depends on must have the ability to respond within an hour, or the help desk's SLA cannot be met when the vendor's product is at issue. Just as in the other aspects of Service Oriented Architecture, the service interface defined between the organization's internal support system and the various vendors must be designed to meet the needs of the service consumer, in this case the help desk.

Custom applications are sometimes the most critical components of an organization's application infrastructure. Since the technical infrastructure help desk is the front line for production problems with custom applications, the escalation procedures must include mechanisms for contacting application teams on an emergency basis. The teams need to have service level agreements with the help desk, so that the escalation procedures can reach the appropriate technical contact in a time period appropriate for the criticality of each application.

Problems that affect large numbers of users and require some time to resolve must be managed so that the help desk is not overwhelmed with multiple reports of the same problem and requests for status updates on the resolution of the problem. A status reporting mechanism can free up resources for problem resolution that would otherwise be used for handholding.

The monitoring, auditing, and collaboration tools discussed in other sections are all important to the help desk and integration between the systems used by the help desk and these other services is critical.

Collecting problem and resolution data, along with appropriate metrics like the number of times the problem is reported and the time required to resolve it each time, is invaluable for fine-tuning the operation of the help desk and the entire technical infrastructure. Knowing that a particular vendor component fails frequently could provide the basis for a project to replace the component with a more reliable one. The real benefits of collecting these metrics are realized when the technical infrastructure organization dedicates some level of effort to performing trend analysis of it.

A Service Oriented Architecture can facilitate all of these functions by providing clean interfaces for applications to report exceptional conditions and for the help desk applications to probe the various components of the IT infrastructure to determine the root cause of any particular problem.

Wrap-Up

The components that make up the technical infrastructure are diverse and complex, and although this chapter touched on the most important ones and covered a lot of ground, this is still merely a survey of the technical infrastructure landscape. The importance of a solid foundation to the successful implementation of a service oriented application infrastructure and an enterprise gateway, all key components of an agile enterprise with a transparent IT infrastructure cannot be overstated.

This concludes Part I of this book. In these chapters a holistic framework for understanding IT as three layers of a type of infrastructure was presented and defined. These concepts will be returned to throughout the rest of this book.

In Part II, the concepts learned will be applied to integration within the IT infrastructure. Both horizontal integration (within a layer) as well as vertical integration (between the layers) will be addressed.

In the next chapter, the first in Part II, the ways in which the enterprise gateway should utilize and leverage the business services provided by the application infrastructure will be examined.

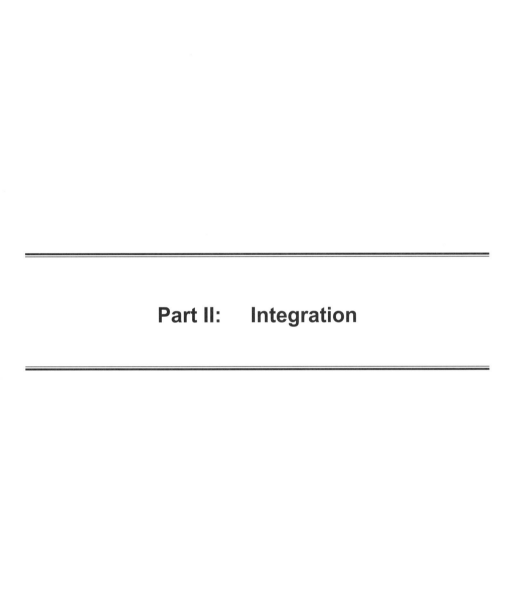

Part II: Integration

Chapter 6: Leveraging the Application Infrastructure

The business services implemented by the application infrastructure enable the creation of agile business processes, high-value composite applications, business partner integration hubs, management dashboards and complex application integration scenarios.

Leveraging these services in appropriate ways can yield market-changing efficiency and agility.

Best Practices for Application Integration

Integrating applications on disparate platforms in a loosely coupled, easily maintainable fashion has been the holy grail of Service Oriented Architecture for at least a decade, and it was the original impetus behind the web services standardization process. It only makes sense that application integration should be the primary area where organizations benefit from the adoption of a Service Oriented Architecture. Leveraging the application infrastructure the right way will yield high levels of integration between the enterprise systems while avoiding brittle interfaces that are costly to deploy and maintain.

Multiple Layers of Granularity

Although business level services are where a Service Oriented Architecture adds the greatest amount of agility and efficiency to an IT environment, many organizations will find a need for other layers of services below the business services, at finer levels of granularity. So long as this design is intentional and managed as part of the overall SOA governance process, it is an acceptable approach and may yield additional benefits. There are tradeoffs, as always, and these should be carefully considered as well, before adopting a multiple granularity service design.

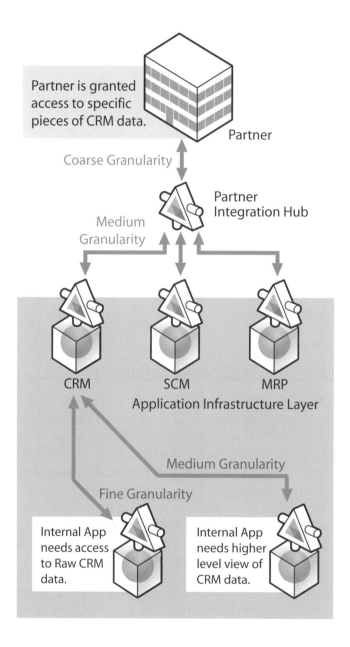

Often the needs of application integration within an organization are different from the requirements for integrating with business partners or composite applications. Such internal integration may require finer-grained services in order to leverage the custom applications developed by the organization to competitive advantage. In the case where internal services are created for application integration within an organization, these services can often be combined or aggregated by other services to provide the coarse-grained business services leveraged by the enterprise gateway layer.

Business services are best thought of from the perspective of business processes. Each service (or more technically, each service operation) implements a single step in a larger business process. From the perspective of an application developer or business analyst, a business service should have the granularity of a single step in a Jacobson-style use-case.[10]

External services, provided to other organizations via the enterprise gateway, often have a different granularity than the business services and/or internal services used within the organization. This is usually because only portions of the organization's business processes are exposed to external partners, so different service interfaces are defined at a very coarse-grained level of abstraction.

Some services used within an organization are not related to business processes at all, but provide some common functions required by multiple applications and business processes. These utility services have their own granularity and their interfaces often look quite different from the business service interfaces.

Sometimes an organization may implement low-level data access services that are a thin shell over the top of a database. Although these may have some value in that they may abstract the application from the physical data model, their associated performance overhead and lack of any true business logic almost always makes this type of service a bad idea. A better approach is to follow the system of record pattern (described later) and allow the system of record to be tightly coupled to its own database, but utilize the services provided by the system of record from all other applications that need access to the business entity.

The technical infrastructure components may provide services as well; these components will necessarily have a different kind of interface granularity. For example, the platform may provide services to interact with the identity management repository or collaboration workspaces. Although these are valuable services to leverage *from* the application infrastructure layer, they are not business oriented and are of a much finer granularity than the services provided *by* the application infrastructure layer.

Business services can be thought of as having three high-level sets of attributes. The first is the interface definition itself, which defines the "signature" of the service's operations and describes how to invoke them and what to expect as a result. The second is the set of policies surrounding the service, such as security and quality of service attributes. The last part of the business interface is the definition of the data structures contained within the messages.

Canonical Data Model

It is imperative that an organization adopt a common set of inter-related data structures for all of the business services within the organization. Without this common schema, the potential benefits of the SOA will be curtailed and development efficiency impacted.

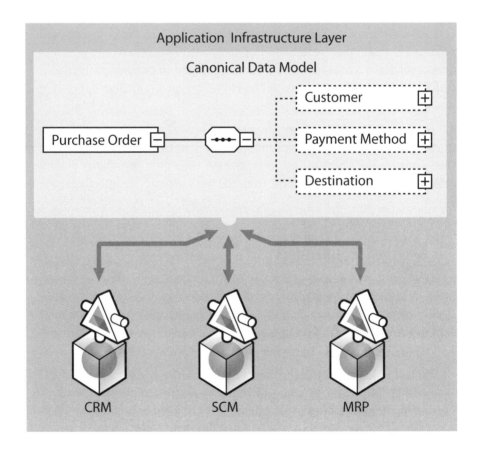

This common schema, often referred to as a "Canonical Data Model,"[11] should define the business domain of the organization. Data entities defined should be in the common language of the business and should be easily understood by everyone in the organization from the CEO to the application programmers. Where applications differ in their definition of these domain entities, a common structure should be adopted that is generic and ignores any quirks present in the individual applications. It is the responsibility of the service implementation to map these generic data structures to the specifics of each application.

If the organization embarks on the path of having multiple layers of granularity, then each layer will likely have a different data model. This is less than ideal, but is sometimes an unavoidable consequence of the appropriate definition of multiple layers of granularity. In these environments the transformation between the different data schema can be performed by composite services, which present coarse-grained interfaces to their consumers while utilizing finer-grained services to accomplish the business operation.

Services exposed to other organizations should follow industry standard message schema whenever possible. In the absence of such standards, the organization should attempt to create industry bodies or consortiums to define and implement them.

Systems of Record

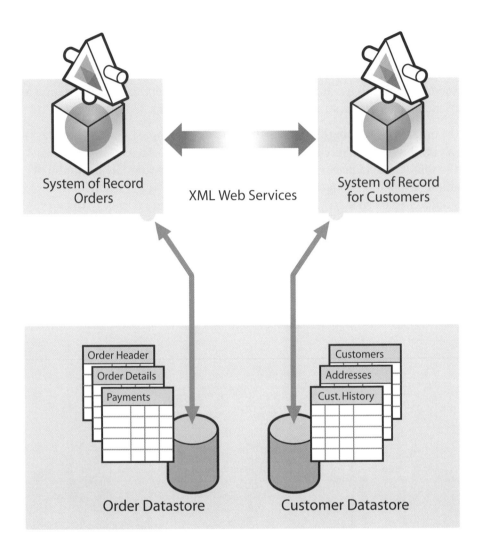

One of the reasons that application maintenance costs have been high in the past has been the habit of replicating data in many different applications, then implementing mechanisms to keep the various copies of the data in synch with each other. The service oriented approach to this type of integration challenge is to develop a system of record for each entity in the canonical data model. This system of record then becomes the sole source of truth on that entity, and any application wishing to access it must go through the service interfaces provided by the system of record. Once applications are modified to access the entity via the appropriate services, the data replication can be removed and the associated maintenance costs will vanish with it.

Composite Applications

As first presented in "Chapter 3: What is an Enterprise Gateway?" composite applications are a completely new class of application that was not possible before the adoption of a Service Oriented Architecture.

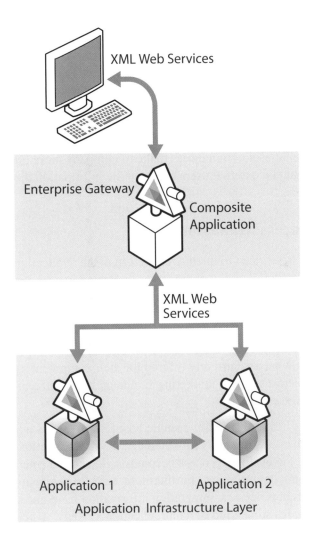

Composite applications include applications that leverage the services provided by the application infrastructure to deliver higher level functionality, potentially to a small set of knowledge workers. These composite applications might be configurable, personal portal sites, smart clients that are based on template documents developed by the IT organization, or even full-blown custom applications that rely on other applications for their business logic

Though composite applications are a form of custom application in the sense that they are developed within the organization, are owned by the organization, and are unique to the organization, they do not implement their own business logic, but instead they depend on services provided by other applications, both custom and packaged. Instead of creating all the application layers from scratch, composite applications merely create the top layers, such as presentation and workflow, and rely on other applications for the business logic. Because they leverage the underlying layers of other applications, they are less expensive to develop and therefore can be used to solve automation and integration problems that could not justify the expense of a traditional custom application development project. The ability to quickly implement composite applications from existing services for specific user communities makes a company more efficient by providing internal and external users with just the information they need in a useful format.

Business Process Management

The adoption of a Service Oriented Architecture in the application infrastructure allows the automation of business processes by leveraging the services from higher level processes. For example, if a cell phone company has service-enabled their CRM system and has the ability to access information on which customers have complained about a particular service, and can combine that with information from the provisioning system to determine what types of services they have versus what are currently offered for their equipment, region, etc., the company can create a targeted marketing campaign to up-sell existing customers to a new service offering.

In monolithic applications, usually a single business process is addressed from end to end, and because it is fully implemented in one application in a tightly coupled manner, the business process becomes rigid and the enterprise cannot adapt to a changing environment. Furthermore, since different applications implement different processes, integrating information from one business process into another requires some kind of data replication strategy, which leads to a brittle interface.

By breaking up these monolithic applications into business services, business processes cannot only be automated, but automation can be accomplished across business process boundaries in a manner that is resilient to changes in the underlying applications. For example, if the CRM system is designed to support the help desk business process in a monolithic way, it may be difficult or impossible to track a customer's visits to the company website or the physical locations in the same system. However, if the CRM system offers a business service for tracking information about any customer contact, that service can be leveraged from the online and physical shopping business processes to track all types of contact with a given customer.

Since business processes cross application, departmental, and even organizational boundaries, the BPM platform must manage transaction context across the business process, effectively coordinating the individual service invocations into a larger whole. This is an area of great complexity and there are several approaches to accomplishing transaction management in an SOA.

Business processes can be optimized for different attributes and the attribute chosen as the focus of optimization will determine the effect the optimization has on other attributes of the process. Software developers are very aware that when a piece of software is optimized for performance, the code becomes more brittle, more complex, and more expensive to maintain. Business processes have the same characteristic behavior. A business process optimized for cost might not be optimal from the perspective of execution speed. When adopting a Service Oriented Architecture, the guiding principal is that constant change is here to stay, and the most important attribute to optimize for is agility, so that business processes can be reconfigured over time as the needs of the organization change in response to internal and external drivers. By implementing business processes as collections of services, they can be reconfigured and reused in different or completely new scenarios.

In order for business processes to change, the business process management layer and the business analysts and managers that control it must support a strategy for evolving business processes. Merely having the ability to change a process does not imply that the change can be made successfully. A core process might be changed in a way that has unintended consequences for the organization, such as drastically lower margins or increased inventory. The organization must institute policies and procedures governing the evolution of business processes and must manage the actual implementation of changes to mitigate risks.

Change management is an important part of the business process evolution strategy. Organizations that adopt an SOA and begin to automate business processes learn early that the mere act of identifying and documenting existing business processes in a formal way adds tremendous value to the organization, and ideas for improvement start coming in from all areas involved. The process of evaluating these ideas to determine business value, associated risk, cost of implementation, and other factors must be formalized and implemented early. By analyzing and documenting the existing business processes, inefficient ones will be identified and changes instituted before the existing process is automated.

Most, if not all, business processes include some amount of interaction with humans and usually work will be handed off from one person to another. There are many ways to accomplish workflow by leveraging the application and technical infrastructure. For example, one employee might enter an order into the order entry application using a smart-client based form hosted in the enterprise portal. Based on the size of the order and the credit history of the customer, the workflow engine might place the order in a held status and generate an e-mail to the account rep for the customer that placed the order to indicate that there is some risk to the company associated with the order. The account rep may then decide that this case warrants some percentage of payment up front and might generate a request to the accounts receivable application to request the prepayment from the customer and release the order once it is received.

Well designed business services are stateless, meaning that they don't manage the state of a business process, though they do manage the persistent data associated with business entities. In order for business process automation to be implemented in an agile fashion, the state of executing business processes must be managed at the process layer, sometimes referred to as the orchestration layer. This allows the underlying services to be re-used in different business processes, which might have very different states associated with them.

The business process execution engine knows and manages the state of all executing business processes and must persist that state in a manner that allows for the restart of business processes after a failure of the engine. This kind of state is not really a part of any one application since it is associated with the business process and the process might span services from multiple applications.

A major benefit to be gained from leveraging the application infrastructure with a business process automation engine is the ability to monitor the execution of business processes and thereby analyze the performance of the enterprise. This business activity monitoring capability is especially valuable in the context of an agile IT environment, since data is being collected across business process boundaries in a consistent, centralized manner, and aggregated at the highest level.

Presenting the data collected from business activity monitoring to management through the use of customizable dashboards gives decision makers a way to monitor the health of the organization and the business processes within it on an ongoing, real-time basis. Having this kind of information makes the entire organization agile and can provide a significant competitive edge.

Dashboards

Dashboard applications utilize the services provided by applications to present real-time business intelligence to decision makers. By implementing dashboards on top of multiple application services, business metrics can be configured and compared in new ways, allowing individual managers to monitor those that are most relevant to their areas of responsibility.

By aggregating metrics from multiple business processes and applications, management is empowered to monitor the functioning of the business in novel ways, leading to new ways of thinking about the organization and new opportunities for optimization.

The best dashboard applications are customizable, allowing management to continually evolve what is measured and how the organization's performance is graded. By making the dashboards independent of the applications and business processes through the use of business services, they can be easily modified by application developers or even business analysts or management.

Dashboards must combine business activity with information from the various applications in the application infrastructure to facilitate decision making. The ability to combine information about incoming orders, for example, with information from the inventory management system and the supply chain management system can help purchasing managers spot potential over- or under-supply scenarios and address them before they become a problem.

Enterprise Portal

An enterprise portal is one of the most common types of composite applications built on top of the services provided by the application infrastructure. The portal provides a single point of access to the entire IT environment for customers, partners, and employees. The portal environment is the ideal place to host composite applications, since each group of users, or even individual users, can have a customized user experience, combining services from different applications into a composite application designed for specific tasks and roles.

In an environment where multiple layers of granularity are implemented in the application infrastructure, the highest level of business services are typically the most appropriate to leverage from the enterprise portal. This is because portals are not the best environment to implement business logic, so the underlying services are the best place for this behavior. It might be more appropriate to leverage the external service layer rather than the internal business services, especially for business partners and customers.

The enterprise portal is an ideal host for smart client applications that leverage the application infrastructure services. Portals typically provide some level of content management, a necessity for document-based smart client applications such as forms, spreadsheets, and text documents.

Portals enable application developers and even end users to develop composite applications inexpensively and quickly. Because of this development efficiency, applications that serve small groups of knowledge workers can be created cost effectively where in the past the cost would not have been justified by a sufficient return on investment.

Applications are usually focused on a cohesive set of functionality conceived to meet the needs of a user community. In many cases, the prime user community of an application also performs other tasks unrelated to the application but part of a larger workflow, requiring access to multiple different applications. In many cases, a business process requires a user to perform steps in multiple applications to achieve one task. Often these employees perform manual integration of applications by copying and pasting information from the interface of one into the other. Not only is this a bad use of human resources, it also leads to ongoing dual maintenance of the data, since the applications are not truly integrated and the system of record is not established and enforced for the business entities.

In these scenarios, integration needs are closely related to the specific job duties of a set of users. These users will typically have a small set of complex workflows that require them to use several applications, pulling specific pieces of information from each and manually integrating them into their workflow.

Higher levels of automation would increase the productivity of these users, but often the increased efficiency cannot justify the cost of extensive application integration or workflow projects. Composite applications can provide a customized workflow for a set of users that relies on services from multiple applications but shields the user from the application domain boundaries. Enterprise portals provide an excellent framework for performing *adhoc* integration via services, so-called "Integration at the Glass." Through this technique, small user communities can be provided with custom portal applications that perform application integration and workflow in the portal server, eliminating the need to work through the application development teams. Once there are significant numbers of users making use of the integration via the composite portal application, the added load may justify moving the integration into the business process automation engine for easier maintainability. Without an SOA, this type of integration is not feasible, because composite applications and the enterprise portal depend on the services provided by the application infrastructure to perform these integration tasks.

Smart Clients

Smart clients present more opportunities to leverage the application infrastructure to enable complex tasks for small groups of knowledge workers. Spreadsheets, for example, are familiar tools for business analysts and managers. Often these are utilized to perform analysis on data from back-end applications for the purposes of generating reports, performing forecasts, and business planning. Instead of making the end users manually pull data into the spreadsheet from various back-end applications, business level services can be invoked directly from the spreadsheet, turning the spreadsheet document into a composite application. Data can be pulled in directly from the systems of record; the spreadsheet can perform the type of calculations that spreadsheets are good at. If desired, the calculation results can even be stored back into applications via other business services.

The creation of documents, such as letters, memos, pleadings, etc., is a large part of the business of many organizations. Often these documents contain information that is stored in back-end systems, such as contact information, account and order histories, and boilerplate text. Composing such documents typically consists of opening the appropriate template, then accessing various applications and copying the relevant data into the document, saving the finished document to the file system somewhere and printing it. This process has a number of inefficiencies, such as the need to copy and paste the information after manually accessing multiple applications, storing the document templates and finished documents in some shared file system where they are difficult to index and search, and manually keeping information in sync if the documents are needed again.

Similarly to the way the spreadsheet templates invoke business services to access numerical data, word processing document templates can be designed to invoke services to retrieve customer information and even to pull boilerplate text from content management services, greatly simplifying the creation and management of the documents. Once they are created, the document can be stored in a content management system, again via services. If the documents are accessed at a later date, the user can re-invoke the services to retrieve up to date information from the systems of record. Because the documents are stored centrally, they can be easily searched to perform business intelligence and data mining activities.

Most applications have a need for some form of manual data entry. By decoupling the data entry forms from the underlying database and instead leveraging the services provided by the application infrastructure, the application development team can freely modify the underlying service implementation, even changing the database schema, without the need to modify and redeploy the data entry forms. Furthermore, the services required by the data entry forms can also be leveraged by other systems that need to add or update the same information.

Another form of smart client that can be used to leverage the application infrastructure is e-mail. Although most people think of these applications as merely a delivery tool for text messages, modern e-mail clients include advanced workflow and collaboration capabilities. Utilizing e-mail clients as smart clients to implement steps in larger business processes is an obvious choice, since everyone is familiar with the usage of e-mail.

Companies such as Google have elevated the browser to smart client status through the use of a set of technologies that go by the collective name of Asynchronous JavaScript and XML (AJAX). In this approach, JavaScript embedded within web pages is downloaded to the user's browser and executed, responding to events generated when the user interacts with the browser. This JavaScript in turn leverages services in the enterprise gateway layer to access back-end systems, allowing a much richer user experience than HTML, which is generated once when the page is requested, and then remains static in the browser until another page request is made.

There is room in the realm of smart clients for custom development, too. Modern application development tools make creating custom form-based applications easy and affordable, even when the numbers of users are small. The presence of form processing frameworks on modern operating systems and platforms, coupled with automatic push deployment systems, means that even custom smart clients can be deployed with a minimum amount of work from the IT organization.

Mobile Devices

Information Technology is increasingly challenged with providing access to the enterprise IT environment to users who are not always physically within the organization but might be traveling around the globe or working out of homes, cars, or airplanes. Supporting these users' needs can be quite challenging; a Service Oriented Architecture in the application infrastructure layer makes it possible to provide advanced capabilities to mobile users, improving productivity for both the roaming users and the back-office processes they interface with. Mobile users access the IT environment using a number of different devices with widely different capabilities and feature sets. The IT organization needs to have different approaches to address the various connectivity, security, and capability attributes of these devices.

The types of networks used by mobile users have important implications both for the services invoked and the applications that invoke them. Many, if not all, mobile devices experience periods where they cannot access the corporate enterprise gateway, yet the users of these devices still need access to their applications and data in order to be productive. For applications to function in a disconnected state, the capability must be designed in from the beginning.

One approach to solving the disconnected challenge is to use cached data coupled with delayed service invocation. When the device is connected, the data needed by the user is identified and downloaded to the device via the services provided by the application infrastructure, where it is cached for later use while off line. Service invocations that would normally occur as part of application usage are delayed if the device is disconnected and are later invoked either automatically or manually when the device is reconnected.

Low bandwidth connections must be considered as well, since coarse-grained services can potentially deal with large messages that would not perform adequately over low bandwidth networks. In these situations, alternate service invocation protocols should be considered to make better use of the available resources.

Service invocations made over public networks must take into account the possibility that the messages could be intercepted, or that the services themselves could be subject to malicious attacks.

Partner Integration Hub

The partner integration hub in the enterprise gateway will likely be a primary driver for an organization to adopt the multiple layers of granularity defined above. This component provides a single holistic view of an organization's entire IT infrastructure for all systems that are out of the organization's control, similarly to the way the enterprise portal provides a single unified view of the IT infrastructure to all humans needing to interact with it.

The service interfaces provided by the partner integration hub to business partners are coarse-grained and almost always composite services. They provide a view of the entire IT environment from the outside in, hiding internal implementations and application boundaries from the external organizations. These services should be designed to view the IT environment as a black box that provides a set of consistent services with a common message schema.

There will be a natural tension between the business services provided by the various internal applications in the application infrastructure and the desired single interface to the enterprise provided by the enterprise gateway to the outside world. The interfaces provided by the applications will naturally be finer-grained than the desired interfaces in the enterprise gateway, and these internal interfaces will also expose some of the differentiating features of the enterprise's IT environment. It is imperative that the partner integration hub adapt these internal interfaces into the desired external interface, encapsulating and hiding the internal complexity, and providing a concise and intuitive industry-standard interface.

Exposing internal interfaces would expose the internal complexities of the organization's application infrastructure and would jeopardize adoption of the service offering. Additionally, there could be drivers from customers and partners to change the internal interfaces to meet their needs in such a way that might jeopardize efficient internal integration.

By providing a set of interfaces appropriate to the outside world from the partner integration hub, the organization is able to relieve this natural tension by adapting the two sets of interfaces and translating between them, providing a single consistent view of the entire IT infrastructure to all applications outside of it. The mapping and translation that must occur to bridge the divide between the internal service interfaces and those that present a single, consistent view of the entire IT infrastructure is performed by the partner integration hub.

Security is, of course, extremely important for the partner integration hub, since the vast majority of these services are exposing critical business processes over public networks. Security crosses all three layers of the IT infrastructure and has implications on each. The most likely authentication model for the partner integration hub will be based upon certificates, which requires the organization to implement a public key infrastructure. Additional security requirements might entail the use of an authorization repository, federated identity management, and web services specifications like WS-Security and WS-SecurityPolicy. The details of implementation are beyond the scope of this book.

Wrap-Up

This chapter examined the common architectural patterns used to accomplish application integration in the application infrastructure layer in the context of Service Oriented Architecture.

Additionally, each of the composite application types identified in "Chapter 3: What is an Enterprise Gateway?" were re-examined in the context of integration, and the ways in which they can leverage the services provided by the application infrastructure layer.

The next chapter will discuss the use of SOA in the Application Infrastructure layer to achieve horizontal application integration.

Chapter 7: Application Integration Strategy

Creating an agile IT environment requires vision, planning, and execution. Without a clear strategy for integrating the organization's application infrastructure, the benefits of adopting a Service Oriented Architecture will not be realized.

An application integration strategy must take into account all of the existing application assets and provide a common approach and associated mechanisms for including them in the service fabric.

Application Integration

Traditional integration usually proceeds by creating a series of one-off integration points between pairs of applications, tightly coupling them to each other, or at a minimum coupling them in a particular deployment. This style of integration is inefficient in terms of development resources and adds significant complexity to the integration point, especially when the two applications have different quality-of-service requirements.

Rather than creating a series of static, brittle, point-to-point interfaces, an SOA allows services to discover and invoke each other in a production environment, freeing the enterprise from the constraints of the traditional develop/test/release cycle of software development. In an SOA, service implementing applications register their service interface with the service registry, where consuming applications can dynamically discover and invoke them. This loose coupling between applications allows them to proceed on different development cycles and with different quality-of-service requirements.

Most enterprises have made significant investments in existing applications, either by purchasing commercial off-the-shelf (COTS) products or by funding custom development. The migration to an SOA does not require the abandonment of any existing applications, but rather sees these "legacy" applications as assets to be leveraged. Leveraging existing applications through service oriented interfaces not only makes those applications first-class citizens of the SOA, but also creates new opportunities to leverage these investments from composite and business dashboard applications.

Most enterprises, even during down business cycles, have a number of new applications that are either being developed or procured at any given time. The maximum benefit achievable from an SOA will be attained when service oriented interfaces are required of new applications. When new applications are implemented in a service oriented manner, their longevity is ensured because their basic business services are exposed to the entire IT infrastructure and their ROI increases by providing additional ways in which they can be leveraged. New application development should leverage the services available from other applications to shorten the development cycle and re-use business services.

What has Changed

SOA concepts are not new, nor are the benefits. Many failed attempts to build Service Oriented Architectures on top of various technologies precede the current wave of successes. The primary differentiating factor between the SOAs of today and those of the past is an inherent dependency on standards. Standards for integration that are agreed to and implemented consistently by all of the platform companies, middleware companies, and COTS product vendors are a necessary prerequisite to the successful implementation of an SOA.

Another way modern SOAs are different from integration strategies of the past is their inherent multi-platform, multi-vendor, and heterogeneous nature. Past SOA technologies required the monolithic adoption of a single platform across an enterprise to achieve the levels of flexibility and efficiency necessary to justify adoption of an SOA. Standardizing on a single platform, however, greatly reduces an enterprise's flexibility, while simultaneously reducing their leverage with the platform vendor. The greatest flexibility and efficiency is achieved when an enterprise is free to choose the right tool for every job, regardless of what tools were chosen for other jobs.

Just building service oriented interfaces into applications is not enough to implement an SOA. In order to reap the maximum benefit from the investment in an SOA, an enterprise must create an infrastructure for managing, monitoring and deploying services in production environments. This infrastructure is vital to the success of an SOA initiative; without it the complexity will quickly balloon beyond the organization's ability to grasp or control. There are several names for this infrastructure, including "Fabric," "Service Infrastructure Layer," and "Service Grid."

Modern services, specifically web services, are built on standard, interoperable technologies like HTTP, XML, and SOAP. These technologies are inherently platform agnostic, making platforms that implement them interoperable. Granted, there are any number of standards and technologies about which the same thing could be said. What differentiates current standards are their adoption by all of the major industry players and a continuing, concerted effort by these companies to ensure that their platforms and products remain interoperable with those of their competitors. Customers play a continued role in this movement by requiring their vendors to plug in to an SOA.

Web service standards define an interoperable way for applications to exchange messages, but not the content of the messages. The message content and semantics are referred to as the service interface. In order to integrate two applications, the development teams must agree on the service interfaces.

Defining the service interfaces for each application is a crucial part of implementing an SOA. These message structures and data formats can be defined within the enterprise or may leverage the work of industry consortiums. The definition of a service interface may include additional aspects such as nonrepudiation, audit trails, compensating transactions, and quality-of-service guarantees. These requirements impact not only the implementation of the service but the consumers of the service and the messages as well. Several industries have ongoing efforts to define a set of common service interfaces. An enterprise that finds itself developing its own interfaces due to a lack of industry agreement should consider forming or joining a standards body to encourage wider adoption of the interfaces.

Historical Application Integration Methods

Every enterprise has requirements to integrate the functionality of multiple applications, and historically, there have been several different mechanisms for achieving application integration. Gartner estimates that 40% of every development project's cost is spent on integration. The goal of a Service Oriented Architecture is to reduce this integration cost until it approaches zero.

In order to understand how this can be accomplished, it is important to understand the existing integration strategies and their associated benefits and drawbacks. In addition to SOA, there are several other fundamental categories of application integration:

- Data Replication
- Tightly Coupled Applications
- Point-to-Point
- Electronic Data Interchange
- Enterprise Application Integration

Each of these will be described in more detail, and strategies for replacing them will be presented.

Data Replication

Data layer integration is the most common, yet it is the least efficient and maintainable application integration strategy. It can be accomplished by having one application directly access the underlying data store of another application, or by replicating the data from another application. This is achieved by using straight schema-to-schema replication or by using data replication and transformation products.

The only redeeming quality of this style of integration is that it achieves integration at all. It is the oldest style of application integration and was born out of necessity, rather than as an elegant or efficient solution to the problem.

No matter how data layer integration is ultimately accomplished, it leads to tight coupling of the applications and brittle, costly interfaces. Changes to the data schema involved always result in ripple effects that impact the integration points of all other applications.

The brittle nature of this style of integration can have a crippling effect on the organization's ability to respond to competitive pressures. Applications that are integrated in this fashion usually require lock-step deployment of new versions, increasing the cost and complexity of any changes, and lengthening the development cycle.

Another issue with this approach is that it is only effective for custom developed applications. COTS applications are delivered with their own schema and are unlikely to support any shared database, whether with custom developed applications or other COTS products, even if they come from the same vendor.

The need to integrate COTS applications with the rest of the IT environment requires a different integration strategy than a shared database.

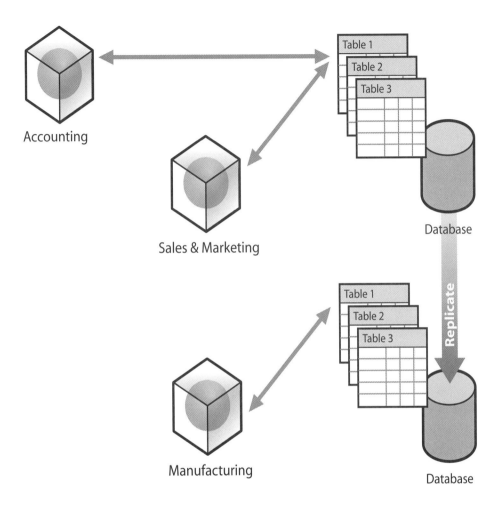

Sharing a database among multiple applications can become a performance bottleneck, especially when the applications have different requirements for performance, availability, and different transactional models.

The shared database approach also leads to duplication of development and maintenance effort. Since the applications share the database but nothing else, the business logic surrounding the data is replicated in every application. As anyone who has ever done application development will point out, duplicated code leads to duplicated bugs and duplicated maintenance effort.

Data replication suffers from some of the same drawbacks as the shared database approach, though it does solve the problems of a shared schema, lock-step deployments, and distributed deployments. Since the applications are free to have different schemas, an additional requirement on the integration layer is the ability to transform the data from one schema and format to another. These transforms are an additional development artifact and suffer from the brittleness associated with the applications in the shared database approach.

Data replication is usually asynchronous and scheduled, rather than in real time, and therefore modifications to the data may not be visible to all applications in a timely manner, leading to inconsistencies and hampering channel integration, as well as other aspects of the real-time enterprise.

Since data replication does nothing to address the need to share the business logic associated with the data, it suffers from the same weakness of duplicated business logic and the associated duplication of development and maintenance effort.

The strategy for migrating from a data replication approach to application integration to a more agile, less brittle approach is to establish a service of record for each entity stored in the databases. The system of record should provide access to its entity or entities through business services appropriate to the entity or entities. Applications other than the system of record should only access entities via the business services provided by the system of record.

Tightly Coupled Applications

Another integration technique used often in the past is the practice of tightly coupling applications to each other in order to achieve high levels of integration. This technique suffers from many of the same problems of data layer integration and is often used in conjunction to address the replicated business logic shortcoming of data layer integration.

One approach to tight application integration is for the applications to share a common library (or libraries) of code. By sharing code, they achieve re-use of business logic. The downside of shared code is a brittleness resulting from the nature of the interface between the applications. Changes in the shared library affect all applications that use it, resulting in a ripple effect for changes.

There are two options for deployment when applications share a common library: the library can be embedded within each application and deployed many times (sometimes called static linking), or the shared code can be deployed as a single library used by each application (dynamic linking). The former deployment model allows the applications to be updated on independent schedules, but uses more system resources (because the same code is deployed with each application) and results in additional development and maintenance overhead, since multiple versions of the library must be maintained in parallel. The latter solves these issues, but at the cost of increased brittleness, as updates to the shared library immediately affect every application when they are deployed, resulting in the familiar ripple effect. Most IT professionals and, indeed, most computer users are familiar with these issues and can relate to the term Microsoft now officially uses to describe the problem; "DLL-Hell" refers to the Windows platform's mechanism for deploying shared libraries of code, called Dynamically Linked Libraries (DLLs).

The strategy for migrating this type of application integration point to a service oriented approach begins with clearly defining the responsibilities of the applications involved and eliminating any overlap. This step should enable the applications to be redesigned in such a way that the shared libraries of code are no longer necessary. The applications can then be augmented to provide service interfaces appropriate to the application's responsibilities. Lastly, applications that require access to the services provided by other applications can be modified to leverage the new service interface to the application, rather than directly coupling to the applications code.

Point-to-Point

Point-to-point integration at the application layer is less common yet equally problematic. There are many different technologies used for this style of interface, and most suffer from the problems of high maintenance cost, brittleness, and limited scalability.

Point-to-point integration has one primary benefit over data layer integration in that the applications are decoupled from the database schema by way of the integration protocol.

Low-level network communication mechanisms are the typical means of achieving point-to-point application integration. In this scenario, applications exchange data via brittle, often binary interfaces that are point-to-point and usually synchronous in nature. Such interfaces are difficult to maintain, problematic in production environments, and rarely if ever reused, leading to a proliferation of integration points as each project implements a new interface.

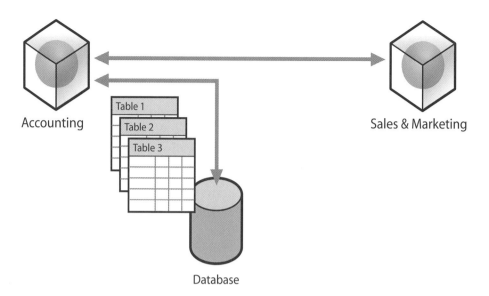

Database

This strategy typically relies on a one-off message format that is difficult to develop and maintain. The underlying socket communication or file transfer communication mechanisms are usually brittle in production, leading to frequent outages.

Since this integration strategy results in an ever-growing number of connections between applications that cannot be leveraged for other purposes, the resulting application infrastructure hinders the organization's agility.

The best approach to migrate these connections to a service oriented approach is to incrementally implement business services where it is justified and then leverage the new services to replace the old point-to-point interfaces.

Electronic Data Interchange

One of the oldest technologies for integrating systems from different organizations is Electronic Data Interchange (EDI). There are standards bodies for defining the data formats for EDI links, some of which are even part of the United Nations.

EDI solves the security issues surrounding the exchange of data between organizations via a physical solution. Rather than depending on a public network for integration, EDI depends on a direct, hardwired connection that only the two endpoints have visibility to. This leased line approach is very expensive, as the telecommunication companies provide this type of always on, physically wired connection at a premium.

The interfaces used over these connections are usually of the sort described in the low-level networking integration section and so have all the same problems. In addition, the standards bodies defining EDI interfaces are slow to define standards and slow to react to market changes.

The best strategy for eliminating EDI interfaces and moving business partners to a service oriented integration approach is to identify the types of interfaces that are implemented using EDI and implement a partner integration hub that offers overlapping services designed in a cross-platform, industry standard way and offered in a secure fashion over the public networks. The high cost of maintaining EDI links and their associated low scalability and brittleness will be incentive enough for business partners to begin utilizing the partner integration hub instead.

Enterprise Application Integration

Enterprise Application Integration (EAI) platforms were created to address many of the limitations of the integration strategies mentioned above. EAI is essentially another data layer integration strategy. Instead of accessing databases belonging to another application, an EAI integration approach introduces a central "broker" in a hub and spoke configuration, with the broker at the hub and a different application at the end of each spoke. The EAI middleware moves data from application to application, performing the transformations necessary along the way.

The additional benefits provided by an EAI approach over the data-sharing approach to application integration are that they decouple the applications from each other by implementing transformation logic in the broker.

EAI platforms are big, costly, proprietary, and difficult to implement. They are big in the sense that there are many components and layers of abstraction. They typically include their own proprietary development environments for working with all the components. They are very costly in terms of licensing and maintenance contracts. They are proprietary in almost every way – they have proprietary APIs and adapter infrastructures, proprietary messaging systems, and proprietary tools. They typically require the help of consultants, either from the vendor or from a partner of the vendor to successfully implement and deploy.

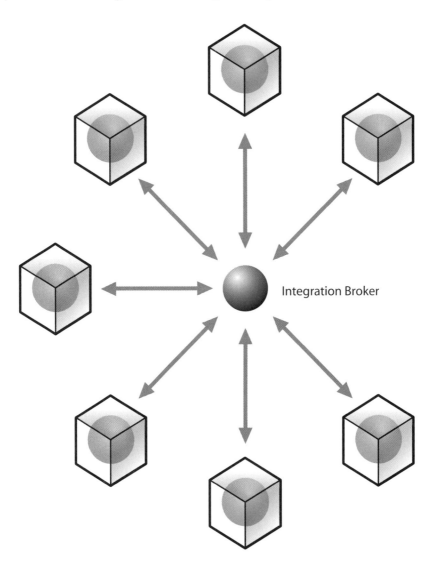

EAI suffers from the high implementation and maintenance costs and limitations of a hub and spoke architecture, where all data flows through a central integration server.

According to Evans Data Corporation's [...] Fall 2004 Web Services/ SOA Development Survey, 4 in 10 Web Services developers feel that Web Services either "absolutely" or "probably" diminish the need for Enterprise Application Integration. Only 10% feel that Web Services "absolutely" does not diminish the need for EAI. In addition, 6 in 10

Web Services developers believe that Web Services can significantly or somewhat lower costs to implement standard EAI implementations.

"EAI used to be a big-budget project that required the building of an entire middleware layer of composite applications that replicated legacy processes. With the standardization that Web Services brings, applications can be linked with fewer lines of code, and often within a much shorter time frame," said Joe McKendrick, an analyst with Evans Data. "The savings potential of Web Services is enormous."[12]

Additionally, EAI doesn't actually remove the brittleness from the IT infrastructure; it merely moves the maintenance costs from the applications to the transformation logic in the broker. The deployed transformation is almost always a hard-coded, tightly coupled point-to-point connection. If one or the other end of the connection needs to be swapped out for an alternative application with the same functionality, the integration point will have to be rewritten as well.

An EAI solution provides marginal amounts of increased agility over a shared database approach by allowing the deployment schedules of the applications to vary independently, so long as the transformations are kept up to date.

As another form of data layer integration, the strategies for replacing EAI are the same with minor variations. The best approach to fixing the brittleness associated with EAI style hub and spoke integration is to gradually replace each point-to-point integration and associated transformations by identifying a service of record, implementing business services in the service of record, and leveraging these services from the other applications.

SOA

Component interfaces such as COM*, CORBA, and RMI were all attempts to solve these integration challenges, but they all shared a common problem: their design was essentially proprietary and platform specific, so they were only useful if the entire IT environment ran on the same platform and was developed using a common technology. Even CORBA, which claims to be platform independent, lacks basic interoperability features between multiple vendors.

Modern SOA technologies and standards address all of these limitations in a variety of ways. The standards and technologies that have been developed in recent years are a direct response to many of the limitations of the older integration strategies and technologies.

There is a significant amount of confusion in the market surrounding the notion of Service Oriented Architecture. The big platform companies tout the importance of SOA while stressing the particular features of their platform that enable an SOA. Each platform company either has or is building/acquiring a suite of middleware products that further enhance the ease with which an SOA may be implemented on their platform, while increasing their customer's lock-in to that platform. The middleware companies focus on building SOA enablement technologies that can be deployed on multiple platforms, overlapping the platform technologies, but providing a common infrastructure in a heterogeneous environment. In the cacophony of marketing messages built around SOA, there is one important fact to remember: a Service Oriented Architecture is not a single product or application; it is a strategy for and approach to application development, COTS product selection, and application integration.

Interface Design

Services should be designed in a manner that exposes a common, industry standard view of business operations, encapsulating the specifics of implementation behind a generic interface.

It is possible to define service interfaces at different levels of abstraction. As mentioned before, the level of abstraction a service is defined at is commonly referred to as the "granularity" of the service. It is important to understand the appropriate granularity of business services.

- Services should encapsulate significant and cohesive business operations and should not merely access or update a database

- A specific operation defined within a service interface should be equivalent to one step or interaction in a business process or strategic use-case

- Services should be defined at a granularity that fulfills business goals of one or more users of the application, often called actors

- Each operation that a service performs should be understandable to all members of the business community, not just the IT staff

Another important factor in determining the appropriate granularity for service interfaces is the scope of potential consumers of the services. An SOA is not bounded by the extent of an enterprise's technical infrastructure, but extends beyond to partners and customers. An enterprise should not expect its partners and customers to adapt their applications to a proprietary, quirky interface that exposes internal data structures.

Enabling Technologies

There are a number of products, technologies and platforms that can contribute to a successful SOA adoption program. Each must be used appropriately though, and no product is an SOA; an SOA describes an entire IT environment. With that in mind, let's look at the product segments in more detail.

The application server market includes heavyweight products that are intended to host applications and are thus endpoints of an integration project. They typically host layered, object-oriented applications that are responsible for supplying the interfaces to a particular set of application functionality or business services. They usually host some form of human user interface and might host one or more machine-to-machine interfaces as well. These interfaces could be based on low-level binary protocols like CORBA, COM, and RMI, or they may be higher level interfaces like web services.

Environments where different applications have radically different views of domain objects require a message transformation capability, which will typically be hosted in an integration platform rather than in individual applications. Environments that require integration between "legacy" applications that do not have native web service capabilities will also require some kind of integration platform.

Application servers are good at hosting applications, but are too heavy for hosting integration points. In an environment where every application publishes a web service interface to its underlying business services, an additional integration platform may not be necessary.

Web service containers are essentially a run-time environment for web services. They are lightweight versions of application servers and are not intended to host full-blown applications, but rather to host business service interfaces to applications. This approach is especially valuable in an environment where legacy technologies are used in business-critical applications, and where a traditional EAI platform is too heavy, too expensive or overly brittle. Web service containers may be included in some Enterprise Service Bus (ESB – see below) products, and are being added to the traditional EAI platforms. Companies should standardize on web services as the preferred integration technology, which may lead them to choose web service containers for leveraging legacy applications rather than buy into the proprietary and expensive EAI products.

The web services monitoring and management space is one of the least mature of all the SOA market segments. The feature sets of these products vary widely, but can be generally summarized as dynamic service discover, location transparency, monitoring of service availability and utilization, message transformation and routing, and quality of service features such as clustering and fail-over.

Governance is another function that can be enabled by technology. The registry of services, for example, can serve not only the consuming applications, but also the development teams that are looking for existing services to leverage. The monitoring of service usage can likewise be utilized to predict future capacity requirements and determine whether service level agreements are being met.

Messaging products focus on the low-level features required by asynchronous messaging. These products typically implement publish/subscribe features as well as one-way messaging. Quality of service features such as reliable/ guaranteed delivery and prioritized messaging are also found here. Most, if not all products in this category provide a Java Messaging Service (JMS) interface to their product, enabling access to the product features from any Java application using a standard interface.

Orchestration platforms provide a means to aggregate services into business processes and to incorporate human workflow into the business processes. These platforms provide some similar features to the EAI platforms but are not as expensive and complex to implement. Furthermore, orchestration platforms seek to leverage services provided by applications, rather than implement the integration logic.

The ESB products are a stripped down version of the EAI products. They implement EAI using web services but without the proprietary application adapters of traditional EAI products. ESBs remove some of the functionality and proprietary capabilities of EAI platforms while delivering much lower cost and shorter development cycles for integration projects.

The evolution of ESBs is and has been driven by the need for standards-based integration (driven by Java) and a phased approach to implementing an integration platform, allowing quicker time-to-market at lower cost.

ESB products exploit web services, intelligent message routing, messaging middleware, and message transformation. ESBs act as a thin universal integration foundation through which services and objects flow. They are essentially messaging with web services interfaces.

ESBs are more aligned with EAI platforms than with web service containers. Synchronous point-to-point services in general, and web services in particular, are only a portion of the Enterprise Service Bus architecture, which also relies heavily on asynchronous messaging, message transformation, message routing, and publish/subscribe patterns of integration, and might include a business process piece as well.

Some people think of an ESB as not having a central hub and spoke system, while others do not make this distinction. They key differentiator here is the "Integration Broker," which is perceived as a "hub" in traditional EAI and a single point of failure. ESBs abandon the idea of a central broker in favor of a "bus" or "fabric" of services that are dynamically discovered and consumed as needed.

Wrap-Up

This chapter has examined the historical application integration techniques, along with their associated benefits and shortcomings. For each legacy integration approach, a strategy for migrating to SOA was presented. The technologies and components associated with implementing a Service Oriented Architecture were examined.

In the next chapter, the dependencies between the application infrastructure layer and the technical infrastructure layer will be discussed and strategies for leveraging the technical infrastructure services from the applications in the application infrastructure layer will be detailed.

Chapter 8: Leveraging the Technical Infrastructure

Applications depend on the technical infrastructure, and there are several strategies for leveraging the technical infrastructure from applications.

Applications must be built on a solid, flexible, and centrally managed technical infrastructure and integrated into a service-oriented architecture.

The presence of technical infrastructure is a given; the ability to leverage it from the application infrastructure is not and must be designed into the application infrastructure.

A technical infrastructure must provide the means for IT operations to provide a secure, connected, managed, and monitored environment.

Leveraging the Foundation

The best technical infrastructure in the world will provide little value to an organization unless the application infrastructure is built in a way that leverages the services provided. Many application development projects take the technical infrastructure for granted and treat it as someone else's problem. Even worse are the application development projects that ignore the current technical infrastructure and build their own for the application, which is the reason most organizations have silos of systems — no forethought went into the introduction of new technologies. Creating an SOA requires an understanding of how applications utilize the technical infrastructure, what limitations are imposed, and how they should and shouldn't interact with it.

Computers

Applications are deployed on platforms, which commonly include physical hardware and an operating system. An organization of any size and with any history will have multiple platforms deployed and in use. In keeping with the philosophy of SOA, the platforms already deployed and running the business should be leveraged and included in the SOA, rather than requiring them to be replaced by a single homogeneous platform. An SOA enables the organization to take a best-of-breed approach to platforms rather than being forced to use a single platform. It should be noted that the savings of standardizing on a single platform from an administration and management perspective can be substantial, if it is achievable.

The way that an application leverages the underlying platform has important implications on how it can be deployed and how best to integrate it into the SOA. Some applications are tightly coupled to the operating system on which they are deployed and utilize proprietary APIs. These types of applications are obviously restricted to the platform they were designed to leverage. Service-enabling these applications can be done by wrapping them in a service layer that abstracts the interface from the underlying application and platform. The scalability of the service, however, will be restricted to the scalability of the underlying platform, since the application that implements the service is coupled to that platform. If the platform becomes a performance bottleneck for the service, then IT will have to reimplement the service on another platform or enhance the hardware of the existing platform if possible. The introduction of a service wrapper will limit the impact of such redevelopment by isolating dependent applications from the underlying implementation.

The ability of an application to make use of additional hardware, such as multiple processors or additional memory, is dependent on the architecture and design of the application. Applications that are single threaded cannot utilize additional processors without significant amounts of rework. In some cases, running multiple instances of the application is a possible solution, but the applications must be designed to support this as well, with mechanisms to avoid resource contention and to synchronize data and processes between the multiple instances. Likewise, if an application cannot be configured to utilize additional memory, it will make no difference when it is added to the machine, unless the application is already memory-constrained[13].

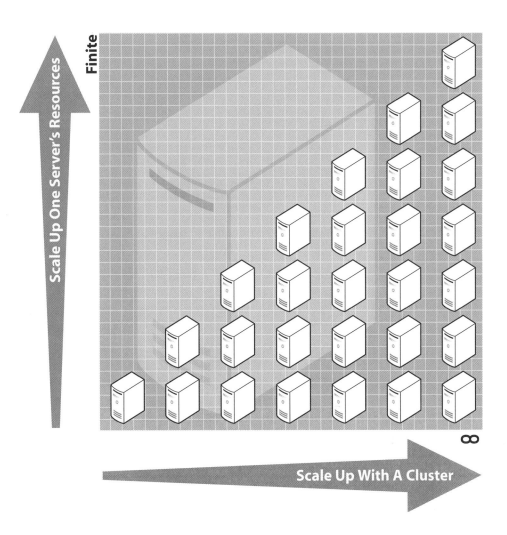

A single machine can only scale to a certain point; beyond that, the only way to add more processing power is to add additional machines. The architecture of utilizing a collection of machines as one logical machine is called clustering. Applications must be designed with clustering in mind or they will not be able to take advantage of this deployment option.

Load balancing is another aspect of clustering; it entails distributing incoming requests to multiple machines in a cluster based on some algorithm in order to distribute the processing burden across the machines in the cluster. Applications that carry on stateful conversations with clients, whether they are humans or other machines, will impact the ability of the load balancer to distribute the requests. This is due to the fact that all requests associated with a particular session will need to be routed to a single machine, or the application will need a mechanism to share session state between the machines in the cluster. For this reason, applications that implement stateful conversations should be carefully designed so that they will function in a load balanced cluster, and so that the additional overhead created by maintaining the statefulness of the conversations will not overwhelm the performance benefit of the clustered deployment.

Hardware failures are inevitable, yet many applications are of a mission critical nature and cannot afford to go down even when the technical infrastructure they depend on fails. This can be minimized through contingency planning and the creation of fail-over mechanisms. In the event of a hardware failure, entire application nodes can be replaced by standby nodes. If this is a requirement for an application development project, then it must be designed into the application from the beginning. Occasionally an application will accidentally support fail-over without any additional effort from the application development team, but this is rare, as many design decisions could have important consequences to fail-over scenarios.

Networks

Network communication protocols are layered on top of each other, with each additional layer providing an additional level of abstraction and functionality to the applications that use them to communicate. In order for the application infrastructure to leverage the network, it is imperative that the applications abstract themselves from the communication protocols to the greatest extent possible. Ideally, the applications are so abstracted from the protocol that the protocol can be changed without impacting the application. Technologies in development now, such as Microsoft's Indigo, will allow the technical infrastructure to swap out communication protocols on the fly based on the most efficient means for each service invocation, and the applications that implement the services or depend on the services will be none the wiser.

The design of applications can have a huge impact on the utilization of available network bandwidth. Applications that communicate using fine-grained services will create much more network traffic and will create performance problems for themselves as well as other applications sharing the network. Legacy integration technologies such as CORBA are well-known for this design limitation, and applications that behave this way are commonly referred to as "chatty," because they "talk" over the network frequently and generate lots of fine-grained network traffic (frequent, small messages). A far better approach is to utilize coarse-grained services (large, infrequent messages) to accomplish entire business operations; even though they will involve larger data transfers, they will occur far less frequently.

Application design must take into account the available network bandwidth. Failure to do so will severely limit the usefulness of many applications. For example, an application design that assumes it will be running on a local area network may hinder or even prevent a redeployment of some components to other locations. Likewise, applications that are designed exclusively for low bandwidth connectivity may not be able to take advantage of faster networks.

An important design consideration for any network communication is network latency. This refers to the time that it takes to transmit data from one machine to another. The network bandwidth capacity and the distance between the communicating machines are the base determining factors, with network traffic and error rate contributing as well. Application designs that fail to account for the range of network latency scenarios that might occur may become brittle, as upstream operations time out while downstream operations are still processing, leading to application failures or usability issues.

Any time data are transferred over a network the potential for the data to be intercepted is present, and when the network is a public one, the risk that the data will be intercepted is significant. Security of network communication is therefore an increasingly important aspect of application design. Security mechanisms must be viewed in the context of the other attributes, such as latency, bandwidth, and geography.

A mobile workforce often requires access to corporate applications and data when a network connection is not available. Designing applications to work in a disconnected mode as well as a connected mode is one of the most challenging problems to tackle in modern application development. The complexities involved include:

- Synchronizing online data with machines that are sometimes connected
- Storing updates made while off line and forwarding them to the back-end application services once the network connection is restored
- Handling conflicting updates

If an application needs to be available in a disconnected mode, then it must be designed to work this way from the beginning.

Identity Management

The technical infrastructure is responsible for implementing the authentication and authorization framework for the enterprise. The application infrastructure should be designed to leverage this framework across all applications. In the past, applications often implemented their own authentication and authorization mechanisms, including storing users and their associated roles and permissions in an application specific database. This process has led to a situation where users must remember different user names and passwords for every application, and administrators must provision users multiple times for each application they use. A more efficient and maintainable solution is to delegate all authentication, authorization, and provisioning responsibilities to the technical infrastructure, where it can be easily leveraged from every application.

Single sign-on refers to a user experience associated with authentication. When users have to sign on to multiple applications using different usernames and passwords, the impression (rightly so) is that the authentication mechanisms are different and not integrated. The opposite of this, where a user authenticates once and their identity and permissions are automatically propagated to all of the applications that they use is the concept of a single sign-on.

One approach to achieving the user experience of single sign-on is to map the separate identities used in all of the applications to one another, essentially creating an uber-user that aggregates all of the identities for any given user into a related set. Although this does create the single sign-on user experience, the administrative cost associated with provisioning users and assigning permissions increases. The increased administrative cost occurs because the multiple identity repositories still must be maintained, and the mappings between them must be maintained as well.

A better and more efficient way to provide the single sign-on user experience is the creation of an enterprise-wide repository for authentication and authorization data. This design creates a single identity out of all the disparate application specific identity repositories, and the applications then leverage this central repository. There are a number of benefits to this approach. The simplification of the user provisioning process is an obvious one. This design also allows for role consolidation across application boundaries, which greatly reduces the complexity of maintaining the authorization information.

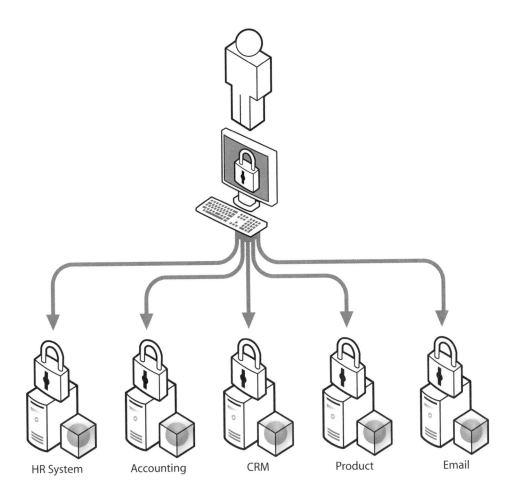

HR System   Accounting   CRM   Product   Email

In applications that are integrated with external applications, such as channel partners or suppliers, identity management becomes a greater challenge. In these situations, it is ideal for each company to retain the authentication and authorization functions for their users, yet allow them to access the appropriate services of the other organizations. This is accomplished through the use of a federated identity management system. In a federated system, each organization maintains its own identity repository using whatever design it wishes, and a limited trust relationship is established between the separate systems. This approach allows identity and permission data to be passed between these systems in a way that creates the single sign-on user experience across organizational boundaries.

Databases

As the repository of all enterprise data, databases are one of the most critical pieces of the technical infrastructure. The ability to leverage databases in a flexible and agile manner requires careful design decisions in the application infrastructure layer.

One of the most important aspects of application-to-database integration is the mechanism the applications use to access the data. This can have important effects on performance, security, and deployment options. Applications that utilize dynamic SQL, for example, have limited options for tuning the performance of queries. Additionally, opening up a database to dynamic SQL allows malicious or defective code to potentially wreak havoc on the data, even crashing the database with queries that are too complex to process in any reasonable length of time. Static SQL is an alternative, as well as funneling all access to the database through stored procedures.

Any application that accesses a database will need to authenticate against the database and will only be allowed to perform the operations associated with the authenticated identity. There are two basic approaches to authenticating an application to a database – application authentication and end-user authentication.

In the former, the application has an identity and a password associated with it that is used for all operations. Although this has the benefit of being simple to implement, it has several drawbacks. First, the identity will need to be stored somewhere, either in the source code (a very bad idea) or in some form of configuration data. This presents a security risk no matter which approach is taken. Additionally, this form of authentication means that the database cannot restrict access to operations based on the actual user of the application, since the end user is not known. If the database needs to track changes to the data based on the end-user credentials, then this will have to be accomplished via a different mechanism.

End-user authentication allows the database to perform granular authorization, but at the expense of connection pooling, since authenticated identities are associated with database connections. There are also various compromises, including:

- An application identity for queries but end-user authentication for updates
- Using an application identity but passing the end-user credentials to stored procedures in the database to allow for fine-grained authorization and auditing

Applications must be designed in such a way that their access to the database takes advantage of the optimizations implemented there, such as logical views and indexes. This requires an understanding of the design of the database on the part of the application development team and an understanding of the application on the part of the database administrator.

Transaction management and scope is a critical function of the database that is under the control of the application. Applications that keep transactions open between user interactions are said to have "long-running transactions." This type of design can cripple the performance of the database and thereby the application because database locks are held for potentially long periods of time. Long database lock times cause contention for database resources and can cause deadlock situations. Application services should be designed so that transactions do not span the scope of a single service invocation. Applications that require transactional semantics that span service invocations should implement alternative mechanisms, such as batching updates or implementing compensating transactions.

Database design follows the rules of data normalization, with exceptions made for performance reasons. Application design follows the rules of domain modeling. The two models for the enterprise data often differ, sometimes drastically, due to the different design criteria of the layers. Bringing these two different models together in an efficient, flexible manner is one of the most challenging parts of application design and has led to an entire collection of patterns and frameworks exclusively devoted to bridging this so-called "impedance-mismatch."

Application Servers

All modern applications are hosted within application servers. Although there are several competing application server technologies, the basic functionality provided is fairly consistent across the spectrum. The application infrastructure layer needs to be designed to utilize the services provided by the application servers in the technical infrastructure in order to leverage the common frameworks implemented there.

An important feature provided by application servers is the ability to pool scarce resources like database connections and re-use them among multiple service requests. This allows a small number of resources to serve a large number of requests, by giving each incoming request access to the resource while it is being processed, then returning the resource to the shared pool where another request can utilize it. Pooling and sharing resources makes the application more efficient by maximizing the actual utilization of scarce resources, while minimizing the amount of time resources are held while not in use.

Application servers typically handle the management and coordination of transactions, especially those that cross component, resource, and even application boundaries. Applications should be designed in such a way that they do not perform their own transaction coordination, but instead rely on the application server container that hosts them to provide these services. This will lead to greater maintainability of the applications and much greater flexibility in the deployment models available to the application.

Processing threads are a critical resource of the operating system and underlying hardware on every platform. Delegating the management of threads to the application server makes the entire node more efficient, since the application server can pool the threads and hand them out to different services as incoming requests are dispatched. This eliminates the overhead associated with either creating/destroying threads on each incoming request or creating a thread for every possible request and letting them all sit idle most of the time. Applications should be designed to take advantage of the thread pooling provided by the application server that hosts them.

As requests come in to an application server, they are examined by the container to determine what service the request is destined for. Once this is determined, the container pulls a thread from the thread pool if one is available and hands off the request and the thread to the appropriate service for processing. This process is known as request dispatching and is a key function provided by application servers that should be leveraged by the application infrastructure layer in order to make the best use of resources.

Application servers should provide the key functionality to make applications perform in a clustered deployment. Rather than handle the complexities associated with deploying an application on multiple machines and making them behave like a single logical node, the application infrastructure should rely on the application servers and load balancers in the technical infrastructure to provide this capability.

The ability for applications to look up services in a directory at the moment they are needed and find a suitable implementation is known as "dynamic discovery." This service is implemented by the technical infrastructure layer and can facilitate many capabilities such as fail-over, load balancing, and location independence. Applications should be developed in such a way that they depend on the technical infrastructure to provide dynamic discovery services and so that they make use of dynamic discovery on every service invocation.

Collaboration Tools

The application infrastructure needs to be integrated with the collaboration tools provided by the technical infrastructure and should leverage these collaboration services to create higher levels of productivity for the organization's knowledge workers.

Applications that have workflow aspects or that need to notify human users of events or changes of status might need to generate automatic e-mail messages. In order to accomplish this, the applications will need access to an e-mail server connected to the enterprise-wide e-mail infrastructure. Service level agreements will dictate how such application e-mail gateways can and should be deployed. Security requirements must be taken into account, since the application will need a means to authenticate against the e-mail server.

Collaboration areas are a fundamental part of the technical infrastructure that will become increasingly valuable in the future. The application layer utilizes these spaces to store documents that are being developed or accessed by a team, to maintain meeting notes and schedules, and to organize and store all of the artifacts associated with various types of projects. While most applications fail to leverage these collaboration spaces today, others treat them simply as file systems where documents are stored. More advanced applications are capable of being deployed inside these spaces and to become a part of the collaboration environment.

Instant messaging, text paging, and text messaging have become important communication tools and are increasingly finding uses in the application infrastructure layer, as applications need mechanisms for contacting human users that are mobile and don't necessarily have access to e-mail. As these tools become more important to the business processes of the organization, the reliance on the implementations in the technical infrastructure increases and more attention will need to be paid to these components.

Voice response systems are maturing and can be found in many enterprises' IT environments. Voice mail is generally treated as an island of information. With the advent of voice over IP and the continued deployment of this revolutionary technology, voice mail systems will become increasingly integrated with the rest of the application infrastructure. Outgoing voice calls generated by applications are also an important capability of the technical infrastructure, as applications need to alert users and customers that may not have any other means of contact of important events.

For example, credit card companies have implemented advanced artificial intelligence systems to detect fraudulent use of their credit cards. In fraud cases, the speed with which the fraudulent usage is confirmed can mean the difference between approving the charge or denying it, recovering or losing the issued funds if the charge was fraudulent but approved, and catching the perpetrator or letting them escape to commit further fraud. Making the fraud alert system capable of placing an outgoing voice call to the cardholder's cell phone, informing them of the potential fraud, and asking them to confirm or deny the legitimacy of the usage can reduce the time between detection and resolution from days or hours to minutes or even seconds.

Management Tools

The promise of Service Oriented Architecture lies in the ability to re-use business services across multiple business processes and in the agility that comes from decoupling the services from the business process, allowing the process to change as the competitive landscape demands. As an SOA matures, the management of the application infrastructure and the services provided there become an increasingly important function of the technical infrastructure. Tools specifically designed to manage this environment must either be developed or purchased. Effective management tools allow the operational IT organization to catalog, manage, deploy, and monitor the application infrastructure.

Service Registry

One of the most important components of the management toolset is the registry of service interfaces. This registry serves several purposes:

- It implements the runtime operational directory used by applications to perform dynamic discovery of services

- It provides the development teams with an inventory of existing services from which composite applications can be built

- It serves as an important part of the IT governance process and an important tool to the governance body

The service registry contains metadata about the services provided by the application infrastructure, including:

- Messages associated with the interfaces

- Policies that apply to the messages and to the services

- Security attributes of the interfaces

- Endpoints where the services are deployed

The registry must be searchable by applications looking for an implementation of a particular interface to support dynamic discovery. The repository also must be searchable by the people in the IT organization. This allows development teams looking for preexisting services to leverage an SOA governance body to support ongoing management of the enterprise's SOA.

If business users are to define business processes that leverage the services provided by the application infrastructure, then they will require modeling tools that are geared towards nontechnical skill sets. Without the ability to visualize existing business processes and develop new ones without embarking on a development project, the organization will not be able to realize the potential of the SOA, especially the ability to make the enterprise more agile. These modeling tools are an important component of the technical infrastructure that has a high level of visibility to the business, since they will define the face of the business processes that the enterprise implements.

Modeling can also help the IT organization determine the dependencies between applications, services, business processes, and the services that implement them. Understanding the dependencies is a necessity when defining the service level agreements of the applications. This has a tremendous impact on the technical infrastructure that is ultimately responsible for deploying an environment that can meet the requirements of the business with regard to performance and availability.

Information in the service registry will become more critical to the organization as the roll out of the SOA continues. As this information becomes more valuable, the ability to extract and summarize it into reports will similarly increase in value. The nature of the service registry is different from traditional relational databases, so standard reporting packages might not provide the necessary functionality. Ideally, the vendor that provides the service registry should design and implement customized reporting capabilities as well.

Dynamic Systems

As IT environments have grown increasingly complex and applications increasingly distributed, the cost of managing the technical infrastructure, on which these distributed systems depend, has increased dramatically. Initiatives to address this increased complexity and associated management cost fall under the general umbrella term of "grid computing." An extension of the grid computing concept known as the Dynamic Systems Initiative (DSI) is an industry-wide effort led by Microsoft. DSI has as its primary goal to address increasing management costs by addressing the complexity of the environment:

The Dynamic Systems Initiative exists to create a connection from the design of a system, to the operation of that system, on through to the end users using that system. By creating an integrated feedback loop spanning the entire life cycle of a system, we can facilitate the ongoing improvement of IT infrastructure with software. The Dynamic Systems Initiative is about maximizing people resources and delivering software that can decrease labor costs through the entire IT life cycle. For this effort to succeed, systems must be designed with operations in mind, with management a core attribute of the underlying platform.[14]

A key component of this strategy is to develop applications with deployment in mind. Too often the application development team writes software without thinking about production environments, then "tosses it over the wall" to the technical infrastructure team to deploy, manage, and maintain. This approach results in design flaws and inefficient use of the technical infrastructure or organization, which adds cost to the IT budget. By making deployment decisions part of the application design process, operating costs are ultimately decreased and development teams are responsible for the production deployment model as well as the application.

Application development teams can take deployment options into account while they design and develop distributed systems. The process of modeling the operational environment and actually deploying the software to it needs to be integrated into the tools used by the application development teams. Through providing this functionality directly into the integrated development environment that the application team uses on a day-to-day basis the need to design for deployment is reinforced and ultimately made more efficient. The tools should not only model the deployment environment, but they should automate the actual process as well. This approach ensures consistency across the development, quality assurance, and production environments.

Once applications are deployed, the ongoing operational characteristics of the applications are communicated back to the application infrastructure organization. This communication is done by the operational technical infrastructure organization with the assistance of various monitoring and reporting tools. This allows the application development teams to make modifications that will increase the efficiency of deployed applications, as well as helping them to make better design decisions on future applications.

Capturing the experience of the actual users of the system and feeding that back to both the application development team and the operational organization can provide valuable insights into both the application and technical infrastructures. This additional feedback loop can serve to focus the efforts of the IT organization on those projects that will yield the most business value.

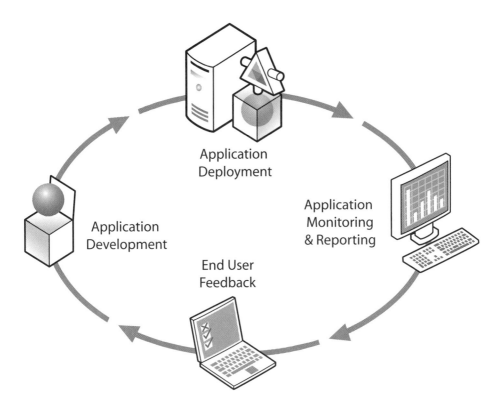

Effective monitoring solutions track metrics for performance, utilization of systems, and monitor server and service functionality. Issues occurring in the environment are either reported to the IT organization, or actions can be taken to automatically resolve specific issues. An effective monitoring infrastructure needs to be centralized, standardized, and should aggregate data from different applications, platforms, and technologies. Monitoring solutions aid in problem determination and resolution and can facilitate ongoing capacity planning. Monitoring the infrastructure for security risks can prevent the loss of data to malicious users, whether within the organization or outside of it. Monitoring data has the most value when important information is communicated to the appropriate people within the organization in a timely manner and at an appropriate level of detail.

Wrap-Up

This chapter looked at the ways that the application infrastructure should utilize and leverage the services provided by the technical infrastructure. Tools for monitoring and managing the technical infrastructure were also discussed.

This completes the second part of this book, which has been about integration. The ways that an SOA enables application integration, the ways in which the application infrastructure layer leverages the services provided by the technical infrastructure, and the ways that the enterprise gateway leverages the application infrastructure were all discussed.

In the next section a roadmap for migrating to an SOA will be presented, including techniques for building it, how to execute the program, the business case for doing so, and the organizational impact of the process.

Part III: Service Oriented Architecture Roadmap

Chapter 9:   Building a Service Oriented Architecture

The decision to adopt a Service Oriented Architecture is the beginning of a journey for the entire organization. The approach taken may vary for each company, but the goal of building an agile, loosely coupled suite of business services and leveraging this application infrastructure from the enterprise gateway remains constant. Executing an SOA strategy is a process of adopting practices and tools that implement this vision.

The various strategic and tactical decisions and processes a company can implement to arrive at an SOA can be divided at the highest level into two categories, "bottom-up" and "top-down."

Bottom-Up

Many organizations begin this journey without knowing it. Application integration projects are undertaken in the absence of an overall integration strategy and the technical staff leads the way by opportunistically using web services for new interfaces. These environments often have one or more application or system architects that are familiar with the promise of services and understand that building interfaces using this technology is the best alternative, especially in the presence of heterogeneous platforms.

This approach often occurs in the context of point-to-point integrations of existing applications. Because of this, the services might not be developed to the appropriate level of granularity for broader use and may not take advantage of a service registry for location independence. Although this is a less-than ideal approach to SOA adoption, it is at least a start in the right direction.

Application integration projects have existed for a long time and there are many existing integration techniques, technologies, and deployments in any enterprise. As the number of differing interface styles proliferate, the management of these integration points increases in complexity. Many of these integration projects probably resulted in tight coupling between applications, resulting in brittle interfaces that require maintenance whenever either application changes.

As part of the migration to an SOA, these existing interfaces should migrate to, and new integration projects should take, a service oriented approach. The SOA adoption program should develop a comprehensive survey and inventory of existing applications and integration points, identify those that are strategic, and develop a plan for the migration, retirement or replacement of each with service oriented interfaces.

Benefits

Since the bottom-up approach is driven by the technical organization and is associated with existing integration projects, this strategy can be pursued with little or no executive buy-in. The technology champions convince their peers and immediate management that services are a good approach for each individual project and over time more and more interfaces become service oriented. This can be an important benefit of the bottom-up approach in organizations where there is significant resistance to change or where executive buy-in for strategies can be difficult or lengthy to obtain.

An important benefit from this approach is the additional experience the IT organization gains in the technologies and tools associated with services. As technology champions mentor others in the organization, knowledge is transferred among team members and across team boundaries, building momentum for an SOA integration strategy within the technical organization as more and more people become familiar with it and the associated benefits. As knowledge grows, so will the desire within the organization to follow some of the more advanced techniques that come with the adoption of an SOA mindset.

Because the bottom-up approach is executed in the context of existing integration projects that are already planned and budgeted, it delivers value to the organization in an incremental, iterative fashion. This avoids the potential resistance to an approach that requires an upfront investment in time and resources and a lengthy planning and design phase before any business value is delivered. In most environments this is a near necessity, unless executive management includes a technology visionary that can sell the organization on the benefits of an SOA strategy.

The bottom-up approach to wrapping existing applications in service layers to facilitate application integration means that the business logic is re-used, rather than re-developed. Since the cost of reimplementing it would usually be much higher than the cost of implementing the service wrappers, the return on investment for implementing the wrapper services will be higher as well.

Shortcomings

While the bottom-up approach has several important benefits, it has several shortcomings as well, some of which are serious limitations to following the bottom-up approach for more than just the initial phase of SOA adoption.

One of the immediate problems with this approach is that the service interfaces are designed in isolation from each other, in the context of individual application integration projects. The development team only takes into account the needs of the current project and only designs the service interface from the perspective of the two applications being integrated. Because a broader approach is necessary to design interfaces that can be reused across the entire IT environment, these early services will likely have little potential for long-term reuse or for being leveraged from the enterprise gateway. Often these interfaces will expose application-specific attributes that should be encapsulated within the application and will yield brittle interfaces easily broken when changes to the underlying application are made. This brittleness can be visible and can be seen as a reason that an SOA is not delivering on its promise.

Since the interfaces are designed in a vacuum, there is little chance that they will take into account an overall canonical data model that should be used across all service interfaces. Once the analysis is performed to determine an appropriate enterprise-wide model for the business entities used in messages, the services that were developed in the early phases will need to be modified to fit into this model, requiring changes to the applications that depend on them.

Another inefficiency of this approach is that the teams undertaking the implementation of these early services may be unaware of each other's work, and may end up duplicating effort or redefining the same business entities in different ways. These overlapping services and models will need to be merged once an enterprise-wide model is developed.

Early service implementations used for point-to-point application integration are usually developed without any thought about a larger service fabric; the potential flexibility is limited. Usually the consuming application is "hard-coded" to a particular endpoint. Although this is easily rectified at a later date when the rest of the infrastructure to support the Service Oriented Architecture is in place, re-use and flexibility will be limited in the interim.

The lack of an overall strategy for implementing services may lead to inappropriate use of technology in certain cases. For example, the lack of standards for implementing the security aspects of services may lead to one-off identity repositories that are disconnected from the larger enterprise context and will need to be replaced later. If an SOA is a strategic element, the choice of implementation technologies needs to be strategic and not left to individual project teams.

One of the worst potential problems with taking a bottom-up approach to SOA adoption rests with the potential for failure. If isolated integration projects that are utilizing services are unsuccessful, the failure may be blamed on the technology, or worse, on the service oriented approach, giving the strategy a blemish that may delay or prevent later efforts to adopt a more comprehensive strategy.

A common misconception on projects that utilize services without an overall SOA strategy is the belief among the team that they need to create a complete set of services for the application. Since the environment is not ready for the consumption of most of the services an application might provide, the development of them is a very significant waste of development resources. Furthermore, since the service interfaces are designed in the absence of both an enterprise-wide canonical data model and an identified consumer, it is highly unlikely that the service interface will be appropriate at a later date when a need is identified, meaning that the development effort is spent on writing services that will never be used.

Organizations that decide to follow a bottom-up approach, or discover an existing web service integration project following a bottom-up approach should develop mitigation strategies for each of these shortcomings.

As the bottom-up approach reaches a certain critical mass, both the value of services and the pain of not having an enterprise-wide plan and approach to development, deployment, and management will inevitably lead management to begin a top-down effort. Often, the security infrastructure required to handle cross-application identity management will kick-off the top-down initiative.

Top-Down

In the top-down approach, management leads the way by clearly setting SOA as a strategic direction and creating initiatives to implement it. Given the up-front costs of adopting an SOA and the inevitability of the top-down approach, it is highly desirable that companies take this approach initially.

The first and most important step in implementing an SOA using the top-down approach is deciding to do so and communicating that decision throughout the IT community. As with any enterprise-wide initiative, active executive sponsorship is critical to success in implementing an SOA.

Management, working with the IT organization, the user community, and outside vendors and consultants, should develop an SOA roadmap justifying and describing the company's approach and planning the rollout to the entire organization. For most organizations, the scope of the adoption program will span multiple years; IT must work together with executive management and business units to prioritize the effort, ensuring that the organization focuses on near-term projects that contribute to the bottom line while still moving incrementally toward the envisioned architecture.

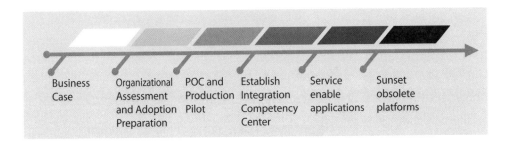

| Business Case | Organizational Assessment and Adoption Preparation | POC and Production Pilot | Establish Integration Competency Center | Service enable applications | Sunset obsolete platforms |

The executive mandate to implement the SOA roadmap initiates many activities. First and foremost, an SOA is implemented in phases and is inherently inclusive and evolutionary. It is important for the strategy to be clearly thought out and communicated, and a plan for adoption should clearly address what priorities are highest, and why and what aspects are best left for later phases. Ongoing development projects should be included in the adoption program, rather than treating them as irrelevant to the SOA strategy. This inclusive approach will help guide the organization and get everyone on board with management's direction.

The top-down approach to SOA adoption is much more of a program than a project and will encompass many different projects, initiatives, teams, and organizations. Each project should be developed iteratively, and iterations should be planned based on strategic direction and risk-based project management. These techniques don't eliminate the potential for failure, but they minimize the impact of failures on the overall organization and the program. They also ensure that false starts are corrected sooner rather than later, minimizing wasted effort.

Ensuring that all projects adhere to the enterprise SOA strategy is one of the biggest challenges facing organizations that take the top-down approach to SOA adoption. The responsibility for managing, monitoring, and enforcing the practices and policies of the SOA program cannot be distributed among the various teams within the organization; it requires the creation of a centralized governance body that can oversee multiple projects and perform a consultative role on each. Although this group may go by various names, "Integration Competency Center" (ICC) is a reasonable choice and has some momentum in the industry.

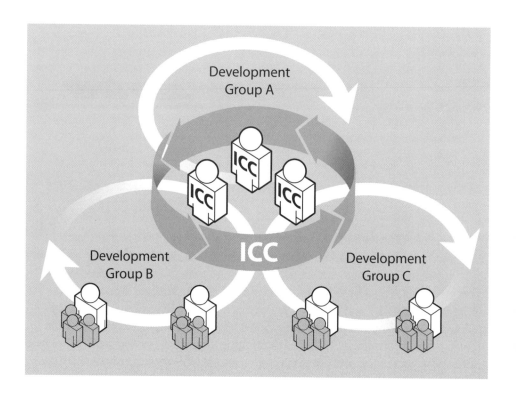

The ICC is both a governance organization and a center of expertise related to the SOA adoption program. These two objectives must be balanced, since the governance duties will take some authority away from the project teams, yet the ability of the ICC to facilitate the projects will require significant goodwill, communication, and cooperation from those same teams.

It is unlikely that most project teams in a medium sized IT organization will have the necessary expertise initially to adhere to the SOA strategy of the enterprise and successfully implement services based on it. The ICC should provide architectural consulting services to each project team to ease the transition and adoption of the new technologies and techniques.

Defining the best practices related to service design, implementation, and usage are a key responsibility of the ICC. Best practices should not just sit on a shelf in a three-ring binder; to be effective they must be communicated to the project teams and made part of everyday activities. A combination of communication channels should be used in most environments, including formal training, mentoring and coaching, self-motivated learning, and reviews.

In the top-down approach, the coordination of a comprehensive inventory of applications, and their integration points to other applications, is the responsibility of the ICC. For each of the identified applications, a strategy should be put in place for service-enabling the application or for replacing the application with services provided by other applications, either existing or new. For each identified integration point, an appropriate approach, priority, and timeframe should be identified for moving it from the legacy integration technology to a service based approach. For each business entity identified in the canonical data model, the ICC should establish an appropriate system of record for the entity and define the service interfaces the system of record should implement relative to it.

Overcoming cultural challenges is as critical to success in rolling out an SOA as the technical issues. The standard approaches to large-scale organizational change are applicable. The organization should actively identify and address cultural impediments to implementing the SOA roadmap. Statements like "our problem is special," "that won't work in our environment," or "this is just like <insert technology failure of the past>" are often symptoms of an underlying fear or a poor understanding of the strategy. Identify and create a plan to address the underlying root cause of these roadblocks. Integrating a feedback cycle into the performance evaluation and compensation models can help mitigate these cultural challenges. Key educational gaps should be identified and an appropriate training program created to address them. The influence of outside expertise can be a crucial and necessary force for change in an organization.

One of the first and most important service offerings of the ICC should be to identify any relevant industry standards that should be utilized in the creation of the suite of business services. Most industries have some standards bodies that have started the process of creating canonical data models and interface definitions. Others have legacy standards that can be adapted to the new technologies. In most cases companies that are interested in adopting one of these standards will want to join the body that defines and controls the standard so that they can gain access to implementation details from other companies using it and potentially influence the direction of the standard's development.

Some companies will find that there are actually multiple industry standards that could be adopted, and they should carefully evaluate the appropriate usage of each, define a common policy for choosing between them, and agree upon on a common model that embraces all aspects of the enterprise.

Organizations that purchase large application suites with a Service Oriented Architecture are adopting the vendor's interface definitions as a *defacto* standard. When custom applications are incorporated into the SOA, the vendor's interface definitions should usually provide a starting point for the definition of new services.

The ICC should work with COTS vendors whose products are already deployed in the enterprise to ensure that they implement service oriented interfaces in future versions and are able to consume the services provided by other applications. When evaluating applications for purchase and deployment within the organization, the ICC should require that all products implement an appropriate service oriented interface.

As the SOA is implemented and rolled out to the production environment, the infrastructure necessary to manage, monitor, and maintain the SOA will become critical to the success of the program. The ICC should evaluate all of the various products that might assist the organization in these areas, and select the ones for usage based on the criteria identified by management working in close association to the ICC and the various project teams and stakeholders.

Commitment to an SOA strategy has implications for all current and future development. Most, if not all, development should be done on service oriented platforms (like .NET and J2EE) and with an SOA mindset. For legacy platforms that are strategic to the enterprise, a technology and strategy should be developed for integrating them into the SOA. Application development groups should wrap existing applications in business service interfaces to leverage past investments and achieve maximum re-use. It may be necessary to port certain applications that have legacy maintenance concerns.

Enterprise portal applications should be implemented as service consumers whenever possible. This provides the greatest level of flexibility for portal applications and lowest degree of coupling to back-end applications. It also serves as an important driver for the implementation of business services.

Benefits

One of the biggest benefits of following a top-down approach is that the executive buy-in and prioritization allow the organization to focus early on delivering the functionality most critical to the success of the business. This sponsorship can result in appropriate funding for the ICC and active change management. By addressing service development strategically instead of opportunistically, the benefits gained from adopting a Service Oriented Architecture are recognized earlier, and the overall ROI of the program is higher because the return curve is accelerated and compressed.

Because the top-down approach focuses on the entire strategy rather than individual point-to-point integration projects, it forces the organization to focus on enterprise architecture. The side effects of this, such as identification and documentation of the business processes that support the enterprise and the associated steps and workflows associated with each, create additional opportunities for improvement and automation across the business as a whole. In many cases, the move to an SOA causes companies to really take a close look at what they actually do for the first time, which can lead to some big surprises among management when they see just how inefficiently they are doing business.

Shortcomings

Although the top-down approach is clearly the best, and indeed the inevitable approach for a successful SOA adoption program, it too has its shortcomings. Each potential problem area should be planned for in the SOA adoption strategy and appropriate mitigation strategies put in place to avoid them.

One pitfall to avoid in any top-down, management-driven effort is the risk that the organization will get stuck in analysis paralysis and spend endless effort in meetings and generating documents, without ever building anything of value. Iterative and incremental management techniques should be used to mitigate these risks. Time-boxing in particular is an excellent way to ensure that just enough analysis and design occur, without risking the development of "complete" designs that try to take into account eventualities and scenarios that are too speculative.

The possibility that the IT organization could slide into a waterfall approach to development is high, especially if an iterative and incremental approach is new. Unfortunately, if this occurs then the risk of analysis paralysis will return, since the mitigating factors were based on abandoning the waterfall approach in the first place. For this reason, the ICC must provide ongoing project management and software development process consultation and oversight to ensure the organization's various project teams continue to adopt and follow the best practices of modern software development methods.

A lesser risk is that the organization will fall victim to political in-fighting or cultural impediments, as different project teams and departments fight over control of the SOA vision and implementation. This risk must be addressed by executive management, who alone can put in place incentives and barriers to this type of organizational dynamic. To accomplish this, management must translate the technical aspects of SOA into a business value proposition for the organization.

Wrap-Up

This chapter addressed the two basic approaches to SOA adoption. The bottom-up, opportunistic approach was discussed along with its benefits and shortcomings. The top-down, management-driven approach was also examined, along with the initiatives appropriate to this approach.

Every organization that embarks on the SOA journey must eventually end up following the top-down approach if they are to recognize all of the promised benefits of an SOA. The earlier an organization adopts this program, the better will be their return on the SOA investment.

In the next chapter, the business case for adopting a Service Oriented Architecture will be examined in greater detail.

Chapter 10:   The Business Case

Understanding the business case for the new IT infrastructure
will enable the champions to sell the program to management
and investors.   The costs and benefits come from several
sources, and understanding each will help convince the various
stakeholders of the business value to be recognized by adopting
an SOA.

Show me the Money

The purpose of technology is to make the business more competitive. Since technology serves the business, it makes sense for the business to lead the technology. Too many organizations allow the IT department to lead the way when it comes to technology adoption. Business stakeholders should not only be involved in the identification and prioritization of technology projects, they should ultimately be responsible for the successful implementation and rollout of IT projects, taking credit for the successes, and assuming responsibility for the failures. Only then can the organization be relatively sure that the technology is serving the business rather than driving it.

In the past, IT has done a poor job of justifying technology spending based on business needs and business financial models. It has often been said that productivity gains are difficult to measure and assign value to, so traditional models for determining the potential benefits of a project don't apply to IT. This is essentially the whining defense: "It's too difficult; I don't want to do it."

Technology investments should not be treated differently than other types of investments like plant and equipment. They have costs associated with them and (hopefully) benefits that will result. Over time, the benefits should pay for the cost of the investment, or the project is not worth undertaking.

Implementing the IT environment presented in the previous chapters has costs associated with it as well. Some of these costs are merely reallocations of existing IT costs, and others are unique to the process of building an agile IT environment. The following sections will take a look at these costs first and then the benefits associated with this approach.

Technology Costs

One of the primary costs associated with most SOA implementations will result from product purchases. There are many components that must be put in place, and most are available from outside vendors and support standard interfaces and protocols, allowing each organization to mix-and-match various tools and products to come up with a best-fit approach unique to their environment.

Some of these costs will be hardware costs, since these new components of the agile IT environment will require hosting horsepower, and some are software licenses. In the technical infrastructure layer, foundational hardware and software will need to be put into place and incorporated into the larger technical infrastructure. Centralized management and monitoring software will need to be installed, and the associated staff to administer it will need to be trained or hired. In the application infrastructure layer, service-enabling technologies may need to be put in place, such as enterprise service buses, web service containers, or asynchronous messaging products. In the enterprise gateway layer, business process management and orchestration products will need to be purchased and deployed, as well as the enterprise portal solution.

In the context of an overall enterprise IT strategy, the cost of the enabling technologies need not be borne by individual projects. If there are multiple projects on the agenda and each requires a given enabling technology, or could at least benefit from it, then the cost of the product may be spread across all the projects and thereby ease the cost benefit scenario for each.

Abraham Maslow warned of a possible pitfall in this approach when he said, "If the only tool you have is a hammer, you tend to see every problem as a nail." Organizations that have purchased a given enabling technology often try to shoehorn every IT project into the capabilities and development model of the enabling technology, even when the requirements of the project are a poor fit. There are always tradeoffs to make, but the IT organization must be able to determine when a technology is appropriate for use on a project, and when it is more appropriate to build or buy a new capability.

Organizational Costs

Implementing a Service Oriented Architecture will require development effort from the application infrastructure team and this effort has costs associated with it. Although in some cases implementing functionality using services is just an alternative design, in other scenarios the creation of services constitutes additional incremental effort. There are costs to not adopting an SOA as well, and these can be calculated and seen as benefits to the approach, justifying the additional effort required up front by savings and additional capabilities in the future.

Any change of the magnitude discussed here will touch most, if not all, of the IT organization, as well as other parts of the business that rely on IT. Whenever organizational change is undertaken, there will be organizational friction created, as people and groups struggle to adapt their current ways of thinking and working to the new paradigm. This organizational friction hurts productivity in the short term, since the time spent trying to adapt to the new way is time not spent doing things the old way. Just as it is possible to measure the benefits associated with productivity gains, it is likewise possible to measure the costs associated with productivity losses. The cost of the organizational friction created by the adoption of an enterprise Service Oriented Architecture should be factored into the overall financial justification for the adoption program.

The new technologies, products, approaches, and techniques associated with the new IT vision will most likely be foreign to much of the organization's IT staff. Educational programs will need to be put in place to bring the appropriate resources up to the desired levels of competency. Just as in any scenario involving educating a diverse group in a broad range of subjects, a one-size-fits-all approach will be inefficient and potentially counterproductive. A combination of formal classroom education, individual mentoring, and other approaches should be used appropriately to achieve the goals of the adoption program. A just-in-time approach to all education is encouraged, since people will tend to gain the most from learning things that they can immediately put to use. All of this education has costs associated with it, from the tuition charged for classroom courses to the licensing for intranet-based web courses to the time it takes the employees to actually complete the various educational programs. These costs are all part of the SOA adoption program.

A necessary part of SOA adoption is IT governance. Without strong governance processes and an associated governance body, the services implemented by the various projects and application teams will be inconsistent and will not leverage a common data model. Lack of a strong governance body will also hamper the ability of the application infrastructure teams to make good use of the underlying technical infrastructure assets in a consistent way. The governance process and the associated governance body required for the successful adoption of an enterprise SOA are a cost associated with the adoption program.

Return on Investment

Again, technology in and of itself never provides any benefit. In order for it to benefit from an investment in technology, they must apply the technology to the business. The successful application of technology investments to business processes will provide benefits to the business that will (hopefully) yield a positive return for the technology investment.

The most important measure of the success for any IT project is whether the investment shows a positive return, how big the return is relative to the investment, and how long it takes for the benefits to outweigh the costs. These attributes are collectively referred to as the return on investment, or ROI.

A financial model that takes into account all of the estimated costs and benefits for an IT project and forecasts the associated return on investment should be required before any project is officially launched. Such rigorous financial models are an important part of the executive decision making process and have become standard operating procedure for approving other types of investment, such as in new plant and equipment.

IT organizations that continue to resist the need to create financial models that justify technology spending are putting the entire IT budget at risk. They have no way of determining whether they are actually helping the business perform better or are merely spending money on technology that may or may not have any value.

The implementation of Business Process Automation, Management, and Monitoring actually enables the organization to measure the ROI of IT by providing important metrics on the performance of business processes. By using these metrics to identify areas of inefficiency, the organization can target IT projects at those areas with the highest potential return. Continued monitoring of these metrics will allow the organization to determine whether any given project actually created the projected return.

Measuring Value

It is often said that the value associated with IT projects cannot be quantified and measured, so the creation of an ROI model is impossible. If it is true that the value of a given project cannot be quantified and measured (in the vast majority of cases it can, but the IT department does not want to put forth the effort required to do so), then it is also true that the value cannot be realized and therefore has no impact on the bottom line. Since the project will have costs but no benefit, it should not be undertaken.

When calculating the benefits associated with a given project, it is extremely important that the organization take care in which metrics are used. Measuring something will almost always have consequences, and the law of unintended consequences is in effect for measuring activities just like all others. Measuring the wrong thing can result in organizational incentives that are counterproductive to the overall business goals of the enterprise.

Financial Models

The financial model is a tool that helps management decide whether or not a project should be undertaken and how it should be prioritized against other projects. Projects whose financial model never shows a positive return should obviously never be started. Projects that show a lengthy period before the investment is returned should be weighed carefully before initiation, especially given the short lifetime of many IT investments. In these cases, it is often possible to break up the project into multiple projects or phases that can be made somewhat independent of each other, allowing the organization to tackle the high ROI portions first. By the time the low ROI projects are due to be tackled, the priorities may have changed or alternatives may have surfaced that eliminate the need for them all together.

A point that is often missed in ROI models for SOA related projects is that an individual project may benefit the organization several times over. A human resources portal, for example, requires the implementation of a portal server and product, but that same implementation can be used as a place to access customer information or to allow business partners to access data about their orders. There are multiple benefits to include in the model:

- Reduced maintenance costs
- Reduced integration costs
- An incremental milestone in the overall SOA adoption program

Financial models are just that – models. They are based on estimates, projections, and assumptions. Although it is imperative that they be created to justify IT spends, it is equally important that they not slow down the adoption of valuable technology in the interests of completeness. The IT organization and the business stakeholders should focus on creating models quickly, then iterate on them as more data become available. In many cases multiple financial models should be created to help the project management decide between alternative implementations. The realities of actual costs may result in an ROI model that starts out looking rosy, but turns south once the project is underway. In these cases, the management must be prepared to take a close look at the model and possibly to cancel the project and cut the organization's losses.

Given that the business should own the project and take responsibility for successes or failures, it makes sense for the business to also own the ROI model, unless the ROI is specifically related to IT (for example, by making IT more manageable). The division of labor between the business stakeholders and IT can be negotiated and will likely vary from project to project and organization to organization, yet the ultimate responsibility for building the financial justification and selling it to management lies with the business, as does the determination of success and the associated credit or blame.

In the context of the reshaping of the IT environment, it is important that the financial models for various projects take into account opportunities to completely reshape the business processes, rather than merely automating existing processes or making them more efficient. This is where the agility associated with a Service Oriented Architecture built on a solid technical infrastructure offers opportunities for the business to leapfrog the competition, redefining their business and potentially entire industries. The costs of this type of business process reengineering can potentially be higher than merely fine-tuning existing business processes, yet this is exactly where the largest benefits can potentially be realized.

Very few business models are designed to shrink the organization or to keep it the same size – growth is usually the goal. The ROI models created to justify technology spending should therefore take growth projections and goals into account, potentially recognizing larger benefits in the future due to projected growth of the enterprise.

Prioritizing Investments

It is impossible to tackle all projects that have a positive ROI at the same time. Some means of prioritizing projects is necessary. Once the organization is in the habit of requiring financial models for every project, it becomes much easier to prioritize projects relative to each other. One obvious way is to prioritize projects with the highest return in the shortest period of time above projects with lower return and/or longer return periods. Although there are undoubtedly other aspects that affect project priority, this should be one of the basic consistent means used by management.

We can safely assume that there will always be more potential projects than there will be resources to accomplish them. Focusing on smaller projects and prioritizing them both by their relative risk and their return on investment will have the effect of eliminating wasteful projects, since these will consistently be prioritized lower and may never even be initiated.

There are multiple ways to measure return on investment and to quantify it in financial terms, but for the purposes of prioritization, a metric that combines the cost, benefit, and time aspects into a single number that can be compared across projects is invaluable. For example, the net present value of the project brings all of the time based costs and benefits into the present and gives each project a value in present-day dollars. This "net present value" number has the added benefit of being easy to understand even by people with no background in finance. An alternative measure of project value is the internal rate of return, which gives the project a percentage rate of return per year, much like a mutual fund or certificate of deposit will have a rate of return per year. The metric used is not as important as that a single metric is identified that allows projects with different ROI models to be prioritized against each other in an objective fashion.

The availability of investment capital should also be an important part of the project prioritization process. During economic or industry downturns, companies will naturally cut back on IT investments, as they do all types of investments. When IT budgets shrink, smaller projects with lower cost will naturally have higher priority than large expensive projects.

Market demand can have both a direct and indirect affect on project prioritization. In industries where a company gets out ahead of its competitors with a Service Oriented Architecture, enterprise portal and partner integration hub, the customers and partners for that industry may demand similar capabilities from the other players. Companies that are not able to catch up to the leader in a reasonable amount of time face loss of market share, increased supply costs, and potentially risk their continued existence.

Opportunity cost should not be ignored in the prioritization process. The cost of investing in one project and not others should include the potential benefits that will not be realized as a result of foregoing the other projects. These missed opportunities are a cost of pursuing one project at the expense of another.

Just as financial models should be continually revisited as actual costs and benefits are realized, project priorities should be revisited as well. If actuals cause a shift in priorities, the management must be willing to make tough decisions to reallocate resources appropriately, even going so far as canceling or shelving projects whose actuals cause their priorities to drop precipitously.

Incremental Investment

The importance of making technology investments in increments and continually delivering value cannot be overstressed. Multi-million dollar multi-year projects that deliver a big bang at the end almost always fail to deliver a positive return and often are made irrelevant by changes in the economic or competitive climate before they ever deliver any value at all. The fast-paced nature of technology and the goals of the agile enterprise are antithetical to large IT projects.

Service Oriented Architecture is a strategy and set of guiding principles; it is not a project or set of deliverables that should be planned and executed. Having said this, many planning decisions (particularly those made to satisfy the "top-down vs. bottom-up" argument) have direct bearing on the organization's ability to incrementally invest in SOA. As a rule of thumb, SOA adoption should be broken down into projects that yield incremental value and are prioritized based on their financial models and return on investment, just like all IT projects.

Organizations that are taking the bottom-up approach to SOA adoption are following an inherently incremental path, though there are certainly drawbacks that make the bottom-up method less desirable than top-down. Since services are only implemented in the context of existing integration projects, the IT organization is unlikely to get sucked into a big bang service implementation that may yield little value.

The top-down approach has an inherent risk that must be managed and mitigated. Since the organization has a strategic objective and the objective is supported by upper management, there will be a tendency to incorrectly try to deliver the "entire SOA" as a single project. This is not the goal of the top-down approach, and efforts to turn the SOA adoption program into a single project and deliverable must be resisted and corrected.

Often, product licensing costs can be made incremental through accurate predictions of load and good capacity planning. By purchasing licenses incrementally, the costs can be aligned better with the benefits associated with them, thereby yielding a higher overall return for the project(s). For example, a project may require fifty servers spread over a wide geographic area, each with associated software licenses. If the production rollout is staged over three years, then the purchases of both hardware and software can be similarly distributed over time, minimizing the impact on the project's initial cost and spreading it over multiple year's IT budgets.

Technology for Technology's Sake

It has been said already but cannot be overstated – technology by itself does not yield value; only the application of technology to business processes yields value. IT organizations that are focused on technology for the sake of technology are misguided and must be refocused on business value in order to achieve the goals of the agile enterprise.

Too often technologists discover a new whiz-bang gizmo and then go looking for problems that it might solve. Although this approach occasionally yields value to the organization, more often it results in "toys" for the IT department that no one else in the company uses or wants. The better approach is for IT to look for ways that technology can make the business perform better and then evaluate the available technical solutions against the business challenges, looking for an alternative with the best overall return.

Although technology champions are an important part of organizational change and are essential for SOA adoption, they must often be reigned in by management and the business stakeholders. The technology champion risks being blinded by the light of the technology he or she is associated with, and losing his or her focus on the underlying business problems and challenges that the technology needs to address. The responsibility of project stakeholders and the IT organization is to balance the business needs against the strategic objectives of the IT organization, and to meet both the tactical needs of the business and the strategic objectives of the enterprise.

Whenever IT is at risk of falling in love with a technology, management and business stakeholders should ask, "What business problem does this solve?" The lack of a coherent or consistent answer is a dead giveaway that the project should be stopped. Even the presence of a good answer is not enough, though. Good follow-up questions are "What are the alternative technologies that could solve this problem?" and "What are the business benefits of this technology over the alternatives?"

The overriding consideration in technology selection, as well as project prioritization, should be the business and the associated business processes. The business leaders must try to instill in the IT department the need to think about the business processes rather than technology and to make decisions based on the needs of the business around the business processes.

Leverage Previous Investments

Adopting a Service Oriented Architecture and implementing an agile IT environment is not about throwing away prior investments and implementing new applications in their place. Rather, it is about leveraging existing and previous investments and bringing them along into the new world of business services, where the investment can be leveraged appropriately in new ways. Wrapping existing applications in service interfaces is an inherent part of this strategy. Older application technologies may need a fairly robust service layer built over the underlying business logic to accomplish this, while applications built on newer technologies may need only a thin service layer that can be built right into the existing applications. It is difficult to imagine an application in production today that cannot be wrapped in services and brought into the new Service Oriented Architecture in some way.

Rip-and-replace strategies should be carefully weighed against leave-and-layer approaches, since a complete replacement of an existing application that is supporting the business is a costly endeavor and inherently more risky than leveraging the preexisting business logic. Often rip-and-replace strategies are the result of technologists that are enamored with new technologies and disinterested in supporting older ways of doing things and are unable to see the benefits inherent in continuing to leverage IT assets that have already been depreciated.

ROI Scenarios

The ways in which the new agile IT, built on a solid technical infrastructure and integrated using loosely coupled business services, creates added value for an organization are myriad and diverse. In order to construct financial models that justify the various projects that will fall under the SOA adoption program, the business leaders need to understand all the ways that the new IT environment might benefit the business.

Every potential project should go through a business benefit analysis phase, where the business leaders identify all of the ways that the project might help the organization. Some of the essential questions asked during this benefit analysis are:

- How will this project improve the business?
- What business processes will be affected?
- What opportunities exist to reengineer existing business processes?
- What other opportunities will be created by this project?

- How will this project help prepare the business for growth?
- What competitive advantage might this project provide?
- What opportunities for cost savings will this project create?
- What new markets will this project open up?

The following sections highlight some of the more common project scenarios and outline how each scenario addresses these benefit analysis questions and provides opportunity to positively affect return on investment.

Cost Reduction

An important area where the new IT environment can provide value to the organization is the reduction of ongoing IT costs. There are numerous ways that costs can be reduced and any given project may result in cost reduction in one or more areas.

The existing integration interfaces present in the IT environment may represent a huge potential for cost savings. Often these interfaces are brittle and tightly coupled, requiring the development teams to continually spend money on maintaining the interfaces as the underlying applications evolve and break the integration. Since these interfaces are often point-to-point and specific to each pair of applications, the number of interfaces is multiplied by the number of consumers for each type of interface. This multiplies the maintenance costs as well, since each point-to-point interface will likely be different, and each interface will be broken by changes in the applications.

Traditional integration projects relied on the proprietary interfaces of each application being integrated. In order to staff these projects, the IT organization had to find individual experts in each application's interface technology. Often these skills were rare, expensive, and difficult to acquire, increasing the cost of integration projects and sometimes even preventing them from starting because of a lack of available expertise. By implementing service oriented interfaces to all applications, integration projects only require a single skill set and therefore are much less expensive and easier to staff.

Legacy interfaces often have high operational costs as well. Some may be designed in such a way that they are replicating large amounts of data over a network, utilizing inordinate amounts of network bandwidth. Polling interfaces may be utilizing processing resources even when there is nothing to process. Interfaces designed to work over leased lines can be expensive to maintain because of the continuing cost of the physical connection.

EDI interfaces are a classic example. These are usually implemented over leased lines that can cost exorbitant amounts of money to install and maintain. Additionally, the protocols used for EDI are low-level, tightly coupled data transfer interfaces that require lots of development effort to create and maintain. They are inherently point-to-point, meaning that the cost of the interface is multiplied by the number of business partners that require it, rather than being shared across all users.

Not only are the costs of maintaining these existing interfaces high, but the additional cost of adding new interfaces using these legacy interface technologies is equally high, as each new connection requires another leased line and the development of new integration code that must subsequently be maintained.

Adopting a Service Oriented Architecture and utilizing the public networks can dramatically decrease the costs associated with these interfaces. Integration utilizing an SOA will no longer require multiple point-to-point connections for each consumer of a particular interface, but instead will implement a single interface in the partner integration hub for all consumers. Additionally, the public networks offer much lower connection costs than leased lines, and these lower cost connections can be shared by many interfaces, spreading the lower cost across multiple projects. The development effort associated with new interface technologies is also dramatically lower, as standard data formats based on XML replace older EDI data protocols based on fixed length records and binary data types.

An organization utilizing traditional EAI products for application integration tasks can potentially save money by eliminating the high licensing costs associated with these products. The adapter pattern used by traditional EAI is also expensive to maintain, since each adapter is essentially translating from some proprietary data or API protocol into another. The central hub and spoke nature of these systems leads to brittle systems with single points of failure.

Additional cost savings can be recognized in the technical infrastructure layer. Once the management and deployment processes are centralized, opportunities for consolidation will usually become apparent. This can lead to cost savings as underutilized and overlapping hardware is consolidated, and duplicate unneeded software and support licenses are identified and eliminated.

Once a solid technical foundation is in place, individual application teams and projects that utilize the services provided by the technical infrastructure can recognize cost savings because they no longer have to implement common infrastructure capabilities in each application. For example, applications that once managed user identities and roles in application databases can instead leverage the enterprise-wide authentication and authorization repository and mechanisms, freeing each application team from implementing this functionality over and over again.

Centralizing the technical infrastructure also provides better opportunities to identify mission critical applications and provide redundant and fault-tolerant platforms to ensure that these applications meet their respective SLAs. By eliminating potential downtime from hardware failures, the organization is theoretically saving the costs associated with lost business productivity.

Automation

Opportunities to automate existing manual or partially manual business processes are still one of the most valuable types of IT projects because existing employees can spend more time focusing on higher value tasks and less time on manual drudgery.

One benefit of business process automation can be speedier execution of the business process from end to end. Once manual tasks in the process are automated and the inherent delay of human workflow is minimized, business processes that took days or weeks may execute in minutes or hours. Besides the obvious benefits to overhead costs and cashflow, speedier execution may also lead to higher customer satisfaction, which could result in increased market share.

Manual business processes that rely on the repetitive entry of the same data into different applications can be error prone, since each time the data is entered there is the potential for mistakes to be made. The potential for mistakes is reduced to the initial data entry step by automating the handoff of data from application to application rather than relying on reentry of it. The potential for errors can be reduced further by moving the data entry as close to the source of the information as possible.

Service interfaces can be defined for business process steps that require human workflow as well. By implementing these as services and monitoring them in the context of the entire business process, it is possible to identify areas where automation could greatly improve the efficiency of a process by reducing or eliminating delays associated with human workflow. Since the workflow was implemented using a service interface, the IT organization can implement automated versions of the manual processes using the same interfaces and plug in the automated steps into the existing process without affecting the rest of the process. In cases where human intervention is still required under certain exceptional conditions, the business process can be designed to utilize either the automated process step or the manual step, depending on the existence of the exceptional conditions.

Automated business processes can attract new business partners as well. When a partner integration hub provides a cost effective way for different organizations to connect their systems together in a secure and reliable manner, all of the organizations involved have potential cost savings. Given the opportunity to do business with a partner that provides a business partner integration hub versus one that does not, companies will prefer the lower cost solution and favor those business partners that provide it.

Productivity

Improving productivity through IT is not about replacing employees; the goal is to enable employees to take on additional responsibility by making them more productive in their existing tasks.

Most, if not all, organizations have business processes that span application boundaries where the underlying applications are not integrated at all or only partially. This scenario often results in employees that must reenter the same information into multiple systems. By adopting a Service Oriented Architecture and establishing a system of record for each business entity, not only are these employees freed from the drudgery of entering the same data repeatedly, but mistakes and errors are reduced, and the development costs associated with validating the entered data and implementing the underlying business rules in multiple applications are eliminated as well.

Moving data collection and entry as close as possible to the origin of the data can also yield cost savings, as the data collectors who have the most knowledge about the context of the information are made responsible for putting valid data into the system of record, thereby eliminating middlemen and improving the quality of the data. An SOA enables this type of transition by providing business services to smart clients, and mobile devices that can be taken into the field by the employees and used to directly enter collected data into the system of record. These can even be designed to work in a disconnected mode, continuing to collect data while off line and synching up with the back-end systems when a connection is available.

When data collection is pushed to the origin of the information, it is important that the data collection application be as unintrusive as possible, so as not to degrade the productivity of the employees responsible for collecting the data. If field agents are accustomed to writing information on paper forms, for example, then an appropriate solution might be to give them tablet PCs with a data collection application that simulates the paper forms they are used to and performs handwriting recognition. Alternatively, a digital pen might be used to collect the data written on the paper forms and upload it once the pen is docked at the employee's workstation.

A service oriented application infrastructure layer loosely coupled to an enterprise portal can be leveraged to provide highly customized user interfaces to small groups of information workers in a cost effective manner. This increases the productivity of these workers by giving them exactly the applications they need. Older technologies in the absence of an SOA were not capable of providing such highly specialized applications without significant development costs, which were rarely justified for small groups of users.

An important aspect of all projects whose goal is to improve productivity is that in order to improve something, it must be measurable. The ability to measure productivity is an area of active research and advances in productivity metrics will provide more impetus for using them as justification for future IT projects.

Whenever IT sets out to improve the productivity of some group within the organization, the input of the actual users should be the driving force behind the design and implementation of any resulting application. The users who do the job understand it best and they should provide the basis for making a given task easier to perform. In the context of business process reengineering, it is more important to get the input of higher level subject matter experts that are able to think outside the box of individual steps within a business process.

Some of the most powerful productivity improvements are discovered by groups of people who are able to collaborate in ways that were previously difficult or impossible. These types of changes are seldom anticipated, but rather they emerge from the behavior of groups of people working together to accomplish a common goal. In order to enable this type of productivity enhancement, IT should provide the organization with a set of general purpose collaboration tools and then let the organization determine how best these can be used.

Self Service

The benefits of providing self-service capabilities to employees, customers, and business partners can deliver cost savings, improved productivity, improved satisfaction, and speedier execution of business processes. Although there are many different types of self-service projects, each with different benefits to the organization, some common ones are detailed here.

Much of the effort in most human resource departments is utilized to communicate all of the various aspects of employment arrangements with the employees. Ongoing communications related to compensation, benefits, retirement plans, open positions, and outside activities can occupy multiple human resource staff full time in a large enterprise. The creation of an employee portal in the enterprise gateway enables the employees to get the information they need and want in a self-service fashion, freeing the human resource staff for more productive tasks.

A primary component of the eBusiness push of the 1990s was the creation of a new channel on the World Wide Web. This allowed customers to perform a few tasks in a self-service fashion, such as shopping, purchasing, and tracking shipments. These presumably increased margins by transferring sales from the high overhead brick-and-mortar retail channel to the web channel, where overhead costs are lower. Most online retailers stop there, but there are still more gains to be made. By fully integrating the channels and providing self-service capabilities to customers across all of the channels, some companies are recognizing even greater increases in margins and reductions in costs.

Customer service, for example, has been integrated into the enterprise portal of many companies and customers can now perform many customer service tasks in a self-service fashion. Even those tasks that require some assistance from the customer service department can be integrated into the self-service portal experience through web based voice calls, text chat, and remote desktop access.

Providing a self-service capability to business partners through the enterprise portal can improve the efficiency of communication and decrease errors in the transmission of business data between the companies. Self-service communication also scales much better than the corresponding people-centered communication mechanisms, and provides a much more consistent level of support to business partners, since the portal will not leave the company to go work for a competitor and never takes a vacation.

Companies that offer a self-service capability to their business partners will tend to attract partners away from their competitors who do not, since the business partners recognize greater efficiency and fewer errors from this form of communication as well, lowering their cost of doing business. Suppliers, for example, may offer a lower cost for their goods to companies that provide higher levels of self-service capabilities, since their cost of doing business will go down.

Ultimately, assuming all else is equal, companies that offer self-service capabilities through their enterprise portal to customers and business partners will take market share away from their competitors who do not. Eventually all companies will need to either follow suit or will likely cease to exist as independent concerns.

Visibility

There are many benefits of providing management with better visibility into the status of all of the business processes within the enterprise. The goals of the real-time enterprise and associated benefits are addressed in greater detail in the paper "Real Time Enterprises: A Continuous Migration Approach," included in the supplemental section of this book.

The idea of "Just in Time" is not new and has been applied to different aspects of business. The goal of a real-time enterprise is to achieve just in time everything, where each business process is executing at the most efficient level possible, and all inputs arrive at exactly the time they are required. This goal will minimize process bottlenecks and backups throughout the entire organization, leading to numerous areas of cost reduction and improved business performance.

Better visibility into the real-time state of executing business processes opens up the door to optimizations that may not have been considered in an information vacuum. Without good visibility into how the business is operating, it is difficult to determine ways in which it could operate better. Transitioning to a real-time enterprise executing on a Service Oriented Architecture enables the implementation of advanced business activity monitoring systems feeding management dashboards hosted in the enterprise portal, providing decision makers with highly valuable data that can be used to continually optimize and tweak the business processes to address changes in the business environment.

Competitive Advantage

Although technology can provide a competitive advantage, it is always short lived. Early adopters gain an advantage over their competition, which lasts until the fast followers catch up to the early adopters. Once the technology has become commonplace in the industry, customers expect it and will force the laggards in the industry to either catch up or cease to exist.

Management should decide which part of the technology adoption curve they are targeting and should periodically perform a competitive position technology analysis to determine where they are in relation to their competitors and the industry.

The early adopter stage of Service Oriented Architecture is already past for most industries. Several industries are already past the fast follower stage as well, though the more mature industries are still in this phase.

The ability to offer customers or business partners services that competing companies do not offer will usually lead to increased market share at the expense of the competitors, assuming that there is a demand in the market for the services offered. The most important benefit of the agile enterprise is the ability to continually offer new services in a cost effective manner, based on the flexibility offered by adopting a Service Oriented Architecture built on a solid technical infrastructure.

Another way to gain competitive advantage is to pass the cost savings achieved through the adoption of a Service Oriented Architecture on to the organization's customers. By lowering the price of the services offered and cutting costs through technology, the agile organization will put price pressure on the less agile competitors, forcing them to operate with lower margins or reduced market share.

Once business processes are composed of independent business services loosely coupled and orchestrated by the business process management tools of the enterprise gateway, the organization achieves a high degree of process agility. Business processes can be continually refined and customized, allowing the organization to do business in new ways and forcing competitors to innovate, duplicate, or disappear. The idea of business process reengineering is the right one, but the limitations resulting from the way it has traditionally been implemented have given it a bad name. Instead of performing a lengthy and expensive analysis process to redefine the business processes, create business services that can be used in different configurations and embark upon a path of continued business process refinement and agility.

In many industries, the idea that one business process is correct for all of an organization's customers and partners is already outdated and most other industries will follow suit. By creating an agile IT environment, management is able to create customized business processes for different customers, opening up new revenue streams and achieving cost savings by eliminating services from the business processes associated with customer bases where the service is not required.

Not only do custom business processes make the organization more attractive to customers, they also attract business partners as well, potentially to an even larger extent. Most business partnerships are based upon a significant volume of business between the two organizations, so the benefits of custom business processes designed around the partnership are multiplied.

An organization that starts the process of implementing a partner integration hub in an industry where standards are not yet defined for inter-enterprise integration will become a thought leader in their industry by defining a *defacto* standard. This will occur to an even greater extent if the organization takes the initiative to create a standards body to define and manage the service interface definitions. Often existing industry bodies can be leveraged for this effort, or consortiums can be formed to lead the effort. No matter what vehicle is utilized to define the industry standard, the respect associated with being a thought leader in an industry usually results in either increased market share or improved margins.

Additionally, being in front of the curve for standards definition allows the company to mold the standards to best fit its needs. The benefits of this are many-fold, because service interfaces are the building blocks of business processes, which are what makes the business run. Adopting interfaces that are not a good fit for existing business processes can entail additional effort and potentially create added requirements for organizational change.

Mergers and Acquisitions

Industry consolidation usually involves the combination of companies that have overlapping IT systems based on different technologies and vendors. The process of rationalizing the resulting combined IT environment can be lengthy, expensive, and risky.

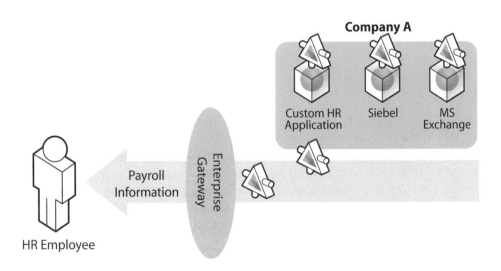

An IT environment based on a Service Oriented Architecture encapsulates the specific implementation of business services behind well-defined, generic interfaces. This approach makes the process of absorbing duplicate or overlapping systems easier. Two systems that provide the same basic services can provide the same interfaces, even though the underlying implementation of the services may be radically different. Applications that depend on those services need not know which application is providing the implementation at any one time. This allows applications to be run in parallel or swapped out independently from all of the other applications in the enterprise.

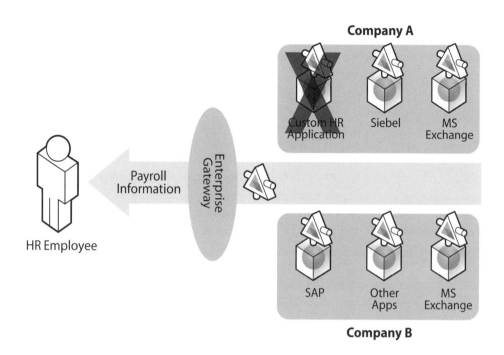

In addition to easing the transition to a single system and allowing an incremental approach to consolidation, services also allow the combined company to take a best-of-breed approach to selecting which systems will be kept and which will be retired. If two systems implement the same service interfaces, then the company is free to select between them based on their individual merits rather than on the dependencies between the other applications within the IT environment on either application.

When combining the technical infrastructure layer of two companies, a centralized system and processes for managing the assets will ease the process of merging the two organizations. If one organization has achieved a high level of centralization while the other has not, then the logical approach is to incorporate the various components of the decentralized technical infrastructure environment into the already centralized environment, eliminating overlap along the way.

An important success factor for any merger is the creation of a technology team whose specific responsibility is to plan, coordinate, and implement the merging of the two IT environments. This team should be created early in the process, before the merger is finalized to ensure that the critical parts of the integration are ready to go on day one. It is also important that this team have broad authority over the organizations and teams that will need to implement the plans, and accountability for the ultimate success or failure of the IT consolidation project.

Wrap-Up

This chapter examined the need for a business case when embarking on any IT project and ways to evaluate the ROI of an IT project and to prioritize projects relative to each other.

The various ways that an SOA adoption program can benefit an organization were also examined.

In the next chapter, various aspects related to executing the Service Oriented Architecture Roadmap will be presented.

Chapter 11:　　　　　*Execution*

A clear vision, a good business case, and adequate funding are necessary prerequisites for becoming an agile enterprise.

Turning the vision into reality takes analysis, planning, and hard work, with many tradeoffs to be made along the way. The agile enterprise is a journey with no final destination – it is a strategy that will continually impact IT decisions and projects.

Assess Where You Are

Once the decision has been made to become an agile enterprise, it is critical to take inventory of the current state of the IT environment. Knowing the current state of the IT infrastructure will enable management to determine what initiatives should get the highest priority based upon associated risks and benefits. Although most IT managers think they understand their current environment, most also hold a number of fallacies about the true nature of what the organization has and is running and how well it is functioning to meet the business needs.

Assessment Objectives

The goal of enabling the agile enterprise rests on taking a holistic view of IT and its place within the organization. Understanding how IT facilitates the business and how it could potentially yield greater benefits is the cornerstone of the SOA adoption program. In order to understand what the current state of the IT environment is, it is necessary to take the same type of holistic view during the assessment of the existing environment.

There are several areas of focus that the assessment should concentrate on within a holistic analysis framework. These key areas of focus are those that have the greatest potential for improvement within the new model that will emerge from the adoption of an SOA.

One of these areas is the overall stability of the existing systems within the IT organization. The goal is to match up the availability requirements of the business processes with the stability and availability of the systems and interfaces that support them. Where systems support multiple business processes, the most demanding requirements should be met. Brittle interfaces and those that are based on batch oriented or data replication styles of integration are areas that should be paid particular attention, since these often do not meet the true needs of the business.

The ability of the existing systems to scale with the growth of the business and meet the needs of business processes that are handling ever higher volume should be analyzed carefully. Systems that lack a strategy for scaling up to higher volumes are candidates for replacement. The adoption of service oriented interfaces over these systems can facilitate their eventual replacement by isolating dependent applications and business processes from the underlying implementation.

The security of the existing systems and interfaces is another area of concern, since the migration to a real-time enterprise based on a Service Oriented Architecture will usually open up new avenues for malicious attack. Environments that rely heavily on the physical security of their systems and networks are at risk when these systems are opened up to outside parties via the enterprise gateway.

In addition to the main focus of the assessment, determining what the existing IT landscape looks like and how it is and is not able to support the requirements of the agile enterprise, there are three other axes upon which the assessment team should evaluate the existing systems and processes.

The first of these is risk. Any environment has components and processes that present various levels of risk to the business. An analysis of what these risks are, how likely they are to occur, and what their realization would mean to the enterprise can be invaluable during the planning and prioritization phase and can help ensure the successful adoption of a Service Oriented Architecture and the migration to an agile enterprise by focusing early efforts on those areas that present the greatest risk to the business.

To the extent that current systems and processes do not meet the needs of the business in one way or another, the assessment team should identify these areas of weakness and recommend strategies for remediation. In some cases the business needs will be supported, but the implementation is less than optimal in one or more dimensions. The assessment team should identify these areas and recommend ways in which the systems or processes might be optimized.

Building and/or buying IT systems is expensive, yet the upfront costs are usually dwarfed by the ongoing maintenance costs, especially when brittle integration technologies are used to tightly couple applications to each other. These are areas of potential cost savings within the IT organization, and, like risk, can be used to help management prioritize projects and initiatives so that the business sees benefits early and often.

Assessment Process

In order to provide a baseline for moving forward, IT should utilize a cross-functional team of senior architects to conduct an architectural system engineering assessment of the IT environment and organization. Ideally, this team would consist at least partially of senior architects from outside the organization, so that a truly objective analysis of the state of the IT infrastructure might be obtained. This team will need broad access to resources and people throughout the entire organization, not just IT.

The assessment team must be given a clear mandate to look in every corner of the enterprise, and its goals and authority should be clearly defined and communicated to everyone involved. The project sponsor must be ready and have the authority to clear roadblocks for the team, as any effort like this will undoubtedly run into an uncooperative individual or organization along the way.

Having authority is critical. Without authority, the assessment team and sponsor will appear ineffective and may not be able to affect the sort of change within the organization required for the initiative to be successful. Management must buy into the recommendations made to feel comfortable giving this authority to the project sponsor.

The assessment team will provide an "end-to-end" technical analysis of the IT infrastructure according to the 5 layers of architecture.

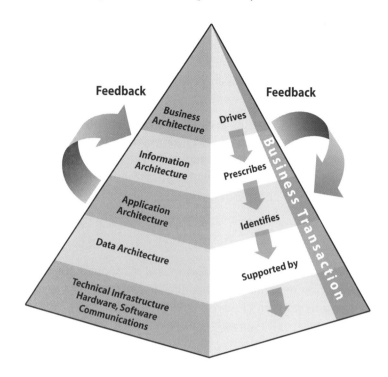

One key member of the team is the business analyst. This individual is responsible for evaluating the organizational and process aspects of the enterprise. Some of the areas this person will be assessing include:

- Business Architecture Layer
  - High-level business goals
  - Business vision and model
  - Business metrics
  - Customer volume
  - Customer expectation metrics
  - Cost model
  - Regulatory requirements
- Organizational Elements
  - IT mission and strategy
  - Resources

- Organizational structure
- Organizational communication
- Organizational performance measures
- Development resources and process
- Operations
- Information Architecture Layer
  - Use cases
  - Sequence diagrams
  - Business policies and procedures
  - Business rules
  - Workflow
  - How business architecture needs are met

The enterprise application architect is responsible for assessing the application infrastructure layer and, to the extent that it exists, the enterprise gateway layer. If the organization is already making use of a business process management and orchestration product in the enterprise gateway layer, then the responsibility for assessing this technology and its application could be divided between the business analyst, who could focus on the business processes, and the enterprise application architect, who could focus on the automation of those processes. Some of the key areas that the enterprise application architect will assess include:

- Overall application architecture
- Design of each application
  - Cohesiveness
  - Distribution of responsibilities
  - Mechanics
  - Packaging
  - Arguments
  - Caching
  - Statefulness
  - Security

- Object lifetime management
  - Initialization
  - Connections
  - Internal object management
- Transactions
  - Scope
  - Applicability
  - Locking
- Other organizations that interface into the systems

The technical infrastructure architect will assess the appropriateness of the existing technical infrastructure layer. Some of the areas this team member will assess include:

- Data architecture layer
  - Bottlenecks in database system
  - Application interaction with database server
  - Administration practices
  - Data architecture
  - Configuration
- Delivery systems architecture layer
  - Detailed analysis of servers
  - Detailed analysis of network
  - Hardware
  - Other aspects of IT

The final key member of the assessment team is the project manager. This person has the normal duties associated with managing the assessment project itself but will also contribute to the deliverable. The project manager, specifically, should assist the business analyst in the area of business process analysis. Additionally, the project manager is uniquely qualified to assess the software development process used by the IT organization and should head up that part of the assessment effort.

Any effort of this type is at risk of becoming bogged down in analysis paralysis, endlessly iterating on the assessment and recommendations and never delivering anything of value. It is highly desirable, if not absolutely necessary, that this effort is time boxed from the beginning and that the assessment team be made aware that the effort is time boxed and will not be extended. Since the ultimate deliverable of the assessment is a report, the only thing that should be allowed to vary from the initial scope and plan is the content of the report itself. Once the assessment is complete, areas that deserve further review can be assessed in follow-on projects, each of which should also be time boxed. An appropriate time period will depend on the size of the organization and the availability of resources for the assessment team itself and those necessary to provide input to the team, but a top end might be in the two- to three-month range.

Assessment Deliverable

The objectives of the assessment are communicated to the organization in multiple ways. The primary deliverable is the assessment report, which summarizes the findings of the assessment team. Each finding will have a set of background data, an identification of the associated risks and benefits, the implications both of following the assessment team's recommendation, and of failing to do so, and the suggestions for remediation. One possible format these recommendations might take is a table summarizing each finding, such as the one on the next page.

Develop a more robust interface between Order Entry and Billing		
Type: Performance, Supportability, Reliability	**Level of Effort:** Develop a more robust, asynchronous interface between Order Entry and Billing	**High Risk**
Category: Application Integration – Order Entry and Billing	**Probability:** 2 - Medium	**Dependencies:** None

Background:

Billing is a legacy accounts receivable product from a third-party vendor that runs on the mainframe. Order entry is a new product from the same vendor that adds order entry capabilities to the billing product. Order Entry relies on billing for all traditional accounts receivable functionality. An interface between Order Entry and Billing provides a means for Order Entry to hand off the billing data for an order to Billing so that the invoice can be generated. This interface between Order Entry and Billing is based on synchronous socket communication and a proprietary command protocol.

Recommendations:

Implement a robust, fault tolerant, message based interface between Order Entry and Billing. Ideally the message content protocol would be based on an open standard like XML.

Justification:

Relying on low level socket communication leads to a brittle interface and limits the flexibility of the relationship between the two applications. The interface is intolerant of problems and is difficult to reset without manual intervention. The synchronous nature of the interface will limit the throughput of the interface.

The assessment process itself facilitates the collection of a body of knowledge through interviews with various people throughout the enterprise, coupled with other discovery activities. This body of knowledge is summarized in the report, but the raw material, if properly categorized and archived, can also prove tremendously valuable to the ongoing adoption effort. Ideally, these artifacts will be collected and stored in digital form in a document repository, and this repository will then be integrated with various collaboration tools, both to facilitate the assessment process and the follow-on remediation activities.

In addition to the document repository, the body of knowledge collected during the assessment is also present in the assessors themselves. These architects and managers should be leveraged in the subsequent SOA adoption program to serve as consultants to the various project teams and form the core of the ICC.

Determine Where You Need to Be

The assessment of the existing IT environment focuses on what currently exists and how it can be made better. The recommendations are focused on risk mitigation and cost reduction. In order to prepare the IT infrastructure for the future, it is important to know what that future state should look like, based on current knowledge and the goals of the business.

Industry trends can be an important part of identifying the ideal future state of IT. The trends within the IT industry can be applied somewhat generically to any organization. Service Oriented Architecture, for example, has been slowly gaining momentum within the technology industry for years and has now passed early adopter status and is entering the mainstream. Enterprise portal technology is another area where the industry as a whole is heading.

In addition to these general technology trends, the trends within the organization's industry can also be an important input into the process of defining the future state. The degree to which competitors are moving toward a more agile enterprise environment is an important driver. Industry trade bodies and consortiums working to define integration standards for an industry can be leveraged as well, and are important indicators of the maturity of the industry.

Once the current state is understood and the future state is identified, the program team can begin to identify the gaps between the current IT environment and the required components to support the future direction. There will undoubtedly be areas where the current architecture does not support the long-term needs and objectives of the business.

Most, if not all, modern IT environments contain a number of different technologies that have been accumulated over time to meet different business needs. Companies that have undergone significant merger and acquisition activities will likely have a more diverse environment and will often contain systems with overlapping functionality and responsibility.

Identifying the technologies that are strategic to the future of the organization will help identify appropriate strategies to migrate the existing environment to one based on a Service Oriented Architecture and supporting a real-time, agile enterprise. Strategic technologies are those that the organization will be making new investments in for at least the next five to ten years. Technologies that are not strategic are not necessarily targets for elimination, but they are are certainly targets for wrapping in a service layer, as opposed to in-depth service-enablement. Additionally, the service wrappers themselves should be implemented in strategic technologies whenever possible, even if the applications they are wrapping are based on nonstrategic technologies. For those technologies that are not strategic, the organization should come up with a plan for the ongoing maintenance and possible retirement or replacement of each, if appropriate.

Technical Infrastructure

Putting a solid technical infrastructure in place provides the foundation layer of the new agile IT environment. All of the basic supporting technologies comprising a company's infrastructure need to be chosen and acquired based upon the strategic technologies, the ability to fit each technology into a heterogeneous environment and manage it as a component of a larger technical infrastructure layer, and its ability to provide the basic services required of the application infrastructure layer.

The identity management system is critical to the implementation of a Service Oriented Architecture in the application infrastructure layer and to the usability of the enterprise portal and partner integration hub in the enterprise gateway layer. Managing the authentication and authorization services for every internal and external user, as well as the applications internal to the organization and in external partner organizations, can be daunting if not impossible without a robust and scalable enterprise-wide identity management solution. Single sign-on functionality should be a basic requirement, with multiple means of authentication supported, including basic user ID and password, client and server side certificates, smart cards, and biometric authentication mechanisms such as fingerprint and voice recognition.

The database is the core of every enterprise's long-term data storage and retention. As such, the database might become the focal point for application integration, which leads to brittle applications built on top of lowest common denominator database schema designed as a compromise to the conflicting requirements of multiple applications. In order to enable the transition to a Service Oriented Architecture, the database schema must be decoupled and partitioned into separate systems of record for the various logical groupings of business entities. Once the brittle data coupling is broken, applications that require access to business entities for which they are not the system of record should access that data via the services implemented by the application that is the system of record for that entity.

In addition to this logical partitioning of responsibility, the databases in the technical infrastructure must be deployed in a manner consistent with the availability requirements of the applications that use them, which is determined by the requirements of the business processes they support. Data backup and retention policies, clustering, fail-over, and disaster recovery must all be considered and designed appropriately for each system of record and the entities it supports.

The application servers that host the applications providing business services reside in the technical infrastructure and need to support the basic frameworks necessary for implementation of a Service Oriented Architecture. These standards and frameworks are a constantly moving target, but those application servers that consistently provide implementations for the latest WS-* standards will make it far easier for the application development teams to provide appropriate business services in a cost effective and timely manner. Application servers need to be appropriately deployed as well, taking into account many of the same attributes as databases including load balancing, fail-over, hot deployment of application changes, and disaster recovery.

Collaboration tools are a big part of the migration to an agile enterprise, since they enable groups of people to work together efficiently in spite of organization, cultural, political, and geographical boundaries. The technical infrastructure needs to provide a robust set of generic collaboration tools, along with high levels of integration between them and the training necessary to teach the rest of the enterprise how to leverage these tools.

All of the components of the technical infrastructure should be managed, deployed, and monitored in a centralized way by the operations department of IT. Putting in place the framework and technological underpinnings to enable this type of centralized management and control is a necessary task of the technical infrastructure team.

Application Infrastructure

In "Chapter 5: What is Application Infrastructure?" a number of architectural patterns were identified that may be in place within any given organization's application infrastructure layer. These architectural patterns require different approaches to service-enablement, whether or not the technologies they are implemented on are strategic to the organization.

Client-server applications usually deploy most or all of the business logic on the client, where it is tightly coupled to the presentation logic of the application. This presents a challenge for incorporating the application into a broader SOA, since services must be centralized and server-based to facilitate deployment, management, and monitoring and to guarantee that they meet service level agreements. In order to service-enable most client server applications, the appropriate business logic will need to be identified and extracted from the client component and then deployed on the server in an application server container. Once this has been accomplished, the business logic can be leveraged by services hosted within the same application server container. It is a good idea to modify the client application components, if they are going to continue to be used so that they communicate with the services instead of accessing the database directly. This will essentially turn the client component into a custom smart client and fully incorporate it into the enterprise gateway layer.

Depending upon the technology used to implement them, server based applications are likely the easiest applications to service-enable. The business logic of these applications is usually already hosted on an application server, and, if they are architected well, the presentation logic is decoupled from the underlying business logic. Services can be easily added as a new presentation layer, leveraging the same business components.

Very few organizations currently have true smart clients deployed on top of a Service Oriented Architecture. Most of the applications that are currently thought of as smart clients are integrated with back-end systems using a brittle, tightly coupled integration technology. To bring these applications into the SOA, they need to be decoupled from the back-end systems and data sources via services implemented in those applications.

Truly distributed applications are difficult to build, difficult to maintain, and prone to failure because of the large number of failure points, each of which can potentially stop the entire application from functioning. There are various strategies for service-enabling these applications and leveraging them within the larger Service Oriented Architecture, including breaking them into multiple independent applications and combining the components into a single larger application. The appropriate strategy will depend on the functionality the system provides, the integration mechanisms between the components, and the design of the system of record for each underlying business entity involved.

A number of technologies and techniques exist for service-enabling mainframe applications, and given the pure volume of business transactions these systems process, it is a good idea to bring them along rather than try to replace them immediately. Even if the strategy is to replace the mainframe and midrange applications in the organization, service-enablement can be an important step in the process, allowing the dependent applications to be decoupled from the implementation so that it can be swapped out for one or more new applications and technologies without breaking the other applications that depend on the services.

Most mainframe environments in production today are capable of running an application server, allowing the mainframe to expose interactive applications as well defined services without the need for additional computing resources. Those that cannot or that do not have spare processing cycles to run the service-enablement logic can be easily wrapped with modern application servers running on separate hardware.

Batch-oriented mainframe applications present a bigger challenge, since they are basically the antithesis of the kind of processing required for the real-time enterprise. The best approach in the short term may be to provide an asynchronous messaging interface to these existing asynchronous processes, basing the message definition on the canonical data model utilized by the rest of the Service Oriented Architecture.

Data entry applications now have technological options for inclusion into an SOA that have only recently become available. Microsoft's InfoPath™, for example, is a generic smart client included with the Microsoft Office™ suite that allows organizations to easily design and deploy form-based data entry applications that leverage a Service Oriented Architecture to store entered data into back-end business systems.

Every application present in the IT environment should have some lifecycle roadmap identified and documented. Understanding how the current implementation of a given business service will be maintained, evolved, and retired will help the service implementation team to pick the right strategy for service-enabling the application.

In addition to identifying all of the applications present, the existing interfaces between applications should be identified and cataloged as well. Some effort to determine the ongoing maintenance effort involved with each interface can provide important indicators regarding the brittleness of each interface. The level of service provided, as well as availability metrics, can be used to identify interfaces that should be replaced early with loosely coupled services. Many environments include multiple interfaces that provide the same types of integration between different pairs of applications. These overlapping interfaces can often be consolidated as part of SOA adoption, yielding an overall cost savings within the IT organization.

It is rare that an IT organization achieves the highest level of integration possible – there always seem to be requirements for ever greater levels of automation. The users of these interfaces will provide important information about the need for additional integration points and they can help the SOA adoption program prioritize the development of new services to satisfy these unmet needs.

Most IT organizations have at least a few packaged applications. Some enterprises have invested heavily in packaged applications and run most of their business processes on packages purchased from independent software vendors. Where packaged applications exist, the vendor's plan for migration to and inclusion in a Service Oriented Architecture should be carefully analyzed. Vendors with no plan, or with inadequate plans to bolt on a few services, should be pressured to give SOA a higher development priority. If progress cannot be made through negotiation, ultimately the organization must be prepared to replace packaged applications with competitive offerings that are service oriented or with a custom solution.

Enterprise Gateway

Since the enterprise gateway is the newest concept within the vision of the agile enterprise, it is probably the least evolved in most organizations.

Business process automation is a large part of the benefit that an enterprise gateway can provide, and modeling the existing business processes within the enterprise is important to achieving this. Although most organizations think they know what their business processes are and how they work, this confidence only lasts until they begin to analyze what is really happening. Once processes are sufficiently documented and modeled opportunities for increased efficiency are often obvious.

The existence of manual business processes are obvious choices for automation, especially where partially manual processes are used to perform integration between systems that are not integrated. This type of project can often yield a high ROI by using a service oriented approach to create a loosely coupled interface that can be leveraged by multiple applications in the future.

Visibility into the functioning of the business processes can lead to better decision making, and can allow the enterprise to react more quickly to a changing competitive landscape and economic situation. Enterprises with high inventory costs, for example, may be able to reduce inventory and save money by providing better visibility into the order and supply chain business processes.

Opportunities to take existing person-to-person communication paths and turn them into self-service applications hosted in the enterprise portal can reduce cost in call centers, human resources, affiliate management, and many other areas.

Determine How to Get There

The most common reason IT projects fail to deliver business value is a lack of planning. With an overarching effort like SOA adoption and the implementation of an enterprise gateway, the importance of planning to the success of each project and to the ultimate success of the program is paramount. The adage "plan early and plan often" is appropriate, since the continuing adoption process will lead to new techniques and a deeper understanding of the business requirements, potentially resulting in new priorities and risks. Rather than resist change, the IT organization should embrace it. Change is the only constant, and an agile enterprise is one that is designed to change.

The process of adopting a Service Oriented Architecture is not a single project with a monolithic deliverable. The program must be broken into smaller projects with short delivery cycles, and the entire development process should be iterative and incremental at the task, project and program levels. Multiple concurrent projects worked by different teams, overseen by the ICC and managed by the Project Management Organization (PMO) as a program of projects will be the best way to ensure that business needs are met and real business value is delivered.

Transforming the IT organization and technical environment into one that enables the agile enterprise is a wide-ranging effort that touches every corner of IT. In order to execute this type of program, a roadmap is critical. The transformation roadmap should lay out the high level goals and objectives of the transformation program, the macro phases of the multi-year project, and the projects that will compose the program according to priority.

The program management must continually ensure that the technology projects are in line with the corporate strategy and that the business processes are supported by the technology. It is impossible to anticipate what all future business processes might look like, so the business services provided by the application infrastructure should be independent and flexible to allow their re-use in multiple business processes, some of which are not yet conceived.

Develop a Roadmap to an Enterprise Architecture

The initial phase of the roadmap should identify opportunities for proof of concept and prototype projects. These will help the organization determine the appropriate technologies and mechanisms for service-enabling the existing applications and will help to flesh out what parts of the technical infrastructure require effort to be able to support the services in the application infrastructure and their use by the enterprise gateway.

The technologies that will provide the framework and technical services upon which the business services are built should be evaluated and tested during the proof of concept phase. The data collected can be used to select appropriate technologies for moving forward with the adoption program. Various attributes should be evaluated for the candidate technologies, including price, viability of the vendor, scalability of the technology, ability of the technology to support a heterogeneous environment, and many other aspects, some of which will vary from one organization to another.

Potential projects for deployment should then be undertaken based on the prioritization process outlined previously. All development should be iterative and incremental, and the tenets of risk-based project management should drive the planning of the iterations. Focusing on projects with short timeframe and high ROI will help give the program momentum and reduce resistance within the organization.

The approach should be rolled out to existing projects through the ICC, with architects from the ICC serving a consultative role to ongoing development efforts, mentoring the team members and ensuring that the applications will play well in the eventual service-oriented environment.

Execute the Roadmap

Responsibility and accountability are important to executing any program, and the transition to an agile enterprise is no different. Stakeholders should take control of the business model and should become champions of the effort. Relevant subject matter experts should be made accountable for delivering information to the architectural assessment team. The key players in the assessment team should be rolled into the ICC, where they should take on governance roles and be responsible for the successful implementation of business services throughout the ongoing projects.

In order to successfully roll out an SOA across an enterprise, the ICC should be formed with sufficient staff and skills to manage the technical aspects of the migration. This organization will serve multiple purposes:

- Set architectural direction and design the key interfaces between the applications

- Serve as consulting architects to each project team, helping them understand the impact of the migration to an SOA and the importance of the change to the company

- Develop, maintain, and disseminate libraries and code templates for use in the various languages and projects

- Serve an oversight and monitoring function, ensuring that the project teams adhere to good design principals, both in the interface design and in the implementation of the interfaces

In order to accomplish these functions, the team will need a core group of individuals with architect-level skill sets. The role of architect requires some soft skills and more hard technical skills. The key soft skills in these positions are:

- Respected and effective leaders

- An ability to see the big picture, both from a business perspective and from a technical perspective

- A solid understanding of the enterprise application suite and corporate strategy

- An understanding of the IT environments where the applications are currently deployed

- An understanding of the types of environments where the applications are likely to be deployed at various points in the future

- A thorough understanding of the technology roadmaps and technology directions and their impact on the technical strategy and hence architectural approach

- Patience and resolve when dealing with organizational politics and an ability to convince various stakeholders of the value of an architecture

- A willingness to listen to alternatives and fairly critique and communicate their relative merit

- An ability to teach and mentor, both informally and formally, possibly in a classroom situation

The hard technical skills the ICC should have in its core group are:

- A thorough understanding of software architecture patterns and design patterns

- A good grounding in the architectures of the platforms strategic to the enterprise

- An understanding of SOA and its implications to application design

- Knowledge and experience in the full software development lifecycle, with knowledge of multiple methodologies preferred

- An understanding of and experience with modeling, and the ability to create meaningful models that communicate important concepts to team members of various skill levels

- An excellent knowledge of web services and the technologies related to them

The ICC must be focused on the business at least as much as the technology. It is a key responsibility that the ICC keeps the IT initiatives aligned with the business goals. Though the business stakeholders own the ROI model, the ICC should have a hand in following up and showing that the benefits forecast were or were not met and should use this information to help build future ROI models. The ICC should also have a strong say in the prioritization of projects, in order to ensure that the projects of highest value to the business are addressed early.

The nature of technology is complexity and an IT organization is made up of people with a wide range of specialized skills. Whenever a shift in approach is undertaken, there will initially be a lack of skills present in the new technologies and techniques. Those that have the skills will be in high demand. The most effective way to use these limited resources is usually to spread them around to many projects. The ICC will be the focal point of this activity, identifying the resources and capabilities that the organization has as part of the assessment and allocating appropriately skilled resources to projects as needed on an ongoing basis.

Business process automation requires ongoing attention to the identification and definition of the business processes. This is started during the assessment, and the models created there are owned by the ICC, where they are maintained and updated. Ultimately these business processes will be defined within an orchestration tool in the enterprise gateway. The definition and evolution of these business processes should also be managed by the ICC, especially from the perspective of change management.

The needs of the business are not always understood by the people in the IT organization, and this disconnect can lead to discord between IT and the rest of the company, which is a waste of energy and effort. Many on the business side sometimes think that IT is not capable of understanding the business, while people in the IT organization often feel that the business people do not understand technology. The key to solving all of this misunderstanding and strife is communication. Management must build communication channels to clearly communicate business needs to the IT organization, which must have a means of disseminating that information throughout the organization. Similarly, IT must communicate the benefits that technology can provide back to the business, so that they can better identify ways that technology might be used.

The creation of a communication plan is critical, along with formulating the strategy for implementation of the new Service Oriented Architecture. The communication plan is a key tool used by program and project managers. The plan should include all stakeholders and their communication requirements, as well as the different communication methods and tools used (status notes, weekly status reports, executive dashboards, etc.) It should identify the audience for each communication channel, and the frequency of communication. This will reinforce the importance of communication and further display the importance of project management and the project manager to facilitate the process.

Once this communication is flowing, the business needs will drive the planning and prioritization process for the rollout, ensuring that business value is gained.

The assessment includes the identification of areas where the organization itself needs to change in order to facilitate the emergence of a new IT infrastructure. Organizational change is in some ways harder to accomplish than technological change. The management of the organization must buy into the need for organizational change and should develop a strategy and plans for making it happen. Change of this type can only happen from the top-down, so executive buy-in is absolutely essential to success.

The rollout of all of these changes, the rationalization of the technical infrastructure, the development of a Service Oriented Architecture, and the creation of an enterprise gateway will not happen without a plan. A change of this magnitude will require careful and ongoing attention from the PMO. It is highly recommended that an organization use a formal project management structure when undertaking such a complex effort. When projects of this magnitude are undertaken without project management experience, PM activities are often delegated to lower level resources, which are ultimately responsible for delivering the project. When this occurs, those resources typically end up ignoring their PM responsibilities (plan tracking, reporting, issue mitigation, etc.

in favor of their daily project tasks (i.e. implementing the solution), thus adding significant risk to the project.

Evolve the Roadmap

The roadmap created early in the evolution of the IT environment will probably be mostly wrong. It is more important for the team to plan for change than to get everything right in the beginning. The roadmap should evolve with the rollout of the technology, and it should be updated on an ongoing basis. The changes in direction must be consistently communicated throughout the IT organization by the ICC.

New technologies are always going to be developed, and every organization will encounter useful technologies that did not exist when the roadmap was created but could provide business value to the company. Once a decision is made to adopt a new technology, the roadmap should provide guidance and best practices for the use of the technology within the IT environment. When such guidance is not provided, projects risk the misapplication of the new technology, as everyone rushes to be the first to make use of it and tries to fit it into places for which it was never designed.

Every project should be followed by a "post mortem" where information is gathered from the team members, stakeholders, and project sponsors. The lessons learned from these can typically be applied across the IT organization, especially in companies with a PMO and an ICC. In order to avoid making the same mistakes repeatedly on different projects, and to apply approaches that proved successful on future projects, the results of each post mortem must be collected and communicated. In some cases these lessons learned will be of appropriate granularity that they should be accounted for in the roadmap.

Metrics should be collected on the efficiency of systems in production, as well as the effort necessary to maintain them and any problems that occur, and these should be fed back to the development organization in a way that they can be easily digested and incorporated into future designs. This is one goal of programs like Microsoft's Dynamic Systems Initiative: to provide a link between the development team and the operational team, so that the development team can design for deployment. In order for this to continue to occur over time and for the application development teams to improve their ability to design for deployment, there must be a feedback loop from the operational environment to the development environment.

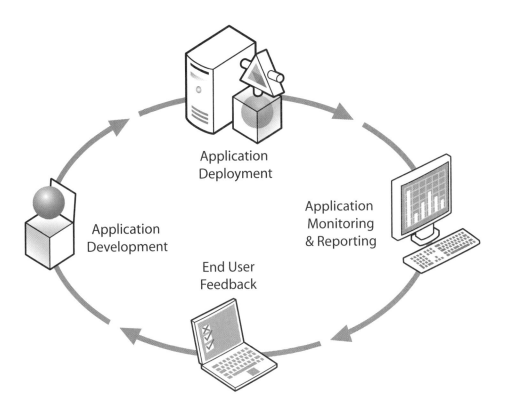

Application
Deployment

Application
Monitoring
& Reporting

Application
Development

End User
Feedback

Industry standards bodies can be an important avenue for identifying industry trends, leveraging the work of others in the industry to construct a canonical data model, and influencing the direction of standards specifications so that they are more closely aligned with the direction of the organization. Over time, most enterprises will incorporate relevant industry standards into their own roadmaps as these standards mature and are adopted.

The most important thing to keep in mind is that change is the only constant, and the purpose of the agile enterprise is to enable and facilitate change. To this end, the organization must continually look for new opportunities to improve the agility of the IT infrastructure and to leverage it in new and novel ways to gain competitive advantage.

Wrap-Up

This chapter looked at various aspects of executing a migration to an agile IT environment based on a Service Oriented Architecture. The chapter detailed the process of assessing where the organization is, followed by an explanation of determining where the organization needs to go and how to get there.

Any change of this magnitude will have implications for the organization as well as the infrastructure. These organizational impacts are the subject of the next chapter.

Chapter 12: Organizational Impact

"Right now, the flywheel is at a standstill. To get it moving, you make a tremendous effort. You push with all your might, and finally you get the flywheel to inch forward. After two or three days of sustained effort, you get the flywheel to complete one entire turn. You keep pushing, and the flywheel begins to move a bit faster. It takes a lot of work, but at last the flywheel makes a second rotation. You keep pushing steadily. It makes three turns, four turns, five, six. With each turn, it moves faster, and then—at some point, you can't say exactly when—you break through. The momentum of the heavy wheel kicks in your favor. It spins faster and faster, with its own weight propelling it. You aren't pushing any harder, but the flywheel is accelerating, its momentum building, its speed increasing."[15]

Navigating Change

There is one thing that an organization embarking on a journey to an agile enterprise enabled by a Service Oriented Architecture can be absolutely certain of: the changes that will affect the information technology infrastructure and the business processes that depend on it will ripple throughout the entire enterprise.

In Jim Collins' seminal work *Good to Great: Why Some Companies Make the Leap... and Others Don't*[16], he identified an organization's willingness to redefine its culture as one of the most important attributes that distinguishes great companies from the merely good companies. There is a parallel here with the basic tenets of Service Oriented Architecture. Just as SOA strives to make the company more agile through IT, so the organization itself strives to be more agile in its ability to absorb and adapt to a changing environment.

Many organizations have benefited from the creation of a change management group. This team has the responsibility to continually identify and plan for cultural changes driven by technology adoption. Often, these groups continue to provide value long after the changes they were formed to address are absorbed into the culture. Since change is the only constant, it makes sense to continually plan for the impact of change on the organization.

It is critical to proactively manage the rollout of the new architecture in order to minimize the impact to the company and its employees. One way to minimize the impact across the organization is to utilize a project-based management structure consisting of a well-defined project management framework and a project manager.

Project Management

The project manager is responsible for driving the project to completion through facilitation of regular communication among key project stakeholders, proactive resolution of project issues, change control and scope management, and hands-on management and tracking of all project activities. More importantly, the project manager's responsibility is to ensure that the company's established management processes are consistently adhered to and that project work reflects management's objectives.

Given the nature of some projects to change focus, increase in scope, and get off track during implementation and rollout, the project manager must monitor what is being done on the project and constantly validate that what is being done is in alignment with the company's objectives.

The purpose of project management is to ensure the success of projects by proactively facilitating the use of a project management framework composed of pre-established processes and tools identified as being critical for project success. The processes and tools comprising a project management framework generally include the areas of communication, project planning, resource planning and allocation, status reporting and tracking, scope management, change management, issue resolution, risk mitigation, and adherence to standards.

The creation and adoption of a project management framework is key to making project management work within any company. In formulating a project management framework, companies must identify appropriate processes and tools that can assist in accomplishing their project goals and that they are willing to support within their organizations. Additionally, it is important to understand the processes and tools created should be unique to the company; what a company requires will depend on its size, culture, and management style.

Some companies prefer more structured processes, while other companies simply prefer to establish generic frameworks that allow for more flexibility in how things are accomplished but still enable them to effectively manage their projects. Whichever direction a company decides to pursue in defining processes and tools is acceptable; however, establishing these processes and tools accomplishes nothing without the practical application of them to company projects. Once the project management framework has been defined, the project manager is responsible for facilitating the use of processes and tools comprising the framework on company projects.

Projects that operate without a project management framework or project manager typically encounter numerous communication, scope, and schedule issues. With no formal structure in place, project team resources are usually responsible for completing their technical tasks as well as performing project management tasks such as status reporting, issue resolution, and scope management. This additional responsibility often distracts team members from their daily project tasks and can easily result in a schedule slip. Once the plan starts to slip, team members typically disregard all project management responsibilities so they can focus completely on their tasks and get back on plan, which in turn can create project management, scope, and communications issues.

Typically, people who have experienced project management in action will attest to the value it brings to projects. There are a number of companies who are not willing to make the investment in implementing project-based management structures with full-time project management resources. Ultimately, a company will have to ask the question: "Is it worth the time, effort, and cost for our technical resources to focus on both project management and technical activities, or are we best served by having a full-time resource manage the project, thus allowing our technical resources to focus fully on delivering their scope of work?" Of course, the answer to this question will depend on many factors, but companies engaging in business critical initiatives that must be delivered as quickly and efficiently as possible are best served by utilizing a project-based management structure, including a project management framework and a full-time project manager.

In the city planning metaphor, an analogy can be drawn in the area of construction. Any major construction project, whether it is a building, a utility or a highway, will have one or more project managers depending on the size of the project. It is easy to see in these disciplines why it would be a mistake to ask the people doing the work to also perform the project management. IT projects are no different and should not be run any differently.

Organizational Readiness

The recognition that organizational changes will occur and a willingness to embrace change will enable an enterprise to reap the most benefit possible from the technology.

> Often the most significant benefit associated with technology comes from its role as a catalyst. That happens when we intentionally use technology to change how we do business – for example, by threatening current core processes, blowing up and getting rid of some of them, changing them dramatically, changing a whole organization.[17]

There is no question that the migration to a Service Oriented Architecture will require new skills within the IT organization as well as the business stakeholders. In order to understand what skills need to be either developed within the existing workforce or brought in from the outside, management must first determine what skills are present within the organization that can be leveraged.

The process of developing a catalog of the relevant skills and experience that can be useful to the program begins with interviews of the IT management, especially at the project level. Once an understanding of the project management skills is gained and the management's perspective of the technical skills present is understood, these interviews should be followed up with the technical staff to validate management's perception and to identify skills that may not have been known.

The software development lifecycle is critically important to the success of all IT projects and different development lifecycles are better at different types of projects. For the transition to an SOA, the presence and utilization of an iterative, incremental development process coupled to risk-based project management is the best combination for sustained success. To the extent that this type of process already exists within the IT organization it should be fostered – to the extent that it doesn't it should be instituted.

The lifecycles of the applications within IT are important to understand, as are the product lifecycles of any and all third party software packages utilized in IT. These development lifecycles will need to be correlated with the ongoing SOA adoption program, and their feature and capability plans will need to mesh with the rollout of business services to support the business processes.

There will undoubtedly be differences between the current state of the IT organization and the desired state; otherwise there would be no need for a program of change in the first place. Following the inventory and cataloging of the present state, a gap analysis can be performed to determine the differences and develop plans for closing them.

Goals

In order to determine what the gaps are between the current state and the desired future state, the future state needs to be understood as well. To understand this, we must look to the basic goals of the agile enterprise.

Strategic Alignment

Management sets the vision for the company, including the mission, strategic goals, and core values. It is becoming increasingly important that IT be applied effectively to achieve management's objectives. In the future, it will be vital to the success of the company.

One important goal of the organizational change is to morph the way that the enterprise views Information Technology. IT should be seen as an enabler of business, and, ultimately, as another piece of infrastructure that the business depends on but doesn't have to think about. Decisions regarding IT projects should be based on sound business reasoning and justified by accepted financial accounting models and metrics.

The transition to viewing IT as an enabler of business processes eases the way to the perspective that IT is infrastructure. A better understanding of the real effect of IT on the organization and its potential as a catalyst for change results from viewing IT as a means to an end, rather than an end in itself.

On the other hand, business people do not necessarily know what is possible at any given time with technology, and they should not be expected to keep up with the changing IT environment and the technology industry in general. The IT organization must remain alert to opportunities to utilize technology to enable the business and it must educate the business stakeholders on the potential uses of technology. The IT management must be diligent and maintain a balance between awareness of potential uses of technology to enable the business and the misuse of technology for the sake of technology.

Since services support business processes, the development of services must be aligned with the continuing evolution of the business processes. This emphasizes the importance of the change control processes and change management. Project management and technical oversight integrate via the ICC to drive the company's adoption program.

The ICC has the unique ability to see into both halves of this dependency, being able to affect the service development and having intimate knowledge of the business processes as they are currently implemented and as they might evolve in the future. The ICC is responsible for aligning these two tracks and ensuring that service development supports the business processes.

It is imperative that the members of the ICC have a deep and fundamental understanding of the business needs, processes, strategy, and goals in order to effectively guide the individual project teams in a manner consistent with the corporate business aims. In order to accomplish this, the ICC must have authority and responsibility related to both the business side and the IT side of every project and must be able to ensure a consistent application of the best practices and tenets of SOA across organizational silos.

Communication

Addressing the organizational change component of the transformation program in the analysis and planning stages can help prepare the way for the projects driving it. Communicating the anticipated changes, their necessity and benefits, and how they will affect the organization can help reduce resistance within the organization.

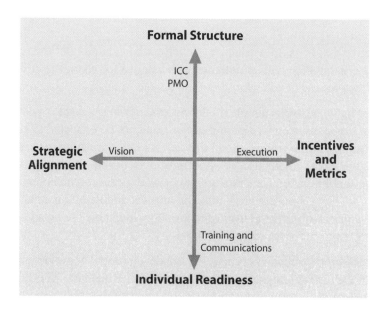

Communication is often a problem for projects that lack a formal project management structure, as project stakeholders will often communicate directly with numerous project team members, which can lead to conflicting or invalid information being delivered in an unfiltered manner to the project team. The effects of such information being passed to the project team could be widespread and include inaccurate scope changes, requirements, and unapproved decisions.

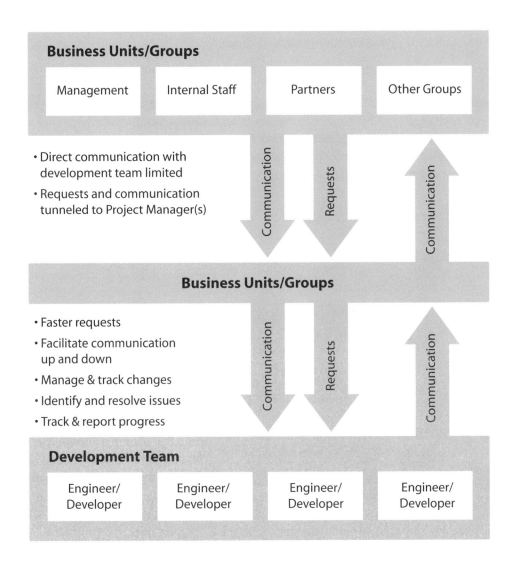

In a project-based management structure, the project manager acts as a layer of communication and process between project stakeholders and team members. The project manager enables proactive communication across key company stakeholders and information workers, including issue resolution, risk mitigation, planning, status tracking, and reporting by facilitating the use of the processes and tools comprising the project management framework. Acting in this manner, the project manager serves as a filter between project stakeholders and project team members, working with both groups and ensuring consistent communication and coordination between them.

Communicating the impact of the organizational shift is as important as identifying the depth and breadth of the organizational impact. Communication and decision channels should be put in place that ensure that the priorities are appropriately driven by business needs and that the projects undertaken match the priorities set by management. In order to avoid problems like low morale and high attrition, the direction of the organization should be communicated to all the employees, and each should be given a clear understanding of how they fit into the plan and how the changes will affect them and their work.

The importance of implementing and utilizing strong PM processes, which include proactive communication across key company stakeholders and information workers, cannot be overstated. Once changes have been communicated, it is important to proactively manage the rollout of changes to minimize their potential impact on the company.

An effective tool that is often used to accomplish this is a project marketing plan. The objective of a project marketing plan is to achieve company buy-in of the project or initiative across all divisions, levels, and business units. The plan is created by identifying the different groups that need to buy into the project and then determining the specific messages that need to be communicated to them regarding the benefits that will be reaped as a result of successfully completing the project. By creating a project marketing plan, management can communicate the appropriate message to each of the different groups in the company. The key decisions for justifying the project should be included in the marketing plan as well.

The ICC and other management bodies must be able to effectively communicate the strategy, goals, and vision down into the organization. Similarly, the activities of individual team members and projects must be traceable back to these same executive level goals.

The ICC is responsible for communicating to the organization the strategic role that IT plays in achieving the company's goals, sustaining its ongoing operations, and enabling future growth. The ongoing governance activities of the ICC ensure that IT projects actually meet the communicated expectations.

Although it is becoming an accepted fact that providing feedback to the development teams about the behavior of applications in an operational production environment improves the overall quality of IT systems, the mechanisms for providing this feedback in an effective way are still being defined. The ICC should facilitate this type of communication wherever possible, and should encourage the application teams to seek out operational data on their delivered applications, while simultaneously encouraging the operational staff to provide feedback to the development teams on the behavior of their applications.

Organizational Structure

One seemingly paradoxical outcome of a successful transition to the desired IT environment is a greater dependence on IT by the business. As IT becomes more flexible and infrastructure-like, the company will depend on it more for execution of business processes. The more transparent IT becomes, the more important it is to the ongoing business enterprise.

A greater dependence on the new IT infrastructure means that there should be greater attention paid to its implementation by the IT organization. The analogy to city planning and utilities can shed some light on how this occurs. Before cities offered basic infrastructure services like water, sewers, electricity, and communication, they grew on an *adhoc* basis, with individual businesses free to erect buildings and factories however they saw fit on whatever land they could acquire. This, in essence, is how most cities came to exist in the first place, with city government only added once the need for a central governance process became apparent.

Once cities began offering utility services, the existing businesses and buildings were retrofitted to take advantage of them, and, in the process, became dependent upon them. As new businesses were built to leverage these utility services, the continued operation and availability of the services became increasingly important. Furthermore, the city needed to manage the usage of the utilities so that they could guarantee a consistent level of services to all customers. City governments created zoning ordinances and review boards to address these challenges and began to plan for land usage by area rather than allowing anyone to use any piece of property they owned title to in any way they wished.

IT shops must undertake a similar process to implement governance bodies to define the parameters for usage of utility services by the application infrastructure. This will become increasingly important as the company's dependence on IT increases, which will be the direct result of the commoditization and industrialization of IT enabled by a Service Oriented Architecture.

The responsibilities and importance of the PMO have already been described. If an organization is embarking on the journey described here without a competent PMO and associated processes, then that will be an important new organizational structure to be put in place at the earliest stages of the adoption program.

The changes within the IT organization will be disruptive, due to the enterprise-wide nature of the change as opposed to the point solutions to integration of the past. It is important that management facilitate this organizational change and the formation of new organizations like the Integration Competency Center. Without proper management support and the authority to make tactical and strategic decisions concerning SOA adoption, this ICC risks failure, irrelevance, and ridicule. The perception of the ICC as a group of architects in an ivory tower handing down impractical edicts must be avoided at all cost.

Management must have the will and the means to set the ground rules for the migration to SOA. The ICC then implements the best practices through a combination of communication, mentoring, oversight, auditing, and governance. The ability to perform these functions depends largely on being granted access to the ongoing IT project teams and the authority to review their work and make changes to the design, architecture, and processes, where appropriate. Visibility into the application and project teams, and the authority to affect their activities, are necessary requirements for success.

The lifecycle of a service, from conception through development, deployment and maintenance, must be managed both from the perspective of the implementation of the service and its consumers. The ICC has a unique view into both halves of the service contract and must carefully manage the lifecycle of all the services within the application infrastructure to ensure that the service contracts are consistently aligned.

The architects that are part of the ICC should act as consultants to the individual application and project teams. Ideally, each ICC architect will consult to multiple projects, each on a part-time basis, mentoring and leveraging the fulltime application architect to implement the policies and best practices of the ICC.

The single most important part of service orientation is the design of generic business services that encapsulate any implementation details and expose a canonical data model to all consumers. The ICC, in its oversight role, should pay particular attention to the interface design heuristics and should enforce the process of contract first service development[18] across all application teams.

Application teams within the IT organization typically have the perspective that they "own" the data that their applications manage. The transition from one in which silo'd development teams own data to one in which the enterprise owns data is a key step along the road to agility.

The idea that each business entity is maintained by one and only one application that provides a set of generic business services related to the entity can be difficult for IT shops used to traditional data layer integration to comprehend. It is the responsibility of the ICC architects, in consultation with the project teams, to determine an appropriate system of record for each business entity and then to ensure that any application needing access to that entity does so by utilizing the services provided by the application assigned as the system of record.

Application teams must adopt an attitude of stewardship rather than ownership, in which they are responsible for providing access to data through standard, generic business services that implement associated business logic. This is another group that will need to be called out in the project marketing plan. Application teams will require a specific message regarding how the change will benefit them, how their roles will change, and how they will contribute to the new organization.

Application teams implement business services and need to understand the design and implementation of their applications, while the developers who assemble the business services into composite applications and business processes do not need to know the application specifics. This differentiation of skills and responsibilities creates agility within the IT organization by allowing higher level application development projects to be staffed with people who might be ignorant of the individual applications, having only an understanding of the services they provide.

Since one goal of SOA is to reuse services across multiple business processes, the level of service (availability, performance, etc.) provided by each business service must be sufficient to support the most demanding business process. The individual application teams implementing and maintaining the business services cannot be expected to understand all of the contexts in which the service is or might be used. The ICC must ensure that the SLAs of each business service are appropriate for all of the business process scenarios in which the service may participate.

Old Way	New Way
Data silos owned by application teams	Enterprise data owned by systems of record
Directly access data managed by other applications	Access entities via services implemented in the system of record
Connect applications to each other	Connect systems to the service fabric
IT is a cost center	IT is strategic to the success of the business
Software developers	Business analysts

Rewards and Measures

The system of rewards and measures that management puts in place for the organization can have an important impact on the successful implementation of the organizational changes identified here.

Whenever significant organizational changes are enabled by technology there will be resistance from portions of the "old guard" of management, who will be skeptical that the new ways of doing business offer any real benefit. Often their subordinates are on board with the direction of the company long before their bosses get it. In these situations, the old dogs will either learn the new tricks necessary to adapt to the changing organization or will leave of their own accord. In either case, there will be a gradual transition within the management structure as employees with more flexibility and imagination are promoted into the spots vacated by their less agile superiors. Promoting the right people into the right positions is the primary reward mechanism available to management.

The technical staff needs to be provided with incentives to improve analysis and design skills to be capable of defining appropriate business service interfaces. Since this aspect is crucial to the success of the SOA adoption program, it is extremely important that the organization have the right mix of skills to define the canonical data model to participate in industry standards bodies to define vertical message schemas and to ultimately implement the interfaces defined.

The skills necessary to meet the responsibilities of the ICC are much more business oriented than technical positions of the past. The system should reward IT staff for learning more about how the business works and applying that business knowledge to IT projects. The company might consider a program that gives the architects in the ICC real-world experience by rotating them through the business units so that they learn the nontechnical portions of the business. Alternatively, business people could be moved into or through the ICC to infuse that knowledge into the team.

The project management office should be appropriately incented to define the organizational change plan and successfully roll it out. In order to determine the success of the program, they should track metrics appropriate to the goals of the program.

One measure of the project management office could be the implementation of the established project management framework across all projects. However the framework is defined, it will include certain activities and tasks, and the execution of these can be measured for individual projects.

Wrap-Up

Clearly, the changes required to transition to becoming an agile enterprise are certain to have a significant impact throughout a company. Appropriate management procedures and organizations can facilitate communications and proactively manage change within the projects and across the organization, the impact can be minimized. The appropriate technical oversight in the form of the ICC can ensure that the project teams enabling the changes are making the right decisions regarding the technical infrastructure and utilizing the appropriate procedures for implementing the company's technical vision.

This book has presented a conceptual framework for thinking about all of IT in a holistic manner. Goals, processes, and techniques for moving IT from the current state to one in which it becomes transparent to the users of it, becoming infrastructure, have been presented and discussed in detail.

The goals of transparent IT and its ability to enable the agile enterprise should be clear, and the steps necessary to achieve it are laid out. All that is left is to begin the journey.

Epilogue

In the Prologue we saw how OG's monolithic systems, brittle interfaces, and lack of collaboration tools caused them to lose a lucrative exclusive distribution contract to a more nimble competitor.

The CEO of OG changed most of his management team and hired a consulting company to fix the problems in the organization and with the IT shop. Let's look in and see how things are going.

Phoenix

Jack looked around the conference room, casually listening into the various conversations around the table as everyone waited for the last couple of attendees to arrive. He made a mental observation that the roles represented were basically the same as that fateful meeting almost two years earlier, when he had asked the assembled team why they were unable to fulfill orders for the season's hottest product. What was the product that year? It didn't matter, every year saw the introduction of new products that were hot for a single season.

The faces in the room were all different, which was mostly his doing. What had followed OG's failure that season could be called a blood bath in corporate-speak, though he had taken his time replacing the key folks in order to make sure that he got the right kind of thinking in his new management.

Ron entered the conference room with a sheaf of papers under one arm, a cup of coffee in the opposite hand, and a convivial smile on his face. Jack recognized for the umpteenth time that Ron was the single best hire he had made in his time at OG and that Ron deserved more recognition for the ongoing success of the Phoenix Program.

"Good morning, Ron."

"Good morning, Jack. Nice tie."

"Thanks. OK everybody, my watch says 8:01, so let's get started. I emailed the agenda to all of you yesterday. The first item is our newest supplier, Bolo Boards. Judy?"

"The new Gladiator snowboard is doing extremely well. We shipped over a thousand in our first week."

"We just signed Bolo two weeks ago! That's really impressive!"

"I have to give a lot of credit to Ron and his team, Jack." Judy smiled across the table at Ron, who demurred. "The consulting architect my team got from the ICC for the integration project had us up and running in a fully automated mode in three days. It would have been faster, but Bolo didn't have anyone with experience in web service technology. Ron's guy had to develop a wrapper for their AS/400 system to accept our orders and put them into their MRP system. He used the legacy EDI tables on their end to get it up and running quickly with zero impact to their systems."

"We should charge them for that." The look on Jack's face seemed to indicate that he was only half kidding.

Although Stephen had only been the CFO for a few months, he was already comfortable with Jack's style and was extremely good at finding creative ways to pay for projects. He was perhaps a little too tight with the corporate expense accounts, but that wasn't such a bad thing sometimes. "Actually, the CIO of Bolo asked us how we had gotten everything integrated so quickly. We referred him to our consulting company, and they are giving us a referral fee, which more than covers the cost of implementing the interface for Bolo."

"So are we able to fulfill all the orders we are getting for Bolo product?"

"Yes. The website referral stats indicate that we are getting lots of hits on the banner ads we ran. We are currently the only online supplier of the Gladiator and the click-throughs from the review in Boarding magazine alone are driving 40 percent of our sales. We're getting a lot of abandoned shopping carts with Gladiators in them, so sales will probably pick up over the coming weeks as the season progresses." Although Johnny's team was doing a great job keeping the web presence up to date and turning changes around quickly, he had a tendency to gloss over details that Jack still found a bit annoying.

"What's a lot?"

Johnny looked across the table at Ron, which told Jack what he needed to know. Even though Ron was technically the head of the Integration Competency Center, he was quickly assuming the responsibilities of a CIO. If he continued to perform as exceptionally as he had for the last eighteen months, Jack would replace Johnny with Ron in that slot.

Ron leafed through the papers in front of him and pulled out a report. "We're getting an average of three thousand hits on the Gladiator page per day, and about 12% of them add the product to their shopping cart. Of those, 42% go on to order the board. That includes the people who come back later and buy it."

"How do the numbers look from your side, Marilyn?"

"Our margins are good, even though we are undercutting all the brick-and-mortar stores. Even with shipping our price is at least 10% below the lowest price we've seen out there and we're getting a 15% margin on that price."

"Okay. Next item – Ron, how is the Phoenix Program coming along?"

"The ICC is starting to function smoothly. I think we've hammered out all of the organizational issues with matrixing our architects into the project teams and we've overcome most of the resistance there. We've finalized the third iteration of the common message definitions that we're using across all of our systems and about 90 percent of our existing services are current with that model."

"Just a second, Ron, is that common message format the one we're basing on the industry standard?"

"Well, Jack, there really isn't one industry standard, but we are leveraging several in different places. We took the best parts of each that is relevant to our business and then tweaked them where necessary and combined them into one model. The technical folks call it a 'Canonical Data Model,' which is a really impressive way of saying a common message format across all our services."

"Is it wise to go our own way on this?"

"Well, it's not ideal, but none of the industry standards really meet our needs. We are staying as close to them as possible and we have an architect from the ICC assigned to each standard. They are responsible for monitoring the progress of the standard and feeding back our changes to the standards body so that hopefully, over time, we will converge. It's important to remember that we're talking about internal services here, so our partners don't see these messages."

"Right, they see the Partner Integration Hub."

"Correct, Jack. The hub implements messages that are as close to the industry standards as we can get. They are really very close, and I expect them to be fully compliant in the next version, which is going to be ready about the same time as the next version of the main standard spec is ready sometime next year."

"Good. Sorry to interrupt your status report, please go on."

"No problem. On the existing interfaces, we've been working through them and replacing them in priority order based on the ROI model for each. We've made it through 12 of the 22 integration points we identified in our initial inventory, and we're getting down to the ones with fairly low return. We're revisiting the models to see if they are still accurate, but if they are we will probably leave most of the remaining interfaces until they start to cause us pain."

"So that project is almost done?"

"Yes. We should wrap that up within the next month or so, depending on what the updated ROI models look like."

Judy looked up from her note pad. "Have we recognized the predicted return on the ones we already replaced?"

"We are monitoring the ongoing cost of maintaining the new interfaces versus the older ones and so far our models look fairly conservative. As far as the integration with our suppliers go, the cost of the Partner Integration Hub has already been covered by the additional sales due to increased order fulfillment and quicker turnaround of new suppliers and products."

"How is that part of Phoenix going?"

"We've gotten very good feedback from the purchasing team on the new smart client solution we gave them for signing up new suppliers. They have taken the average time from closing the deal with the supplier to getting the product on the website to under two weeks, and the trend line is continuing downward, so we expect to achieve our goal there with the new collaboration tools we are rolling out in January. The bottleneck currently seems to be the workflow, which is still being done mostly via email. The new employee portal will include the ability to collaborate in shared workspaces."

"Great. We should have done that sooner."

"I agree." Ron had thought many times that the employee portal should have been a higher priority. "We thought that the integration projects had a higher return, but now it looks like the ROI model for the portal might have been too conservative in estimating the productivity gains and their value."

"Live and learn, live and learn. Excellent work everyone, I firmly believe that this team has turned around OG and saved the company from bankruptcy. The Phoenix Program has been an unqualified success. Remember that this is an ongoing effort. We're adjourned."

Part IV: Supplemental Material

Web Services Infrastructure: The global utility for real-time business by Phil Wainewright

Phil Wainewright is one of the world's foremost authorities on business and technology trends in software-powered services. He is the founder of web services information site Loosely Coupled, and previously founded industry website ASPnews.com, which he sold to internet.com (now Jupiter media Corp) in January, 2000. He serves as CEO of Procullux Ventures, a London-based strategic consultancy for web services ventures, and is contributing analyst with Summit Strategies.

Light dawns

"Computing that is as available, reliable and secure as electricity, water services and telephony."

— Bill Gates, Microsoft, 17th January 2002

Suddenly, people are talking about utility computing again. This time, it's for real.

With the emergence of web services, the convergence of telecoms and computing is finally reaching maturity in a unified platform for doing business in the 21st century:

- The IP-based telecoms infrastructure puts businesses in constant, real-time contact with customers and suppliers.

- Web-based software-as-a-service architectures provide the tools to automate delivery of transactions and services from businesses to their customers.

The delivery of real-time business services over the WorldWide Web is a development that makes business sense of the Internet.

It promises a new era of unprecedented efficiency and productivity — but only if the right infrastructure is in place.

This white paper describes the emerging shape of that web services infrastructure and the nature of the providers who will bring it into being. It sets out:

- The landscape of the emerging global infrastructure for realtime business

- The players who share the task of building and safeguarding that infrastructure

- The contest for new roles and positioning that some of those players will face

Readers will learn how the creation of the global infrastructure for realtime business will add new meaning to the roles of service providers and of software vendors, transforming their relationships not only with each other, but also with many of their most important enterprise customers.

The landscape

In just ten years, the Internet has evolved from an academic curiosity into an integral foundation for doing business. The deployment of web services for real-time business automation marks the culmination of that transformation into the rich fabric of today's Internet.

Network + software

Today, the Internet is more than just a physical network. The software layer of the WorldWide Web is as much a part of the infrastructure as the underlying network components.

- Routers, fibre and cable provide a foundation of IP (Internet protocol) networking

- Servers, databases and application platforms support the web-based software and services that run over the network

Web services run over this software infrastructure. With their emergence, the Internet has ceased to be solely a content transmission network. It has become a computing execution network, processing commercial transactions and business applications.

Network + enterprise

The dividing lines separating the enterprise from the Internet are fading away. Internet technology permeates every network, public or private. Intranets, extranets and ISP backbones all share the same architecture.

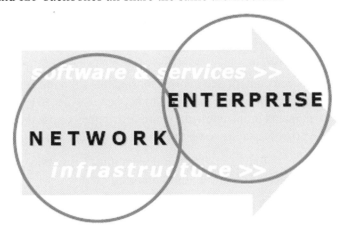

Activities that used to operate in closed separate networks are now starting to coalesce across this common infrastructure, giving rise to new concepts of shared endeavour such as the extended enterprise and collaborative commerce. The difference between a corporate intranet, a shared private extranet and the public Internet is defined today not by their physical extent but by who has access to them.

The common infrastructure is merging to form a single, shared web services infrastructure.

But there was a reason why enterprises used to keep their computing encased within secure, private networks. If they are to have confidence in the shared Web for real-time business, it must operate reliably and predictably to enterprise-class standards.

Shared, end-to-end infrastructure

The shared infrastructure is the foundation for business communication, collaboration and trade. As such, it has to meet much higher expectations than the Internet of old. Delays, interruptions and errors in these activities cost the participants money.

Three prime characteristics raise the bar compared to its predecessors.

Support for applications

The original Internet made it possible to send and receive e-mail and to share access to files. The WorldWide Web added a software layer that made it easier to publish and access other content. The final development has been the emergence of web services, enriching the software layer with application functionality.

The task of the web services infrastructure is to support commercial-grade application functionality.

The difference between content and applications comes from the addition of process — the sequence of events that need to happen in order to produce a result. When participants in the application are distributed across the web, the need to complete processes adds some important new operating requirements:

- **Consistency** — Each separate component must act within certain parameters, such as response times and availability.

- **Authenticity** — There must be some way of assuring the identity of each of the participants in the process.

- **Timeliness** — Each step in the process must execute in the correct order, and promptly — especially if a user is waiting on the result in order to continue with their work

- **Integrity** — There must be mechanisms to avoid data becoming corrupted as it passes between participants

- **Persistence** — Each participant in the process must maintain a permanent record of their part in the transaction.

The web services infrastructure must provide a platform that supports these requirements and more. That demands an array of tools and services to enhance, monitor and maintain quality-of-service.

Multiple providers

Unlike a traditional telecoms or enterprise network, this multi-layered network and software infrastructure is shared by many different providers.

While a select group of dominant telcos provide backbone and last-mile wireline network services, other providers contribute server management, data storage, edge cacheing, security, VPN and wireless services. All are interchangeable on the whim of each individual customer.

Much of the infrastructure, both at the network and software layers, is within individual enterprises. They too thus participate as providers. Note also that an increasing proportion of enterprise computing infrastructure is itself multi-provider in nature. Web-based applications in particular are often hosted at outside providers rather than within the physical network of the enterprise.

Creating an integrated, end-to-end application delivery infrastructure requires close co-operation between these multiple providers and enterprises.

Essential standards

The only effective mechanism to enable co-operation between so many different and varied participants is standardisation.

Many of the standards required for web services are not yet fully defined. Until those standards have been created and put into effect, providers will have to 'plug the gaps' with proprietary workarounds, using one of two alternatives:

- A vertically-integrated infrastructure owned by a single provider or enterprise

- A co-operatively managed infrastructure coordinated by partnership between multiple participants

Many enterprises and providers will prefer the former as being closest to their existing infrastructure and easier to control and manage. Those who opt for the latter will take on a bigger challenge, but will find their efforts rewarded. They will gain competitive advantage through their early investment in the resources and skills required to participate fully in the universal, standards-based shared infrastructure that is destined to emerge.

Software meets business services

Over the past two decades, the word application has become firmly associated with the notion of boxed software packages. That notion becomes obsolete in the era of web services.

The role of software in the business web is to automate business processes.

Those processes do not need to be packaged into discrete applications. Now that the software is online, it has become feasible to dynamically assemble applications by combining individual process components in the form of web services. The resulting applications are not software artifacts but live, software-based business services.

Web services have arisen in response to the network environment, which encourages highly modular software componentisation. Evolving web services protocols allow communications among a web of interconnected, autonomous participants. This enables the assembly of web services applications from multiple providers. The software layer of the web is, in effect, taking on the same standards-based, multi-provider characteristics as the underlying network infrastructure.

But what are web services?

Just like the ASP acronym, 'web services' is a term that has come to mean many different things to many different people. Some use it very loosely to describe any kind of functionality delivered using web technologies. Others have a precise definition relating to the use of XML-based web standards, such as SOAP and WSDL, to enable program-to-program transactions in software.

All the definitions describe emerging techniques for delivering and integrating online functionality. The important unifying theme is a general move towards adoption of dynamic coupling of software-based service components at all levels of the online infrastructure.

Practical applications of web services technologies fall into three groups:

- **Plug-in functionality**. The simplest and most prevalent web services in use today add third-party functions to web pages and portals. Common examples include external news feeds and stock quotes, banner ad serving, and search boxes. Few use XML and SOAP, relying instead on HTML based technologies such as JavaScript, CGI and Java.

- **Remote infrastructure services**. Third-party providers use web services technologies to deliver behind-the-scenes functionality for commercial websites, such as user authentication, payment processing and visitor traffic analysis.

- **Enterprise application integration**. Web services technologies are rapidly finding favour as a solution to the complex integration challenges of linking applications within the enterprise, or across a value chain. EAI implementations are the most likely to use formal web services standards.

Even though the primary purpose of web services technologies is to permit access to remote functions, it is their use for EAI purposes within enterprise or private network infrastructures that is currently attracting the most attention from mainstream IT vendors and suppliers.

A rapidly-expanding band of web services software vendors provide tools and platforms for building web services, including many who specialise in integration wrappers and tools for EAI.

Initially, most EAI projects will remain inwardly focussed. Nevertheless, the use of web services brings the target applications into the same common architecture as the wider shared web. It is the penultimate step on the way to joining the shared web services infrastructure.

Four hotspots

In the era of web services, the networked infrastructure embraces software, and it embraces the enterprise. This focusses attention on four principal areas of activity within the landscape, highlighted in the diagram below.

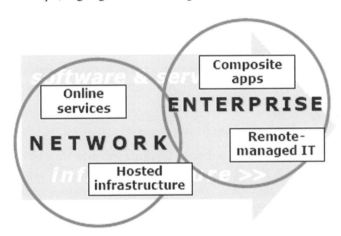

Across all of these hotspots, there is one overriding theme. Having reliable, real-time access to business services makes it easier to outsource non-core activities. Every participant is encouraged to focus on enhancing the quality and cost-effectiveness of their core competence, while tapping the expertise and infrastructure of outside specialists for other elements of their business operations.

Infrastructure: hosted

Hosting is increasingly becoming the norm for Internet and web infrastructure, including web servers and software. In this respect, the web services infrastructure is merely replicating the same progression made long ago by the utility infrastructures of electricity, water and telephony.

Hosted infrastructure is any part of the infrastructure that is owned by providers and operated on behalf of their customers rather than being part of the enterprise.

This encompasses the network backbone, colocation centres, managed server farms, last-mile wireless and wireline connections, and the associated network management services.

Infrastructure: remote-managed

Inside the enterprise sits a mirror image of the hosted infrastructure. It comprises networks, servers, software and client devices. In some cases there are data centres and server farms too.

Much of this enterprise-resident infrastructure is getting too complex and mission-critical for enterprises to be able to manage it effectively using their own resources. They could cope when it consisted of discrete client server networks accessed mainly during the working day. But managing an Internet-connected, wide area network 24x7 goes way beyond their core competence.

Remote management is now gaining acceptance as a means of contracting outside providers to take on responsibility for day-to-day management of the in-house infrastructure, without giving up ownership. Standards-based architectures and ubiquitous network infrastructure have made such services both reliable and cost-effective.

Software and services: component functions

Outside of the enterprise in the software layer are the providers of component functionality. This may take the form of complete application packages or business services, or it may be single-component web services such as Passport authentication, instant messaging, a news feed or a search engine.

The vendors of platform software and packaged applications are players in this part of the landscape. The software they supply is also a component for installation into provider-hosted or enterprise infrastructure. Onetime distribution on a CD is one among several delivery options — many vendors offer the option of hosting or remote management services.

Once they are made available online, business services such as payroll administration, credit card payment processing or courier delivery also become component services. The common web services infrastructure makes it possible to seamlessly assemble traditional real-world services along with software and web services using a single component architecture.

Software and services: composite applications

Web services turn applications, business services and component services alike into standardised building blocks of online functionality. Aggregated together, they are easily assembled into a new generation of adaptable, web-centric composite applications.

Enterprise information portals, content management platforms, public and private trading exchanges, integrated supply chains, customer self-service portals and partner relationship management systems are all converging on this model.

They assemble core application software together with third-party business services and components into a single composite interface. Web services architectures smooth integration between the various components and make it easy to add, subtract or reconfigure individual participants at will within the composite whole.

Engineered by large corporations, or by providers on behalf of enterprise clients, they often target individual users in their millions or small businesses in their thousands. As so often in the first stages of a powerful new technology wave, it is visionaries working in large enterprises who have seized the early initiative to win competitive advantage for their businesses.

Those efforts are now coming to fruition in a gathering tornado of activity.

The players

The major players in this new landscape are not confined to the traditional service provider industries. The extension of the common, shared infrastructure into the enterprise has brought businesses from all kinds of industries into the online service provider arena.

Enterprises become ASPs

In the new always-on web services landscape, enterprises are no longer at the end of the value chain. They are part of it, using the shared infrastructure to automate interaction and transactions with their suppliers, employees and customers.

As aggregators and providers of the online functionality that makes up their composite applications, they effectively act as ASPs to the users of those applications. But this is not a label that gets applied to them, since the applications merely support their core business activities. In many cases too, a service provider remains involved, albeit in a behind-the-scenes role.

Enterprises deploy their composite applications infrastructure in one of three modes:

- **Self-hosted, self-managed**: This is the traditional enterprise computing model, in which the enterprise has complete ownership of the applications infrastructure. It remains a suitable model for enterprises whose operations are large enough to support the high costs of maintaining sufficient resources to meet all of their application deployment, delivery and management needs.

- **Self-hosted, remote-managed**: This model maintains substantial in-house investments in applications infrastructure, but subcontracts outside expertise and management infrastructure to supplement the in-house skills base and help meet day-to-day operational requirements.

- **Private-label hosted**: In this model, the application infrastructure belongs to and is operated by an external provider, who delivers it on behalf of the enterprise and under its brand. In this type of relationship, the enterprise is sometimes referred to as a "virtual ASP" or V-ASP.

Similarly, the component software and services that make up the composite application come from three sources:

- **In-house**: These are normally the components that reflect the enterprise's core competence, and are originated by in-house resources.

- **Packaged software**: Automation of routine functions is often best implemented using conventional packaged software, particularly when tight integration with the organisation's core operations is required.

- **3rd party services**: Supplementary content, functions and services that are peripheral rather than core, or which rely on specialist outside expertise, are often best implemented using external service providers.

A composite application will often combine all three sources and will quite frequently combine all three of the deployment modes. For example, a bank might build and operate its own online small business banking service, while using remotely managed CRM software to automate user support for the application, and delivering a third-party payroll management service under its own brand as an optional extension to the core service.

Infrastructure operators

Hidden behind the aggregated façade of the composite application lies a thriving community of providers. Once hyped under a dazzling array of xSP acronyms, these providers are barely noticed now, and yet the scope and influence of their activities continues to grow.

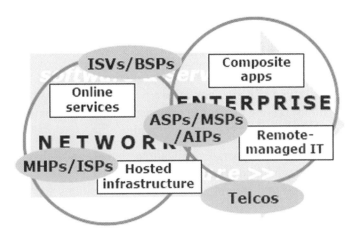

Even an enterprise that remains intent on keeping all of its applications infrastructure in-house still relies on external providers for elements of the underlying architecture.

The majority of enterprises will increasingly seek to outsource as much as possible of the infrastructure, since they will find themselves unable to achieve sufficient scale to compete with the lower cost and higher operating efficiency of dedicated providers.

Among the infrastructure operators, providers fall into two main clusters. ASPs, MSPs and AIPs focus on enterprise-facing, application-level infrastructure, while MHPs and ISPs look after the physical, networkcentric infrastructure.

Telcos form a third group, with a crucial role to play in co-ordinating the delivery of reliable, end-to-end network services.

ASPs/MSPs/AIPs

These are the providers that operate elements of application-level infrastructure for the enterprise. For clarity, they are divided here into three separate types, although in practice many of the companies operating in the sector blend various functions into a composite offering. But it remains possible to define some core characteristics for each of the three types.

- **ASPs** (application service providers) are the application software experts. Many companies in this group prefer not to use an ASP or xSP label, instead describing themselves as outsourcers, solution providers, or some other form of service provider. Nevertheless, their core competence is the same: deploying and managing applications to deliver reliable business functionality. Within this group, there are several distinct variations worth highlighting:

- **VSPs** (vertical service providers) tailor their application offerings to suit the needs of companies in specific vertical markets. Their portfolios usually include a high proportion of proprietary software.

- **Enterprise ASPs** are the best-known (although not necessarily the most successful) type of ASP. They offer a portfolio of thirdparty branded applications, relying on the use of repeatable methodologies and automation to achieve economies of scale.

- **Private-label ASPs** operate applications for sale and delivery by partners under their own brand. The applications offered by this type of ASP range from custom-assembled composite applications and proprietary software to popular brand-name applications.

- **MSPs** (management service providers) are the platform software experts. They leave all the top-level application deployment and management in the hands of their clients, concentrating instead on managing the underlying server platforms such as application servers, databases and operating systems. They'll provide remote management of servers in an enterprise data centre, sending alerts in case of problems or fixing them if the fault's within their remit, and running stress testing on request. Just don't ask them to change the way the application works; that's where they draw the line.

- **AIPs** (application infrastructure providers) are the network software experts. They provide network management infrastructure and services to ensure reliable application deployment via multiple providers all the way to the end user — a kind of MSP for the distributed network. (This is the least well defined of the three categories, and not all analysts agree with this definition. Some use AIP as an alternative name for private-label ASPs, while others use it for high-end managed hosting providers.)

MHPs/ISPs

These are the providers who collectively operate the Internet network infrastructure, made up of the Internet backbone, access points and data centres.

- MHPs (managed hosting providers) operate Internet data centres where they manage servers on behalf of clients, effectively acting as an MSP for the servers on their premises. They often position themselves as AIPs to the enterprise market.

- ISPs (Internet service providers) are a broad category, including both network backbone operators and Internet data centre operators as well as network access providers. They often team up with MSPs to compete with MHPs and can also position themselves as AIPs.

Telcos have a foundation role

The emergence of the shared, end-to-end infrastructure opens up an important potential role for telecoms providers as the co-ordinators and ultimate guarantors of service quality across the network. With a dominant position at the point of physical service delivery at every step of the end-to-end infrastructure, telcos are best placed to execute the AIP function, thereby adding substantial new value to their core service offering.

But they cannot do it all by themselves. They must learn how best to work with providers at other layers of the infrastructure to ensure the effective delivery of applications and services across the network. Co-operation between wireless and wireline providers over the last mile will become increasingly important too, ensuring users maintain seamless access to applications as they switch from office-based to mobile devices and back again.

Software and service providers

Software and services are the raw components from which enterprises assemble deliverable business services. Two main groups of providers create these crucial building-block components.

- ISVs design and build the software that automates the fulfilment and delivery of business functions.

- BSPs employ skilled professionals to perform the specialized business functions that software cannot automate.

ISVs

There are several types of independent software vendor (ISV). Each operates at a different level of software architecture:

- **Application ISVs** form the mainstream bulk of conventional ISVs. They deliver complete packages of software that automate a suite of related business functions. Their application packages are tuned to maximise performance as an integrated whole, and are often poorly adapted for linking to external web services.

- **Infrastructure ISVs** develop platforms and tools that are used to design, build and manage software components and applications. Since their products provide the foundation for the creation and operation of finished applications, they are very influential in aiding or obstructing the adoption of standards.

- **Web service ISVs** develop software components that deliver specific functionality for use either at an infrastructure or an application level.

ISVs have traditionally delivered their software as a packaged product for installation by their customers, but the emergence of a shared connected infrastructure has opened up alternative delivery models:

- Large numbers of ISVs are now offering customers a hosted option as an alternative to installation, either acting as their own ASPs or appointing recognised ASP partners.

- Some ISVs have adopted a "service-assisted" model, in which the ISV acts as an MSP for the installed software. Services delivered under this model may include remote supervision or management of the initial installation and later upgrades, online shadowing and remote fixes during support calls, and continuous monitoring of application performance.

- Other ISVs, particularly those in the web services segment, deliver their software exclusively online, without offering the option of customer installation. In effect, they act as ASPs of their own software. Any client-side code that needs to reside on the customer's machine is installed and managed remotely by the ISV.

BSPs

Business service providers (BSPs) use the web services model to deliver professional service content of some kind. Present-day examples include online information providers, credit card payment processors and payroll processing services.

In each case, there some element of skilled human intervention involved in the provision of the service, even though that professional service core may be surrounded by a great deal of software automation. (Some analysts go further and count as BSPs those ISVs who deliver their own business applications as an online provider).

In the modern world, it is the objective of every business to automate as much as possible of the human element in order to increase efficiency and lower costs. To some extent, therefore, the emergence of the web services infrastructure for real-time business will ultimately mean that every enterprise can become an online business service provider.

The contest

The emergence of a common web services infrastructure will transform the roles of software vendors and telecoms providers, and will revolutionise the business models of many enterprises. Those who are slow to adapt will lose out to nimbler competitors.

Enterprises as online providers

Enterprises recognise the potential benefits of doing business online, measured in such terms as faster time to market, lower overheads, better customer relationships and enhanced responsiveness to changes in market conditions.

Until now, they have held back from attempting to realise those benefits because they saw that the technology simply couldn't deliver. The utilitygrade web services infrastructure finally delivers the assured predictability they have been waiting for.

It is now time for enterprises to master online services.

They must become proficient in composite applications and how best to deploy them to enhance their relationships with customers, partners and suppliers. They must adapt their businesses to an online service provider model, becoming skilled in real-time, always-on service delivery. Existing online service providers already have many of those skills and capabilities. Their expertise will be much in demand.

Web services replace traditional applications

The fact that software vendors deliver applications today as a prepackaged set of functions is an accident of history, not a necessity.

Software applications are simply bundles of software components that automate repeatable business processes. The various components have all been tested together for compatibility and performance, saving the buyer the trouble of doing so.

Web services architectures are designed to allow functional components to operate together on demand. They eliminate the need for compatibility testing, and therefore they eliminate the need for prepackaging of applications.

The only reason buyers will continue to buy packaged suites will be convenience, but they will not want to be locked in by doing so. They will expect to be able to separate any individual component and substitute an alternative should they wish to.

In the context of the composite application, compatibility with third-party components will become paramount. Any failure to adhere to web services standards will threaten the integrity of the entire edifice. When an enterprise has created all of its e-business operations as a series of interlinked composite applications, such a risk doesn't even bear thinking about.

Such considerations make the supremacy of web services over traditional application packages a foregone conclusion.

Applications as infrastructure

Operating systems, databases, web servers and application servers are as much a part of the web services infrastructure as the physical network beneath them. The same applies to certain core applications.

Established business applications such as financials, messaging, sales automation and customer contact are based on a core set of tried-and tested business objects and processes. Leading application packages comprise portfolios of objects and processes that are established as best practice in their field.

Most enterprises installing such an application today do not customise the core components. They simply configure the way the objects and processes interact, and how they are presented to users. The underlying component library has become a stable infrastructure.

Successful ASPs have taken advantage of this trend towards a core application infrastructure. They have built repeatability and economies of scale into their implementation of the core, while retaining their customers' freedom to configure the process interaction and presentation of the application as they please.

Web services architectures now allow those ASPs to deliver their libraries of core application functionality as component services for integration into composite applications.

The automated business functionality has itself become an infrastructure component, and ASPs have become business process infrastructure operators, with a business model based on achieving economies of scale.

The role of telecoms

The content-centric nature of the first-generation web deceived many observers. They concluded that the Internet's primary role would be as a mass medium for content, mainly information and entertainment.

Eager to sell extra bandwidth, telecoms carriers prepared themselves for an explosion in multimedia traffic. They are still waiting. The assumption was a fallacy, based on a failure to recognise the true nature of the web as a platform for computing.

The Internet's primary role is the delivery of function — of automated processes, made available as web services.

Businesses are the main consumers of automated processes, and in volumes that will dwarf the potential demand from the consumer mass market alone. (Indeed, in the context of web services, the delivery of multimedia content to the mass market is just one set of applications within the specific industries of media and entertainment. Focussing exclusively on that single opportunity ignores the bigger picture.)

The opportunity for telecoms carriers is in assuring the utility grade strength of the web services infrastructure.

Carriers are best positioned to maintain oversight of the end-to-end network, providing co-ordination, monitoring and validation services that support the complex needs of the multi-provider networked application infrastructure.

It is up to carriers to become the standard bearers for web services, using their position and influence to ensure the success of the multi-provider infrastructure as a platform for business in the 21st century. They hold in their hands the key to the future productivity and efficiency of global business.

Real Time Enterprises: A Continuous Migration Approach by Vinod Khosla and Murugan Pal

Current market trends, global competition, and technological innovations are driving enterprises to adopt the practices of Real Time Enterprises. Real Time Enterprises are organizations that enable automation of processes spanning different systems, media, and enterprise boundaries. Real Time Enterprises provide real time information to employees, customers, suppliers, and partners and implement processes to ensure that all information is current and consistent across all systems, minimizing batch and manual processes related to information. To achieve this, systems for a Real Time Enterprise must be "adaptable" to change and accept "change as the process".

Any business process within the enterprise, including relevant processes in use by its trading partners (the extended enterprise), must be instantaneously reflected in all enterprise systems. In other words, all INFORMATION is "real time" within a "real time enterprise". All manual or batch processes related to information in an enterprise are inefficiencies in the delivery of products and services – unless the manual and batch mode processes (as in process industries) are required as part of the business nature. For example,

- In a Real Time Enterprise all the systems everywhere could recognize the new product entered in a catalog system so that billing and customer service can be done right from the moment that product becomes available.

- A wireless carrier could activate a wireless phone as soon as the credit card payment is processed with out any time loss or manual intervention.

- A credit card company could improve customer loyalty by automating the dispute notifications starting with the customer, and extending to the credit card company, the merchant's bank, and all the way back to the merchant.

- Last year, Lexmark had $1 million worth of nonconforming material returned to one of its plants in a single lot. Investigation revealed that providing engineers with adequate information online and in real time3 could avoid this situation and future inefficiencies.

- Citibank, to avoid heavy call volume in Poland around paydays, introduced cellular text messaging (SMS) to inform all customers of any changes in their bank balances instantaneously on their cell phone.

Today's business practices and models demand an operational environment acting as a virtual enterprise, with insight into the status of customers, partners, and suppliers on a real time basis while lowering SG&A costs. Cisco and Dell, with better service and higher revenue per employee than their direct competitors, are great examples of leading technology adopters who have leveraged some of these capabilities. At the same time, companies like Lexmark[3] and Cutler-Hammer[7] have realized similar benefits through automation. Still, automation of an end-to-end value chain has not been widely adopted or fully achieved. Even though technologically this has been possible for some time, only now has it become realistic with the advent of Internet-driven standardization. This has led to orders-of-magnitude cost reductions plus the elimination of debate regarding the technical infrastructure to be used. With the advent of Internet technologies such as HTTP, HTML, standardization initiatives around XML, Web services, UDDI, and SOAP, it is now possible. Lexmark leveraged Internet and thin client technology to enable their engineers to monitor production processes at their suppliers in real-time, from anywhere in the world and put defective product on hold at the source. Dylan Tweney in his column states, "Web services will enable companies to link up their enterprise systems with the production processes, bringing executives ever closer to the ideal of 'real-time enterprise computing,' and in turn will make companies better able to respond rapidly to changing market conditions"[7]. We agree.

Cisco's ambition to close their books on a daily basis is the litmus test for a Real Time Enterprise. Consider the benefits of having all information current in all systems such that books can be nominally closed within hours of the close of a quarter (or day!). Cisco does that today, and after adjustments including managerial and auditor input can announce financial results within three days of the end of the quarter. Think of the cost savings in finance alone! Cisco Systems' much-vaunted electronic order-entry system has decreased the rate of errors for the company from 20% to 0.2%[5]. If a <u>majority</u> of the orders come in untouched by humans, think of the sales force efficiency and yield improvements. If most employee information (such as vacation days and 401K's) is "<u>self service</u>" on the intranet, think of the savings in HR. If order status, product configuration, and "available to promise" dates are self-service for customers on the Web, think of the improvements in customer service that are possible, while reducing costs. These improvements are not just about a Website but a structural change to Web enabled IT. The benefit of "self service" is enormous as data will be cleaner when the owner enters it and the process will be efficient because it is outsourced to the end customers themselves. This is how the Internet is being used for information transport rather than a browsing medium. It represents a change in the way finance, operations, HR, logistics, and the whole corporation works. According to Roland Berger's Geissbauer, manufacturers already using the Internet see annual cost savings of 6 percent across the value chain. From procurement to Web-based supply chain management and after-sales service, it may be possible to cut costs by as much as 8 percent to 10 percent[3]. We think the savings are potentially larger. On the other hand, Cisco failed to automate its supply chain deep enough into it's partners, resulting in hundred's of millions of excess inventory beyond what a normal demand forecasting error would have caused in a full real time, full visibility environment.

The reality is that the vast promise of IT, by and large, has been a mirage for most corporations. But does this have to be true? Does the promise only work for some organizations? Are missed opportunities for productivity gains just that, or can they be realized? Are budget overruns, process delays, and "additional costs" to recover the investments already made an unavoidable fact of life? We have gone from MIS departments with large in-house software development efforts, to inexpensive desktop enablement, to large packaged software applications, to productive application development tools, client server applications, portable environments like JAVA, and system integration tools. We have gone through IT consultants, outsourcing vendors, ASPs, the Big 5 and their system integration expertise, but the problems of IT remain largely the same. Even more tantalizing are the stories of "benefits" of good IT strategies. Cisco has substantially higher revenues per employee than its direct competitors, Nortel and Lucent. The cost of doing business is lower at Cisco, and their responsiveness and customer service levels are higher. Geissbauer stresses that many of the top challenges for manufacturers relate to competitive pressure and manufacturers need to respond faster to customers in order to achieve their top-line sales goals. Dell can offer "mass customization" and still maintain much higher inventory turns than its competitors, generating greater profitability in its PC business. Wal-Mart and Amazon have used IT technology as strategic weapons to increase their competitiveness. FedEx could not economically provide the level of customer service that it does without IT. The cost to FedEx of a "package pick up call" or a "where is my package" inquiry have declined substantially (greater than 10X) because of the use of appropriate technology. We guesstimate that each 1% (of sales) of increased IT spending or spending redirected from rigid and outmoded forms of systems integration in a corporation should reduce SG&A spending by 1.5% to 2% (of sales) beyond the improvements in IT productivity. It is important to note that the bigger role of IT is not managing IT functions and expenses, but rather to manage expenses and service levels for the "rest of the corporation". IT can be a strategic weapon and help reduce SG&A costs relative to competitors while improving customer experience. The rate of savings depends on industry sector; those sectors with high SG&A can realize the most significant benefits. This applies especially to business processes, collaboration environments, and personalized applications where the bulk of enterprise activity can be automated. It is clear that every business process, every manual or batch process, and every human touch point that is properly automated and eliminated will result in an economic saving as well as an improvement in quality by reducing the risk of human error and improving the availability of information.

Any astute CEO or CFO will choose to automate and eliminate provided that the risks can be managed and results can be demonstrated in small projects with 90-180 day implementation and payback cycles. IT can become a competitive weapon, with the CIO becoming as critical in reducing costs or improving "product" as the VP R&D, in defining products as the VP of Marketing, in improving customer service as the VP of Customer Support, or in improving operations and reducing operations and administrative costs as the VP of Operation or the CFO. In summary, the CIO becomes a strategic leader.

The goal of this paper is to define the "ground rules" of an IT transformation from the stark reality of legacy applications forward to the promise of the future. In fact, the goal **should not be a radical transformation but rather continuous migration of systems, transforming the organization into an adaptive enterprise**. It is easy to define the ideal "new" world, particularly with the promise of Web services, but harder to achieve a practical reorientation towards such a goal. No magic bullets or ideal solutions exist. However, biases in certain directions and small probing steps do help. Differences in approach can result in a significant impact over a three to five year time frame. Ground rules and technology choices can make environments more flexible, adaptable and pliable over time. It is this paper's goal to highlight these, as well as the "current best targets" towards an ideal environment. Keep in mind we are dealing with first generation attempts at this new model and will run into many "gottchas", issues and practical problems. But iteration towards the above goal is necessary because it is unlikely that we will ever have an instantaneous or ideal tool for the transition. What we will need to do is dedicate an increasing part of our maintenance budget, the largest component of most IT budgets, to approaches that will enable the legacy environment to move towards the new vision.

The inflexible structure of conventional systems has long been the subject of loud complaints by top management. Today's customer expectations, evolving business models and technology trends demand the need for adaptability. It is important to accept CHANGE AS A PROCESS, rather than as an EVENT. IT spending must be evaluated against the total expenditures of an organization, and the potential savings from the effective usage of IT. These evolving business needs demand:

- "Inter-enterprise integration" to shift from Enterprise Resource Planning (ERP) to Inter-enterprise Resource Planning (IRP) and to resolve issues arising from the rigidity and cost of linking systems.

- "Intra-business functional integration" to unify business process beyond what packaged applications capture.

- "Self sufficiency" from a systems perspective, allowing adaptive, low cost iterations, customizations and change isolations, rather than a requirement to get it right the first time.

- Understanding that optimization for adaptability is more important than optimizing for cost, performance or features.

The ability to encapsulate existing systems, automating them as business processes, and letting users collaborate via appropriate interfaces are the keys to Real Time Enterprises as illustrated.

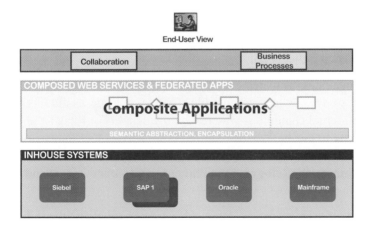

The value of real time enterprises is in capturing the greatest value obtainable from the systems people have created so far, and operating with the same data set that previously existed.

There are a number of philosophical approaches we will discuss later. System integration has been a problem. Customization has made systems static and unchangeable. We will recommend federation, not integration of applications, configuration, not customization, and a bias towards a more dynamic architecture. The big advantage of Web services is that it is inherently open, perhaps even "micro-open and multi-vendor". Web services are inherently multi-vendor, but preserving this may take some conscious decisions. Security, authorization, and entitlement are major issues and hence the very basics of a Web services vision have to include a comprehensive entitlement system in multiple granularities.

Goals

Today's enterprise IT problems are tied to the "islands of information" caused by many legacy architectures distributed across geographies, business units and M&A subsidiaries. The technology evolution has forced many enterprises to buy new software and hardware resources. This has resulted in "best in class", sometimes "most in class", and many times "Try, Buy, Throw" environments. The challenge is to leverage existing operational systems, evaluate "most in class" systems, and reuse the most meaningful. Many times the real problems are legacy processes rather than legacy systems. In such cases, integration is a wrong approach to achieve the necessary plasticity and adaptability. As per Gartner, 70% of all infrastructure efforts fail or substantially miss their objectives. Large integration projects like Boeing's I-Man portal fail to achieve the desired results 60 percent of the time, according to Giga Information Group analyst Julie Giera[6]. She says companies put too much faith in technology's ability to cut costs and fail to adapt old processes to make use of the new technology. There are many reasons that such projects fail.

Our recommendation is to achieve change in small steps. Projects should last from 90 to 180 days, whenever possible. The key to a successful migration is identifying internal champions who realize the benefits of Real Time Enterprises and are willing to evangelize the required efforts. The other dimension of this strategy is to offer end-user configurable processes so that **"iteration" becomes a specification methodology**: getting things approximately right and iterated by the end-user.

Optimization of systems can be achieved in four dimensions: flexibility, cost, performance, and reliability. Our recommendation is to prioritize flexibility ahead of cost, reliability and performance. The evolution from MIS built applications to packaged applications to today's need for more adaptability is a tough challenge. The right answer is found neither in in-house applications nor standardized third party packaged applications; it is somewhere in the middle. A little bit of both allows business to achieve customization via configuration. These are the "composite applications" using processes (pieces) from different packaged applications to assemble (configure) a business process to match how things are really done in the enterprise. But more than any other single factor, flexibility and adaptability are the *most* important selection criteria for new technology given the rate of change in both technology and enterprise requirements. Unfortunately, this tradeoff is seldom made, with features, performance, and price often winning out.

Automation of processes configurable to end user needs is the key (where the end user is defined interchangeably as a human being or a machine capable of understanding specific semantics). This migration can be a continuum and need not be a one-step change. Evolving architecture changes are not only demanded by technology and/or business changes, but also by the rate of adoption. The processes themselves can be assembled from sequence of other processes or can span into a supplier organization using different technology stacks. All these processes operate in a world of common data, semantics, protocols, and translators that we call an "information base" for a Real Time Enterprise. Jeff Jensen[6] of Boeing identifies pulling data together into a single repository as key for their I-MAN project's success. This single repository must be represented as a "virtual" repository — an abstraction for all coexisting data sources based on a flexible schema. Current data repositories, such as relational databases, do not support such a model. We address some requirements under the section "Information Base" (iBase), but as a first step, documents are extracted from the company's various legacy systems and converted to XML as queries are invoked. Boeing plans eventually to move data currently residing in its multiple systems into this repository for easier administration[6].

The challenge is to retrieve data from multiple business units, sort and analyze them. The Web services vision has much of what is needed and we recommend it. It builds on existing Web technologies and accommodates legacy systems to a reasonable degree through a process of node enablement we will define later. It works very well for green-field implementations, but is also workable for real legacy environments. The goal for every enterprise betting on this vision should be to create an "application assembly environment" where end-users can create "composite applications" or "composite Web services" suitable to their personal or corporate work style. This environment operates within the constraints of corporate business processes, often coded into the end user programming environments by business analysts (often as rules or objects, not as computer programs) and to limited extent by programmers to create components and services in languages like Java and C#. Think of an Excel or Visio as the front end for programming Web services to suit the business process modeling needs. Most non-technical end-users can "program" their application into an Excel spreadsheet within the constraints of "macros" that might be defined by sophisticated end-users or business analysts. This creates a "**mass customization environment for business processes, workflow and collaboration**" with sufficient support tools for administration, personalization, versioning, upgrading, and more — allowing end-users to keep their own store of templates and a template exchange to make them productive. The recommended changes should articulate benefits both at macro and micro levels (i.e. each individual project must justify that their value adds individually and as an encapsulated service within a wider scope). This could be a big challenge given the scale of many corporations but planning this migration is *a priori*. For example, changes in an "Order Status" process may benefit all users within a group (micro level), but an organization also can be impacted at a macro level by offering the process as an automated Web service incorporating entitlement and personalization to key customers. Although this migration can be painful in the short term, savings in maintenance costs and the ability to enable end-users to serve themselves will be a huge benefit in a long run. The lack of an ideal environment or too many immediate requirements should not be an excuse to keep doing yesterday's thing. Every organization, to the maximum extent possible, should encapsulate the old world through a process of "**enabling legacy nodes**". These nodes would work in a Web services world, making iterations in functionality, the maintenance spend, the Web services, Java/C#, UDDI, SOAP, XML, XML and schema world of Internet technologies. Many companies who gained their knowledge from Y2K exercises and large-scale system conversions can leverage that experience to abstract legacy functionality as encapsulated modules and expose those modules as Web services — making the migration process easier.

This automation requires all the "point" applications — CRM, ERP, supply chain systems — to provide information and interfaces to business processes that have touch points in other systems or by humans within the extended enterprise. EAI is a first generation solution catering to data synchronization needs, leveraging or extending into the Web services environment by node enablement of much of the legacy world. Many older world tools, often developed for Y2K transformations, will be useful to this node enablement process, as will more modern tools like portals and "Web service publishing tools". Tools like Citrix can encapsulate many legacy environments from the PC world with Web front ends of packaged client server applications. Node enablement is only the start of the solution.

Replacing the many interfaces to older layers underneath the Web services is the key for migration. Imagine a company with 10 billing systems, each dealing with a different customer segment or region, but each offering basically the same services. These systems will have many thousands of interfaces that can be presented as Web services. All of the **business services** offered by those systems can be migrated (possibly as common abstractions) as services that route appropriately to the underlying systems, with every new system talking to the Web service layer. This first step makes it possible to start building new, workflow-driven business processes without reference to systems, but referring to services. Over time, the cost/benefit balance will gradually tilt towards forced migration of all older interfaces. The resulting enormous benefit is the ability to restructure, rationalize, and consolidate those 10 billing systems as appropriate. When this type of migration (occurring over several years) happens in every area, then you are able to completely realize the even bigger benefits of integrating new businesses and outsourced services (such as billing, order management, and data management). The goal is composite applications that leverage legacy applications to model the business processes, collaboration and workflow needs of the enterprise, done in an incremental way.

The grand vision of federated Web services will happen in stages. Security and other practical issues (like billing, SLAs, etc) will constrain most Web services to work initially within the firewall as applications inside the corporation are updated to work together. The level of granularity will test our wits and increase only slowly. Semantic and ontology differences will limit the ideal world of possibilities into a world of very useful but far from ideal possibilities. Think of Web services as the next leap from the Web request architecture (typical HTTP, CGI, and Application Server requests) to a **Web services request architecture**. This goal is as achievable as the transformation from client/server to Web request architectures in the late 90's.

Web Request	Web Service
• Ad-hoc • Stateless • Simple and light-weight to define semantics • No Encapsulation for object transport • Undefined behavior resulting from Exceptions	• Pre-defined, well negotiated, deterministic and reliable • Support for stateful transactions • Semantics can be defined and embedded • Encapsulation supported for XML Schema objects • Infrastructure available to support exception handling behaviors

Example: Cutler-Hammer[7]

With more than 61,000 orders processed electronically last year, Cutler-Hammer realized their design-to-delivery vision by using Bid Manager on complex assembled products manufactured across 26 satellite plants across the U.S. and Mexico. Bid Manager handles small but significant details. For example, it can automatically compose labels that specify capabilities, such as speed and power, of each motor and its components. Then it can direct the nameplate engraver to print the label. In the past, a technician would type the nameplate information, increasing the likelihood of error and slowing the process. Cutler-Hammer's customers, field reps, and distributors are able to electronically design and place 95% of their orders remotely, bypassing plant engineers. One such customer, Grove Madsen Industries, a supplier of equipment to Las Vegas casinos, feeds their design directly to the Cutler-Hammer assembly line 2,050 miles away.

Over time as this subset of corporate processes migrates or infiltrates into the whole corporation and forces migration of legacy systems, the fusion of new technologies and legacy systems with rigid processes may pose a paradigm mismatch, thus complicating the migration process. In such instances, we recommend encapsulating those areas and abstracting them via well-defined interfaces and behaviors.

Why Now

Many will ask why an enterprise should transform into a Real Time Enterprise now, and how IT can play a role in this process. Changing business models, evolving market, competitive pressure, and cost benefits of leveraging existing systems drive the need for this transformation. The balance between Return On Investment (ROI) and Risk Of Not Investing (RONI) is the key factor in answering the "why now" question.

Return On Investment (ROI)	Risk Of Not Investing (RONI)
Infrastructure renovation in an evolutionary way	Legacy systems not matching current dynamics as in Boeing example[6]
Cost savings + real time adaptability	Expenses, both cost and competitive losses
Improved responsiveness, customer loyalty	Lack of real time insight, process overheads
Leveraging technological improvements	Dwelling on past accomplishments

Five years ago, if someone quoted a scenario such as our Cutler-Hammer example, it would have raised many eyebrows regarding infrastructure for communication, consensus on semantics, and agreements on exception handling, encapsulation and implementation mechanisms. Today, one can model a solution using HTTP (S), SOAP, XML, Rosettanet, XMLschema, Web services, and language-independent abstracted interfaces for this seemingly intractable problem.

Some Guidelines

There are four golden rules and corollary implications vital to the IT transformation process:

- Plan on being wrong.
- Adopt thy partners.

- Design thy architecture.

- Implement thy solutions in steps.

Our proposal is based on our experience with the IT industry and technology evolution. Interestingly, similar recommendations and guidelines can be found from *The Forrester Report's* "Start Using Web services Now"[13] and "The Web services Payoff"[14], and the *HBR* article "Your Next IT Strategy"[12].

Plan on being wrong

As previously discussed, it is important to identify the IT customers, their expectations, behaviors, usage trends and future needs. Cutler-Hammer enlisted not only software writers, but also experts at the plants, sales engineers, and many others to compile the requirements. It is also important to consider various types of customers such as:

- Interacting customers via browsers, bandwidth constrained devices, and voice access systems.

- Machine-based connectivity via XML2XML, EDI, Partner Interface Processes (PIPs), and other client environments.

Beyond the obvious attention to users (customers) is the far more important and often ignored fact that most requirements cannot be fully specified prior to actual use. Often 30-50% of the cost of a new implementation goes into specification of screens in a hypothetical environment. It is much more reasonable and feasible in the Web services world to only attempt an approximate solution to the business process. Through actual use, the end user can modify the "application Web service", personalize it, and compose it with informal practices and processes. These modifications can be based on the idiosyncrasies of each user or practice group and subject to the continually evolving constraints placed on the user by the business decisions (through a business analyst). This process leads directly to the need for a mass customization language for business processes utilizing the Web services environment. Enabling real use of IT because of increased relevance to each user may be the single biggest benefit of the Web services architecture. It is important to understand the variations and evolutions (e.g. multiple and customized versions with different granularity) that the customer community will demand. For example, Applied Materials (AMAT) could have a generic selling process that has to be customized specific to Intel and Motorola's needs and derived from the generic process. Change and adoption are more critical in dynamic environments than getting today's environment exactly right. For example, end user modifications/programming at the level of Excel programming is very desirable in a system where end-users fine-tune the environment to fit their needs.

Ground Rules:

- Assemble a virtual team of people (not exceeding 3 or 4) to identify and compile the requirements. The team should represent a cross section of the customer community along with developer and business analysts, and have a senior techno-functional person as the moderator, as well as clearly defined deliverables, and specific timelines. Qwest Communications gets these teams together for intense 3-4 day "sessions" before a 90-day implementation cycle commences.

- Understand existing current solutions, their gaps, and what end-users actually need. For example, a trading broker using Excel would not want to use a browser interface even though it gives real time capability. The right solution is to provide an Excel interface with real time capability.

- Implement a prototype (with stubbed interfaces) that can be quickly customized for end user needs to understand real caveats of the proposed functionality.

Adopt thy partners

The Real Time Enterprise must span the physical boundaries of an enterprise and should extend as a virtual enterprise through the entire end-to-end value chain. For example, Colgate-Palmolive trimmed its inventory 13% and saved $150 million by attaching its order planning systems to thousands of Wal-Mart and Kmart[9] cash registers. This extension includes the collaborative partners, suppliers, sub contractors and vendors (all referred as "partners" hereafter). Each one of these partners may vary in size and have their own infrastructure for implementing their IT systems. Certain partners may exceed the expected enterprise guidelines and some vendors may not have any infrastructure at all. Your enterprise and your IT organization should adopt all these partners and adapt infrastructure support to their level. This eases the paradigm mismatch in information flow across partnering organizations and helps transform your enterprise into a Real Time Enterprise. The goal is to create a partner eco-system around your organization — helping them help you become successful. A successful eco-system allows the partner set to be easily and rapidly changed based on evolving business needs and level of sophistication. Partner collaboration is another important aspect from design to implementation, as well as during execution. The usage model, user management, rich security model, and transparent seamless processes across enterprise boundaries are key factors of a collaborative application environment. Web services are a great way to implement partner collaboration systems: they abstract the interfaces across partner systems, do not depend on the implementation language or object types, and provide loosely coupled connectivity (unlike RMI, CORBA or RPCs).

Ground Rules:

- Identify short-term projects; with incremental value added and well defined loosely coupled interfaces (initial iteration).

- Identify candidate value chain companies (customer, tier 1 supplier, sub vendor, contractor), going 3 or 4 levels deep "into your close partners13", as suggested by Frank Gillett.

- Pick the right type of projects and partners for your domain needs15.

- Define semantic interfaces, exceptions, and data types for information flow across the chain (Rosettanet PIPs); provide pre-implemented plugins that can run within a standard runtime (servlets or Web server plugins), if necessary.

- Agree on periodic iteration updates and be willing to spare your own resources to help implement partner solutions.

- Include partners when talking to solution providers and create usage scenarios and proof-of-concept environments based on real partner needs.

Design thy architecture

Once you identify your customers' needs and connectivity requirements to your partners, the right architecture must be designed. Your architecture's mindset, belief, and vision should cater to the short and long term goals of your enterprise. The architecture should be based on:

- Open standards and multiple vendors.

- Flexible, loosely decoupled interfaces considering rapid changes and evolutions of underlying systems.

- A production system that can manage, monitor, and support versioning of the Web services life cycle.

- Ability to leverage existing systems and reduce cost.

- Flexibility as more critical than optimization for cost, performance or features.

The designed architecture should not tie you into any proprietary environment and should accommodate all software lifecycle phases without the overhead. The right architecture will be modular and abstracted, with simple and consistent interfaces. Good architects are the scarcest resource and using existing talent is the most common and most significant mistake made in IT. To quote *The Forrester Report[1]*, "Projects succeed or fail because of software architecture". Adaptability and flexibility is often determined by architectural choices. Allowing for a complex set of diverse suppliers (possibly two in each critical category) and forcing these disparate choices in the current implementation may be the only way to accommodate the unforeseen needs of the future.

The traditional architectural approach integrates runtime environments for data synchronization and information flow, without consideration for how user management, globalization, and personalization (key elements of Internet solutions) can be supported across various integrated point solutions. For example, consider a business process that touches a CRM system built as client-server system, a supply chain (SCM) system built as Web based solution, and a sales commission system built in mainframe using COBOL. Each system has its own user management system: CRM using Windows NT authentication; SCM system using an LDAP solution; and the mainframe using case-insensitive passwords. One challenge is to map the user password information from the Web solution to a different backend. Another challenge is language translation (globalization) for various level solutions since the SCM system may support Unicode, the CRM system may support Windows globalization, while the mainframe may not support any globalization.

The goal here is to design a

- Reasonably flexible system that can adapt to future needs — i.e. it can embed any type of future application environment.

- Cohesive framework — i.e. provide common methodologies (open standards based) for business object modeling, process definitions, and data source mappings.

- Utility-based service architecture for authentication and authorization (entitlement), globalization, personalization, monitoring, caching, presentation, business rule definition, and execution that can coexist with existing legacy systems in an evolutionary manner.

- Comprehensive framework to support various types of users (Intranet, Extranet and Internet) based on their entitlement within different administration models (self managed or delegated administration).

The design must account for existing systems; for example, globalization utility service must not only be based on Unicode, but should map underlying systems such as Oracle, SAP, and other functional components seamlessly in multiple levels (data, business object, API and business process levels). It should address globalization in multiple layers (data schemas, formats and styles like currency, menu systems, messaging components, presentation templates, and locale based rules). Every one of these subsystem layers must be locale aware, automatically detected during runtime based on a user's preferred locale, and pre-generated and cached where and when possible to improve performance. All these locale specific components must be abstracted and encapsulated in the development framework so that translations are performed in a scoped manner and narrowed to resource files, directories, and definitions.

The concept of configuration vs. customization is a key to end user enablement. Many solutions claim to support configuration but in reality do customization. Configuration is, by definition, something you have changed to adapt to your business needs and is guaranteed to upgrade without any modifications. Configuration can happen in many levels.

Building Blocks

- Providing basic building blocks (e.g. e-mail notification, approval routing, file attachments etc.) and let the user assemble a business process.

Development Configurations

- Re-implementing the functional logic for the same interface, more towards the end of customization, with upgrades guaranteed.

Deployment Configurations

- Declaratively rerouting functional or control flow or changing the presentation components.

Runtime Configurations

- Rule Based, depending on different user roles and authorization levels.
- Data Driven, depending on data loaded or derived based on specific calculations.

The architecture must separate programmer level customization from business analyst level configuration. While there are some performance impacts, the configurations at the development and deployment levels can be converted to a byte code level (Java classes) and cached after the first invocation. Only the runtime level configurations are left to the interpretation mode.

Ground Rules:

- Be open to customer needs, to technology infrastructure changes over time, and be flexible on reiterating the design, since architecture is the key to adaptability.

- Design a cohesive reference architecture that can adapt to future needs or can be extended. The architecture should be modular — "what you need is what you use", portable, and standards-based as much as possible.

- Clearly demarcate between the roles of programmers and business analysts. Stress the importance between configuration and customization.

- Define a common object model and data-modeling environment that enables a flexible schema (refer to iBase section in building blocks) to extract and operate on data from various systems underneath (ERP, SCM, Mainframe, client-server systems).

- Define a sand box of data types, exceptions, process interfaces, application integration methodologies, and development models (covering a wide spectrum) across the enterprise.

- Decide on make vs. build and focus on your core competence. If you can find a product catering to your needs, even with reduced functionality, you should adopt it since it can take care of future maintenance and support costs.

Implement thy solutions in steps

The solutions and implementation roadmaps should be phased in over 90 to 120 day increments, whenever possible. This is possible more often than is generally assumed. The development of LINUX is proof positive of the feasibility of this approach. The solutions must be scoped in such a way that the incremental implementations over a period of time result in the ultimate solution, but every phase should result in meaningful and useful addition of functionality. Every deliverable becomes trackable, modifiable, and implementable. Avoid the large multi-year system integration projects whenever possible, even when you are told incremental implementation cannot be done. The promise of Web services guarantees migration in small and evolving steps. One can abstract the interfaces and the implementation can grow in modules. The assembly or orchestration of these modules, resulting in a more meaningful business process, can take place in the future. For example, a traditional Order Management ERP system can expose Order Status (O/S) as a Web service today. It then can link the O/S Web service with the Order Entry (O/E) Web service that will be implemented at a later point of time as an automated Order Management Web service. An implementation beyond twelve months is likely to be wrong by the time you get there, as the business requirements will have [changed]. When lifecycles for applications are short spending 12 months in the evaluation phase while a reasonably usable solution could have been built in 3 months is imprudent. As a minimum, the shorter process will clarify system requirements and caveats, which in itself is a success.

Ground Rules:

- Decide on enterprise-wide adoption time lines and plan on coexistence in diversified system implementations.

- Identify and scope candidate application areas for individual vendor exercises. The life expectancy for these applications should not exceed 9 to 12 months.

- Have vendors provide a migration strategy describing how they would migrate to other vendor's solutions or to the entire enterprise.

Pick the right vendors and a phased implementation approach, migrate other existing solutions to the right approach, and use the new approach as a nucleus to extend the base functionality.

Approach to Transformation

The transformation to enable Real Time Enterprises becomes smooth when the following areas are approached properly.

- People.
- Architecture.
- Meta-Architecture - Architecture to connect architectures.
- Node Enablement & Legacy Encapsulation.
- Shifting the maintenance environment to the new vision.
- Composite Apps and application assembly environment.
- Building Blocks.

People

People are very instrumental in the success of a project. A strategically diverse team ranging from field service individuals that interface with customers, to line of business managers, key architects, and candidate programmers should be assembled. Often IT organizations are more conscientious when choosing the technologists than when involving the broader constituent base. This increases the likelihood of mismatched expectations. The gene pool for this team is very important. The constituents should be open and aware of evolving technologies and standards, and be willing to take a shepherd approach rather than a sergeant approach in testing new solutions. Qwest forces three-day intensive interactive, offsite sessions before the start of a project where all the business users, vendors, and IT participate and iterate the needs, statement, build prototypes, and otherwise hone in on expectations. Every IT organization should change the mindset from "Consultants" to "Resultants" — i.e. the implementers (especially the system integrators or vendors) must be paid after the results are delivered, not for their consulting hours. The notion of "fixed scope of work" rather than "solutions" creates disincentives for the right, iterative approach, increases the upfront cost of specification needlessly, and sets up a conflict between the vendors need for billable hours and the clients need for iteration at low cost.

Architecture

- Federation NOT Integration

  Focus the application assembly on how each application can be federated rather than integrated. The difference between federation and integration is in the meaningful sequencing of processes loosely coupled with best possible efficiency to implement the business process, while preserving ADAPTABILITY. This is different from traditional integration of connecting point-to-point solutions for synchronization, thus resulting in high-level abstraction and coarse-grained process automation. A simple analogy is how an automobile differential gear engages the wheels with the motor. The differential gear drives the axle with the best possible efficiency, accommodating the speed difference between wheels, and is adaptable to varying conditions by coupling "loosely". Some efficiency is lost but a large degree to flexibility is gained. Web services hold a similar promise.

- Configuration NOT Customization

  The assembly of these coarse-grained processes must enable the business analysts and business users to be self-sufficient, serving their own needs rather than depending on an IT person or a Systems Integrator to the maximum extent possible. Loose coupling allows Web services to cater to the need for configurability.

- Reliable and Self Recovering

  The implemented systems should be capable of handling failures on their own and of failing gracefully. Low consequence failure mechanisms (e.g.

backup or skeletal operation) are more important than "high availability" in many situations. For example, if two different processes are assembled and if the down stream process fails, the former process should be capable of recovering from all known and unknown exceptions (generic handler), as defined by the behaviors established by the business user rather than the programmer.

- Evolutionary NOT Revolutionary

    The choice of architecture should allow modular components that can be implemented in an evolutionary way. Having a creative way of assembling existing applications in a meaningful manner is more desirable than simply having one more new way of developing applications. The architecture choice should enable various degrees of solutions and bridge all potential point systems rather than sticking to certain religious choices. The Asera[18] system, based on meta-architecture approach, and the general process of node enablement, discussed later, are early attempts at this. Layers of abstraction as an architectural feature are key to preserving evolutionary capability for systems.

Meta-Architecture - Architecture to Connect Architectures

Automation of processes across multiple systems and applications requires a flexible multi-layered architecture. This meta-architecture is a simple layer rather than dedicated platform. This layer will provide large-scale reusability rather than fine-grained component model architecture. In addition, this layer will provide semantic abstractions and well defined and agreed interfaces to bridge into legacy systems. This layer will also automatically reduce instances of redundant systems within an enterprise. No single vendor can meet all needs (be best-of-breed) across varying application areas over many years and product versions. Plan on a multi-vendor architecture and avoid spending 3x-5x the cost of the system with system integrators. The nature, orientation and characteristics of Web services rightfully fit this model. Web services and SOAP protocol inherently support loosely coupled interfaces independent of language implementation and transport protocols. XML's interchangeability and SOAP's capability to abstract HTTP or asynchronous queues enables building a seamless value chain spanning inter, extra, and intra enterprise systems. Web services may not be the only way to solve these problems, but it is the one that naturally fits the model and is available now. We paid special attention to this set of needs when founding Asera. Asera builds solutions by first inserting this "abstraction layer" and tailoring solutions as "composite applications". This approach enables the world of new business process orientation by leveraging both the processes and information embedded in existing IT infrastructure. In addition, Asera provides common services around these legacy and composite applications, such as globalization, entitlement, and personalization, among others.

Node Enablement

The software choices you make should provide systems (node) and process enablement at the right levels of granularity, synchronization, and behavior. Corporations should strive to transfer as much as possible of the maintenance spend on legacy applications and environments into new paradigms as they evolve, instead of doing the patches and enhancements in the old world. If nodes are encapsulated, abstracted, and thus enabled to participate in the new world, maintenance can be gradually shifted to the new paradigm - currently, the Web services paradigm. The purpose of this enablement is to improve self-productivity and to re-leverage existing systems and processes. The process should include identifying the areas to automate, partners to include, information islands to connect, and end-users needs. The new "process enablement" should result in morphing linear and sequential processes into collaborative processes accommodating today's business needs. Each legacy application should be published as a Web service that can be used in a "composite business process". This way, users do not have to traverse 50 screens across 5 applications to do order entry; workflow and collaboration can happen easily on these legacy processes and information, independent of departmental and corporate boundaries and restricted only by the entitlement system.

The level of granularity depends both on what needs to be reused and what the end user community can handle. For example, if a mainframe data object is extracted as an XML object and merely presented as an HTML table, it may not make sense for the end-users since they may not understand how to interact with the table. At the same time, if that particular data object needs to be fed into another process, it cannot be fed as a COBOL object in that runtime environment. The granularity can be in multiple levels, purely in the data attribute level (data types), in the business object level (XML format), in the business process level (APIs or process invocation entry points), or in user interface levels (screen emulation). There are no right or wrong levels. It depends on the level of functionality that needs to be leveraged, time and budget available for integration, life expectancy of the underlying system, and the new integration layer.

Reuse of legacy systems depends on what has been already implemented, and what needs to be leveraged. For example, there could be a generic pricing rule with manual overriding capability implemented as part of the ERP implementation. In order to adapt and leverage, all "generic selling" processes may call into an existing pricing rule within ERP. But, when it comes to a privately negotiated exclusive relationship, you may want to add a business rule in a different layer that can "simulate" the manual overriding capability within the underlying system. This enables the existing process to adapt to specific needs by adding additional business rules in a different layer. The existing process is encapsulated with well-defined interfaces and behaviors.

An open approach should be adopted for legacy enablement. For example, if the user community is comfortable with existing user interfaces (mainframe screens or client UI), the goal should be to reduce the operating costs rather than migrating the users to a new interface. A suggested migration path is to have the screen interface exposed in a portal environment (a Citrix enabled emulation) with other portal objects available in the same Web page. Using the same screen increases user comfort and acceptance while reducing client operating and license costs. In addition, the user community will be able to adapt their learning pace to the capabilities of other portal objects and the power of Internet. This will facilitate the adoption of new technologies over time and ease migration of legacy user interfaces to either thin client interfaces or "native" client interfaces. We refer to "native" client interfaces as productivity application suites such as Microsoft Office™ that communicate to the backend through the Internet.

Application Assembly Environment and Composite Applications

The design time environment for process assembly (i.e. to build end user centric business processes assembled from pre-defined components or sub processes) is the key to end user enablement and leveraging of existing IT investments into higher ROI's. This approach meets the custom needs of the enterprise while minimizing custom software code. The resulting business processes can be called "Composite Applications" or "Composite Web Services". The design time environment should provide an intuitive interface (e.g. Visio) for the business analyst using services provided by the IT programmer. This environment should include graphical modeling of the business process-flow (e.g. a drag and drop interface) and tools for process assembly. A robust design environment should also include emulation tools that validate assembled process flows and translators that generate common repository formats suitable for the runtime environment (i.e. workflow languages like BPML, WSFL or XLANG, though transparent to the business analyst). Design time environments that generate common repository formats do [not] limit future design changes in runtime platforms. The design time environment should support multiple versioning (configurations specific to custom needs derived from basic versions) and support role-based entitlement capabilities for automatically picking the correct version during runtime. The key challenge here is to identify the common repository format for specifying user interfaces common to HTML, WML, XML2XML, XML2EDI that can also accommodate sequencing of screens and declarative interfaces to define UI elements for the design time environment to generate. There is not one standard that can support all these requirements. This provides an opportunity for picking a key vendor and actively participating in the definition of standards. Solving this piece of the puzzle is a critical step toward enabling real time capabilities through the composition of underlying "application Web services". The utility of current packaged applications will be increased by enabling participation in the composite application that services a corporation's business process, as practiced by each group.

Shifting of maintenance investments to the new visions

Identifying and projecting the life expectancy of applications and systems is very important for the real time enablement of an enterprise. For example, a mainframe system requiring end-users to process many of the logistics prior to data entry loses an opportunity for providing real time capabilities. Instead, a plan for migrating functionality to the new system with a retirement timeline should be established. An alternative to investing in the maintenance of old systems is the building of a parallel new system providing the same capabilities. Y2K exercises provide good case studies for this approach. Providing "native" client interfaces to Internet-enabled back-ends will be the next wave of paradigm shift within enterprises. Think of having Excel, Word, and Outlook replacing browsers while providing the advantages of Internet without the thin client element. Case studies from MSDN provide good examples for using office documents[10].

The majority of IT expenses in most corporations are on "maintenance spends" on old IT systems. If some of these expenses are used to encapsulate old IT systems and enable Web services that can participate in "composite applications", then there will not be a need to rewrite or modify these applications and the business process/logic they incorporate. A "continuous migration" of legacy applications, "maintenance spend", and "extensions" to legacy will evolve in the Web services world resulting in maintenance money going to the "right" side of the legacy/new equation. This is achieved through node enablement. The common argument that there is no choice in adopting the new because most resources are spent on extending and maintaining legacy systems is replaced by the possibility of enabling participation in new processes and automation by extending the legacy systems through a series of small steps.

Building Blocks

The building blocks for the transformation can be categorized into five categories:

- Node Enablement.

- Information Base.

- Applications Enablement.

- Process Enablement.

- User Enablement.

These building block layers in fact resemble the evolution of IT systems over the past 3 decades as illustrated in *The Forrester Report[13]*.

Node Enablement

Node enablement is the process of re-using existing systems and applications without any modifications or additional expenses. The stress should be on encapsulation and legacy reuse. Key characteristics of this process should be predicting the obsolescence of the application over time, choosing the right granularity for encapsulation, reuse vs. restructure vs. rewrite of the process logic and representation, and in defining the invocation interfaces and semantics for invocation. Technologies exist today to provide legacy node enablement, as do software vendors who specialize in this area.

As explained in the previous sections, the key decisions to node enablement are:

- Cost justification – evaluate costs by hardware, software licensing, new extensions, performance impact and training for new interfaces.

- Life expectancy - project the life expectancy or obsoleteness of the underlying system over a period of time before investing in node enablement.

- Reusability factor for legacy systems – based on the current business model compared to the original time of legacy system implementation.

- Level of desired integration - depends on the kind of interaction needed for other systems relying on the legacy node. This can range from data attributes, business objects, business processes and UI levels.

- User community readiness – to accept new systems and interfaces. Continuous migration with a phased deployment approach will be helpful.

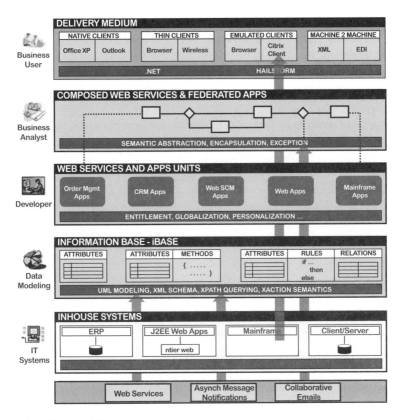

Information Base – iBase

Information Base (iBase), also known as XML database[2], is the key differentiator for the proposed model. iBase provides [a] universal schema for all types of data objects and models in a loosely coupled way. iBase introduces the notion of "Beyond Databases to Data Sources". As explained by Scott Dietzen[2] (CTO of BEA), much Web data is not in a database and service-based architectures have to hide the data model. iBase, in our opinion, is not a radical concept. A long standing requirement is that each enterprise must choose an approach to implement and accommodate changes in object/repository specifications, business partner interfaces, and communication modes for achieving federation across partners and competition-turned-partner or vice versa. iBase will be based on XMLschema for object definitions, meta-data structures, meta-schema, meta caching, and some extensions for simple rule and relationship definitions. iBase will provide a language independent environment to define and implement methods associated with object definitions in an encapsulated way. iBase will support encapsulated object models comprehensive enough to support data objects from various sources including RDBMS, ODBMS, flat files, Web services and sites, main frames, EDI, or any data source. The need for basic object level services such as synchronization, translations, messaging, security, and entitlement and the importance of metadata will drive the migration from database to information base for corporations.

Applications Enablement

The goal of this block is to bring packaged applications into the Web services/ composite applications world. Web-enabled client-server applications and new Web solutions have matured, making this a reasonable building block for leverage by IT environments. The only abstraction that is essential for transformation is to package the building blocks as "apps units", or "**application Web services**" that have well defined encapsulation and delegation for entitlement, globalization, and personalization for use in "composite business processes". The higher-level building blocks can delegate requirements with respect to collaboration, intra-application state management, entitlement, and globalization to this layer. For example, a portal page with Siebel's CRM object should be able to delegate the user locale and process information to the underlying Siebel application rather than translating the rendered contents in the portal layer. Here the portal component should assume the role of aggregator rather than translator. Companies like Asera, BEA, and Bowstreet, in combination with application server and EAI vendors, can be used to implement this block. Again, the granularity of integration or enablement depends on what level of integration is needed and what resource and time commitments are available. The application enablement can be achieved in various levels ranging from the data level, object level, API level, business process level, Web services level, and presentation level. The level of granularity to use will be a critical decision in this enablement. At the same time basic services like entitlement, globalization and personalization may not be available as the levels move from data to presentation level.

A typical process for application enablement includes:

- Deciding on the functionality to be exposed.

- Modeling right business objects in the common object format (ex. XMLSchema).

- Mapping business objects to data source formats (ex. Trading object to Auction System's native format).

- Writing connectors and adaptors to the underlying system.

- Mapping delegation interfaces to the underlying system with respect to application services like globalization, entitlement, and user management. If you want to provide missing services, you may have to write in the new layer.

- Processing business objects by routing them to a process-enabled workflow, then through delivery medium.

Process Enablement

Process enablement, also known as "Federated Applications Environment", allows business analysts to assemble process sequences for "their end user" needs using intuitive design-time environments like Visio or Excel as well as custom business rules that can be expressed declaratively as in Excel macros. The process sequences should support standard branching rules, parallel execution capability, event monitoring, and trigger facilities interfaced with collaborative e-mails. This is a lightweight layer built on a standard application server's runtime platform or other application runtime platforms to automate and manage processes in a coarse-grained environment. This block will provide collaboration, inter-application state management, semantics encapsulation, abstraction and exception handling for assembled business processes. In addition, it will support fine grain version control in order for the end-users to maintain their own versions of customized business processes. This block transparently and appropriately delegates error handling, business intelligence tracking, access control, monitoring and reliability to all the underlying blocks.

Process enablement is the key paradigm shift from traditional environments and evolving requirements. Internet-enabling 24x7 assistance to customers, vendors and suppliers, and automation of end-to-end value chains require end-users to configure their own services to meet their needs. Self-productivity and configuring/assembling business processes from a number of possible permutations are very important. A declarative-based design tool, which can support multiple versions, different granularity levels, entitlement-based customized versions, a publishable repository for the enterprise, and Extranet partner to leverage are just a few characteristics of this block. Semantics for encapsulation of "application Web services", exception handling, and interface abstractions are essential requirements. For example, let us assume Applied Materials (AMAT) is defining a basic spare parts selling process. Any small customer would go through this generic business process. An AMAT rep working on the Intel account may want to derive this generic process and customize to a new version specific for Intel or for Motorola. The system should support different custom needs for each of these AMAT customers, but at the same time be confined to sand box definitions of exception handling and interface signatures, while providing mutual exclusivity between these two processes (Intel process hidden from Motorola customers). In addition, the discount calculations for each one of these customers may be different and hence the need for the system to support declarative business rules. These simple declarative rules (sometimes complex) have to be associated and managed with either generic workflows or with each customized version of the business process flow.

There are evolving tools and standards available today to implement this block. It is not a matured area, but it is an opportunity for your enterprise to adopt one of these early vendors to influence them and the standards to cater your needs, making it a win-win situation.

User Enablement

This is the top-level building block that provides user interfaces to the end-users and personalization capabilities with respect to content rendering. This block should provide interfaces via native clients (Office, Outlook) for power users, thin clients supporting multiple devices, emulated clients for legacy users, and faceless clients with machine-to-machine automated connectivity. Portals, Rosettanet PIPs, and UDDI interfaces are good examples of faceless clients.

"Mass Customization" is a process that enables end-users to "**configure**" their processes and to tailor their "**custom**" needs into their "**native**" format or environments. Although this may appear to be paradoxical, the following example provides clarification:

Today's energy trading brokers retrieve their base data from mainframe computers via ftp, copy it to their disks, go to their desktops, use Excel to process the cost model, derive recommendations, execute them, and repost the data back into mainframes via ftp. The need for these business users to leverage their "**native**" Excel tool (power environment) and run "**custom**" macros developed individually to process or dissect their data to achieve a "**configurable**" solution is a good example of **Mass Customization**. Obviously, there exists a need to connect the front-end power user environment (Excel) to the back-end systems (mainframes). We propose this as the goal for the user enablement block.

The user enablement block should provide a rich set of design-time tools, a version control environment, a template store, an exchange environment, and an emulation environment for legacy systems and interfaces to "native", thin, wireless, and machine-to-machine interfacing clients.

Building blocks in future

How will these building blocks evolve or adapt to the needs of IT in the future? IT could move in the direction of "bandwidth aware" smart applications, "live document" embedded applications, and "scenario optimized" automated applications. The user enablement block addresses the first two types of applications, while usage tracking, combined with a rule-based personalization within the process enablement block, addresses the last one. Even though all usage types cannot be anticipated, it is interesting to have these building block layers evaluated for growth and change. In his report[13], Frank Gillett indicates the growth stages of Web services will follow those of the Web itself.

Vendor Landscape

Open Standards, Emerging Technologies, and ISV Offerings are three key dimensions that influence the migration towards Real Time Enterprises. Several vendors who enable implementation of the building block layers are listed below. Even though this is not a comprehensive or an exhaustive list, it is a good selection of vendor candidates. Detailed vendor studies can be obtained from Gartner and Forrester materials (References 10, 13, 14, 16, 17). The characteristics of a comprehensive e-business architecture are described by Daryl Plummer in the "Technology Drivers for E-Business and Global Computing"[17]. Daryl's commentary on "4 Web services platform"[16] categorizes Web services platforms into 4 different types: to produce, consume, manage and provision Web services.

Node Enablement

- System Vendors – include IBM, Microsoft, Sun, Oracle and BEA. They provide execution environments where the basic threads of execution are managed and monitored.

- Legacy Access Vendors – include SEEC, Microfocus, Sapiens, Most Software, Netron, and Jacada. They provide access to legacy systems and expose them as Web services.

iBase

- Tools and Modeling Vendors – include Metamatrix, Enosys, Excelon, Right Order, Rational Rose, and Together Soft. They provide XML repository, caching, object modeling, and code generation tools.

Applications Enablement

- Enterprise Application Vendors – include SAP, Siebel, i2, and Matrix One. They provide packaged applications for enterprises, including ERP, CRM, SCM and PLM solutions.

- EAI Vendors – include Webmethods, Tibco, Vitria, and See Beyond. They provide integration capabilities such as messaging, queuing, transformations, collaboration, etc.

- Core Service Vendors – include Netegrity, Entrust, Oblix, ATG,

Epicentric, Plumtree, Savvion, Versata, Core Change, and Mobile Q. They provide essential services such as security, directory services, portal, personalization, business process management, wireless device access, etc.

Process Enablement

- Web services Platform Vendors – include Altoweb, Avinon, Bowstreet, Cape Clear, Grand Central, Infravio, and Iona. They provide a production platform for Web services.

Given all these components, there is a need for a meta-architecture (architecture connecting architecture) to house different systems and to federate them, which we will call the **Generic Purpose Production Platform**. This platform provides basic services including globalization, personalization, workflow orchestration, monitoring, caching, and business object management. These services must be available as standard services and the platform must offer more ways to interface (beyond Web services). Microsoft has attempted to provide these services via .NET, while IBM and BEA propose their own equivalent stack on J2EE. A preferred approach is to use a multi-vendor approach like Asera's generic purpose production platform, based on a referenced meta-architecture and partnered with some of the above listed vendors, enabling customers to develop, deploy and manage composite business process.

Challenges

The following are some challenges you could face during the transformation.

- How do you find people with the right design experience?

- How do you define correct semantics, interface contracts, abstraction and encapsulation?

- How do you make systems fail gracefully when spanning different systems?

- How do you model human intervention as automated processes during node enablement?

- How do you incubate your partners or suppliers while not exposing the competitive edge to their other customers?

- How do you stay ahead of the leading edge on technologies but not get caught in the hype?

- How do you define Quality of Service and Delivery to guarantee deterministic behaviors in a loosely connected world?

It is important to reduce the risk of obsolescence by making change easy enough so that you are not constrained to using only larger, entrenched vendors. This almost always will also coincide with lower total cost.

Conclusion

As we understand the importance of Real Time Enterprises and how IT strategies can enable transformation into Real Time Enterprises, it is important to consider the following:

- Select your platform, development environment, standards strategy, and vendors/partners based on your architecture.

- Small implementation steps result in incremental efforts.

- Insure your chosen eco-system does not lock or tie you into a proprietary environment.

Intentionally, this document did not cover issues with regard to

- Cost of ownership.

- Environment management.

- Details of workflow and collaboration.

Our focus is on technology and architecture for continuous migration of software infrastructure.

Our recommendation is to adopt this paper as a guideline for modeling your architecture and migration path based on your specific needs. It is important to identify your organization's steering committee, which will agree upon plans to implement the strategy. We defined the "ground rules" for an IT transformation (to facilitate continuous migration) and an approach to implement them. We suggest adapting to biases in certain directions and taking small probing steps to help migration. Again, we are dealing with first generation attempts at this new model. There will be challenges during implementation, but the reward is worth the effort to migrate into this exciting path. These guidelines will help you automate your business processes in a collaborative environment and provide you an economic saving as well as an improvement in quality. The savings in SG&A spending, quality improvements, and time spent serving your customer needs are the crux of the benefits you will realize from automating IT and enabling collaborative business processes. IT migration strategies should include ease of change management and evolution as a managed process. Many times, cutting edge technologies come out of startups, while IT shops too readily adopt large software vendors. Before one can impact the cost structure of an enterprise outside of IT, namely the SG&A costs, IT must be built in a responsive and evolvable way. Many of the promises of IT will become deliverable, and IT will become a strategic weapon for the corporation. Even ambitious goals that everyone can appreciate, like doubling the revenue per employee for a corporation, will become feasible.

Reference

1. Laura Koetzle, "Putting J2EE to work," The Forrester Report, July 2001.

2. "An interview with Scott Dietzen," Infoworld, Nov. 7, 2001. http://www.infoworld.com/articles/hn/xml/01/11/06/011106hndietzen.xml.

3. "Factory floors go online." http://www.internetweek.com/ebizapps01/ebiz031201.htm.

4. "The E-Factory Catches On." http://www.business2.com/articles/mag/0,1640,14874,FF.html.

5. "Where the Web is really revolutionizing business," http://www.businessweek.com/magazine/content/01_35/b3746669.htm.

6. "Boeing links apps via XML." http://www.internetweek.com/enterprise/enterprise111201.htm.

7. "What's going on down at the plant." http://www.business2.com/articles/web/0,1653,34859|2,FF.html.

8. "Know your IT, Know your customer." http://www.businessweek.com/bwdaily/dnflash/oct2001/nf20011023_3424.htm.

9. "Era of efficiency." http://www.businessweek.com/magazine/content/01_25/b3737701.htm

10. "XML Web Service-Enabled Office Documents." http://msdn.microsoft.com/library/default.asp?url=/library/en-us/dnexcl2k2/html/odc_xlB2B.asp?frame=true.

11. Dale Vecchio, "Legacy Software: Junkyard Wars for Web Services," Gartner Symposium, IT Expo 2001.

12. John Hagel III and John Seely Brown, "Your Next IT Strategy," Harvard Business Review, October 2001.

13. Frank E. Gillett, "Start Using Web services Now," The Forrester Report, December 2001.

14. Simon Yates, "The Web Services Payoff," The Forrester Report, December

2001.

15. Simon Yates, "Which Industries Will Adopt Web Services," The Forrester Report, December 28, 2001.

16. Daryl Plummer, "4 Web services platforms," Gartner Research Note COM-15-1387, January 2002.

17. Daryl Plummer, "Technology Drivers for E-Business and Global Computing," Gartner Symposium, IT Expo 2001.

18. www.asera.com

Situated Software by Clay Shirky

*I teach at NYU's Interactive Telecommunications Program (ITP),
where the student population is about evenly divided between
technologists who care about aesthetics and artists who aren't
afraid of machines, which makes it a pretty good place to see the
future.*

*Part of the future I believe I'm seeing is a change in the software
ecosystem which, for the moment, I'm calling situated software.
This is software designed in and for a particular social situation
or context. This way of making software is in contrast with what
I'll call the Web School (the paradigm I learned to program in),
where scalability, generality, and completeness were the key
virtues.*

*I see my students cheerfully ignoring Web School practices and
yet making interesting work, a fact that has given me persistent
cognitive dissonance for a year, so I want to describe the pattern
here, even in its nascent stages, to see if other people are seeing
the same thing elsewhere.*

Users By The Dozens

We've always had a tension between enterprise design practices and a "small
pieces, loosely joined" way of making software, to use David Weinberger's
felicitous phrase. The advantages to the latter are in part described in Worse is
Better and The Cathedral and the Bazaar. Situated software is in the small pieces
category, with the following additional characteristic -- it is designed for use by a

specific social group, rather than for a generic set of "users".

The biggest difference this creates relative to classic web applications is that it becomes easy to build applications to be used by dozens of users, an absurd target population in current design practice. Making form-fit software for a small group of users has typically been the province of banks and research labs -- because of the costs involved, Web School applications have concentrated on getting large-scale audiences. And by privileging the value that comes with scale, Web School applications put other kinds of value, particularly social value, out of reach.

We've been killing conversations about software with "That won't scale" for so long we've forgotten that scaling problems aren't inherently fatal. The N-squared problem is only a problem if N is large, and in social situations, N is usually not large. A reading group works better with 5 members than 15; a seminar works better with 15 than 25, much less 50, and so on.

This in turn gives software form-fit to a particular group a number of desirable characteristics -- it's cheaper and faster to build, has fewer issues of scalability, and likelier uptake by its target users. It also has several obvious downsides, including less likelihood of use outside its original environment, greater brittleness if it is later called on to handle larger groups, and a potentially shorter lifespan.

I see my students making some of these tradeoffs, though, because the kinds of scarcities the Web School was meant to address -- the expense of adequate hardware, the rarity of programming talent, and the sparse distribution of potential users -- are no longer the constraints they once were.

Teachers on the Run

The first inkling I got that the Web School rationale might be weakening was an application written by two of my former students, Paul Berry and Keren Merimeh. In November of 2002, as a project for a class on the feeling of online spaces called Social Weather, they created an application called (alarmingly) Teachers on the Run.

Teachers on the Run was essentially HotorNot for ITP professors, to allow students to describe and rate us in advance of spring course registration. Every professor was listed in a database; students could come by anonymously and either enter a comment about a professor or cast a vote agreeing or disagreeing with an earlier comment. The descriptions were sorted in vote total order, so that a +5 description (5 more students had agreed than disagreed) was displayed higher than a +2 or a -3. And that was it -- a list of names, a list of comments, click to vote, and a simple sorting algorithm.

They launched it on a Friday. By Saturday night, another student called me at home to tell me I'd better take a look at it. There are only 200 or so students at ITP, but Teachers on the Run had already accumulated hundreds of comments, most positive, some negative, a few potentially libelous. More importantly, though, there had been over a thousand votes in 24 hours. By Monday morning, I had students telling me they knew what was on the site, not because they'd seen it, but because it had been the only topic of conversation over the weekend.

The curious thing to me about Teachers on the Run was that it worked where the Web School version failed. RateMyProfessors.com has been available for years, with a feature set that put the simplistic write/read/vote capabilities of Teachers on the Run to shame. Yet no one at ITP had ever bothered to use RateMyProfessors.com, though the weekend's orgy of rating and voting demonstrated untapped demand.

Despite the social energy it unleashed, I missed the importance of Teachers on the Run. I told myself that it had succeeded for a number of reasons that were vaguely unfair: The users knew the programmers; the names database had been populated in advance; the programmers could use the in-house mailing list to launch the application rather than trying to get attention through press releases and banner ads. Most damning of all, it wouldn't scale, the sine qua non of successful Web applications. DOA, QED.

Then I saw the design process my most recent class went through.

The Class

In a class called Social Software, which I taught last fall, the students worked in small groups to design and launch software to support some form of group interaction. To anchor the class, I required that whatever project they came up with be used by other ITP students. This first order benefits of this strategy were simple: the designers came from the same population as the users, and could thus treat their own instincts as valid; beta-testers could be recruited by walking down the hall; and it kept people from grandiose "boil the ocean" attempts.

What I hadn't anticipated was the second-order benefits. Time and again the groups came up against problems that they solved in part by taking advantage of social infrastructure or context-sensitive information that wouldn't be available to adherents of the Web School. Two strategies in particular stand out.

The first had to do with reputation systems. One project, The Orderer (designed by Vena Chitturi, Fa-yi Chou, Rachel Fishman, and Cindy Yang) was for coordinating group restaurant orders, common in late-night work sessions. The other, WeBe (Brandon Brown, Yoonjung Kim, Olivier Massot, Megan Phalines) was a tool for coordinating group purchases of things like chips or motors. Because money was involved, a Web School approach would require some way of dealing with the threat of non-payment, using things like pre-pay or escrow accounts, or formal reputation systems.

Instead, in both projects the students decided that since all the users were part of the ITP community, they would simply make it easy to track the deadbeats, with the threat of public broadcast of their names. The possibility of being shamed in front of the community became part of the application design, even though the community and the putative shame were outside the framework of the application itself.

Communal Attention

The other strategy had to do with communal attention. Two other projects, Scout (Karen Bonna, Christine Brumback, Dennis Crowley, Alex Rainert) and CoDeck (Mark Argo, Dan Melinger, Shawn Van Every, Ahmi Wolf) ended up being situated in the community in a more literal fashion. Scout indicates physical presence, by allowing students to register themselves as being present somewhere on the ITP floor, and displaying that information. CoDeck is a community-based video server, designed to allow video artists to share and comment on each other's work.

Both groups had the classic problem of notification -- getting a user to tune in requires interrupting their current activity, not something users have been known to relish. Billions were spent on Web School applications that assumed users would bookmark for a return visit, or would happily accept e-mail alerts, but despite a few well-publicized successes like Schwab.com and eBay, users have mostly refused to "check back often."

Both Scout and CoDeck hit on the same solution: take most of the interface off the PC's dislocated screen, and move it into a physical object in the lounge, the meeting place/dining room/foosball emporium in the center of the ITP floor. Scout and CoDeck each built kiosks in the lounge with physical interfaces in lieu of keyboard/mouse interaction. Scout used a bar code reader to swipe in; CoDeck gutted a mid-70's BetaMax chassis and put a Linux machine inside, then used the BetaMax buttons to let the user control the video stream. Both Scout and CoDeck have web sites where users can enter or retrieve data, but the core piece of each is location in physical space that puts the application in a social context.

These projects all took the course's original dictum -- the application must be useful to the community -- and began to work with its corollary as well -- the community must be useful to the application.

Group Capabilities

We constantly rely on the cognitive capabilities of individuals in software design -- we assume a user can associate the mouse with the cursor, or that icons will be informative. We rarely rely on the cognitive capabilities of groups, however, though we rely on those capabilities in the real world all the time.

In brainstorming sessions, a group can generate not just more ideas but more kinds of ideas than the same individuals working in isolation, and a group consensus is often more accurate than the guess of the group's most knowledgeable individual. Groups also know a lot about themselves. People in work groups know who to go to for design advice, or who is unreliable in a pinch, without any formal designation of those roles. Members of social groups know who it's fun to go drinking with or who you shouldn't lend money to (often the same person) without needing that knowledge to be spelled out in a FAQ.

Web School software ignores this kind of knowledge, because it is hard to make explicit. On most large mailing lists, for example, only a handful of posters start discussions, while most posters simply follow-up; and, at a higher level, only a handful of the members post at all, while a most simply lurk. We've known about these patterns for decades, but mailing list software still does not offer any features specific to starting vs. continuing threads, nor does it treat high-volume posters and lurkers differently.

There is another strategy, however, analogous to asking the user to recognizing icons; the designer can simply assume the group has a certain capability, without needing to recapitulate it in code. If you have an uncollected payment in a communal buying pool, the software can kick out a message that says "Deadbeat alert. Deal with it." A real world group will have some way of handling the problem, usually through moral suasion or the threat of lost reputational capital, or even, in extreme cases, ostracism.

This is no different than what happens in offline groups every day, but the solution feels wrong, in Web School terms, because those web applications can't assume there is a tacit reputation system. By relying on existing social fabric, situated software is guaranteed not to work at the scale Web School apps do, but for the same reason, it can work in ways Web School software can't.

Outside Eyes

I finally started regarding situated software as a practical development strategy, rather than as a degenerate case of "real" application development, when I invited outside reviewers into the Social Software class for a mid-term critique. These were all people who work with social software for a living, and the critique session was enormously valuable. Two of the recommendations made by the reviewers, however, struck me funny.

The first was the suggestion, made to the CoDeck group, that they should make all the features of their video tool available over the web -- upload, download, comment, and so on. The second recommendation was an exhortation to the WeBe group that they should look at Web School group-buying sites like Mercata and MobShop as guides to their own work.

This was the moment for me when cognitive dissonance finally became unsupportable. Each of those comments was a) exactly what I would have said, had I been an outside reviewer in someone else's class, and b) obviously wrong, given the problem the respective groups were attacking.

The suggestion about general web accessibility for the CoDeck interface came in the form of a rhetorical question -- "Why not make it as broadly accessible as possible?" In the Web School, of course, the answer is "No reason", since more users are always A Good Thing, but for CoDeck there were several good reasons for not simply turning their project into a Web video app.

First, the physicalization of the interface, using the gutted BetaMax deck, provides a communal affordance that it is impossible to replicate over the web. Second, since CoDeck serves a tight community, the density of communication among ITP video makers would be diluted by general accessibility. Third, having the video deck in the lounge makes it self-policing; the cohesion of the community keeps it largely free from abuse, whereas a generally accessible and password-free "upload and critique" video site would become a cesspool of porn within hours. Finally, serving a local community maximizes use of free bandwidth on the local network, enabling features that would saddle a public system with crippling costs.

WeBe Small

Similarly, the recommendation that WeBe should look at Mercata and MobShop carried with it the assumption that the goal should eventually be to operate at large scale. However, Mercata and MobShop failed because they were built to scale.

Those sites required a virtuous circle, where more users meant more savings meant more users. Alas, the thought that somewhere, someone else was saving a bundle on Tupperware was never enough to attract users, and without critical mass, the virtuous circle turned vicious. Like RateMyProfessors.com, the mere existence of a Web School app wasn't enough, and having been built for tens of thousands of users, it couldn't operate for dozens or even hundreds.

WeBe, on the other hand, was copying a small-scale pattern they first observed when a fellow student, Scott Fitzgerald, orchestrated a 30-license discount purchase of Max, the multi-media editing software. He used the ITP mailing list to recruit buyers, and then walked around the floor twisting arms and collecting checks. This required real social fabric to work -- everyone knew and trusted Scott.

As the instigator, Scott also benefited from the good karma -- everyone who participated saved quite a bit of money, enhancing his reputation. Unlike actual capital, reputational capital is easier to accumulate in smaller and more closed social systems. The idea for WeBe came about in part because Scott said the purchase, though successful, had required too much work. Whatever the WeBe group could do to make ITP group purchases easier, they didn't need to build identity or reputation systems. Because the software was situated in a particular (and particularly tight) community, they got those things for free.

Old Scarcities Fade Away

Where the Web School works well, it works because it is the right kind of response to some sort of scarcity. There's scarcity of funds: Servers are expensive, not to mention load-balancing routers, tape backups, and the other accouterments of serious uptime. There's scarcity of talent: Good programmers are hard to find; great programmers are scarce as hen's teeth. And there's scarcity of use: Users are busy, they are creatures of habit, and there is significant competition for their attention.

However, addressing these scarcities can give Web School design a kind of merry-go-round quality. You need to scale because building a useful web application is so expensive, but much of the expense comes from the requirements of scale. Furthermore, these scarcities amplify one another: You need a big hardware budget to build an application that can scale, but you need good programmers and system administrators to handle the load, whose salaries require an increased marketing budget, to attract enough users to pay for it all.

What I think I'm seeing my students do is get off that ride. They can do this because none of the scarcities the Web School addresses are as significant as they used to be. First of all, Moore's Law and its equivalent for storage, plus the gradual improvement in operating systems, means that an $800 desktop machine can also be a pretty good server right out of the box.

Second, user attention was scarce in part because there were so few users at all. In the 90's, launching an application on the Web meant forgoing any direct connection with a particular real world community, because internet users were spread thin, and outside the IT industry, most real world groups had only a sub-set of members who were online.

Those days are ending, and in some places they are over already. In the US today, if you are under 35 or make over 35,000 dollars a year, you are probably online, and if both of those things are true, then most of the people you know are probably online as well. You can now launch an application for a real world group, confident that all of them will have access to the internet.

The Nature of Programming, and the Curious Case of MySQL

Finally, the practice of programming is changing. Gartner recently caused a stir by saying there would be 235,000 fewer programmers in the US ten years from now. This would have been like predicting in the 80s, that there would be fewer typists in the US by 2004. Such a prediction would be true in one sense -- the office typing pool has disappeared, and much data entry work has moved overseas. But actual typing, fingers hitting the keyboard, has not disappeared, it has spread everywhere.

So with programming; though all the attention is going to outsourcing, there's also a lot of downsourcing going on, the movement of programming from a job description to a more widely practiced skill. If by programmer we mean "people who write code" instead of "people who are paid to write code", the number of programmers is going to go up, way up, by 2015, even though many of the people using perl and JavaScript and Flash don't think of themselves as programmers.

A variety of technologies are driving this -- perl, PHP, ActionScript, DHTML -- with a lot of mixing and matching and no one core tool, with one curious exception. Every application of this pattern I've seen has used a MySQL database.

There's an analogy here with web server software. In the mid-90s, getting a web server running was such a messy endeavor that it was a project goal in and of itself. Then Apache came along, and so simplified the process that the web server became a simple building block for larger things.

MySQL does this for databases. This matters for the development of group applications, because the ability to sort is a public good. If Teachers on the Run had simply been a list of professors with attached comments, it would have been a write-only application, like those worthless "Tell us what you think!" comment forms on the bottom of news articles. One of the critical things any group wants to know is "What does everyone else think?", especially if there is reason to believe that the group in aggregate knows more than any individual. Adding the 'users rate comments' system, and then pulling the data out by rating instead of time, made the system valuable.

You can of course build these kind of features in other ways, but MySQL makes the job much easier, so much easier in fact that after MySQL, it becomes a different kind of job. There are complicated technical arguments for and against using MySQL vs. other databases, but none of those arguments matter anymore. For whatever reason, MySQL seems to be a core tool for this particular crop of new applications.

Software for Your Mom

Situated software isn't a technological strategy so much as an attitude about closeness of fit between software and its group of users, and a refusal to embrace scale, generality or completeness as unqualified virtues. Seen in this light, the obsession with personalization of Web School software is an apology for the obvious truth -- most web applications are impersonal by design, as they are built for a generic user. Allowing the user to customize the interface of a Web site might make it more useful, but it doesn't make it any more personal than the ATM putting your name on the screen while it spits out your money.

Situated software, by contrast, doesn't need to be personalized -- it is personal from its inception. Teachers on the Run worked this way. Everyone knew that Paul and Keren built it. You could only rate Clay and Marianne and Tom and the other ITP professors. You didn't even know it even existed unless you were on the ITP mailing list. The application's lack of generality or completeness, in other words, communicated something -- "We built this for you" -- that the impersonal facade of RateMyProfessors.com doesn't have and can't fake.

One of my students mentioned building a web application for his mother, a schoolteacher, to keep track of her class. If you were working alone, unpaid, and in your spare time, there's no way you could make an application that would satisfy the general and complete needs of schoolteachers everywhere. You could make one for your mom, though.

Small, purpose-built apps have always existed, of course -- learning BASIC used to be a rite of passage for PC owners, and data intensive institutions like investment banks and research labs write software for small groups of users. Now, though, the combination of good tools, talented users and the internet as a social stage makes the construction of such software simpler, the quality of the result better, and the delivery to the users as simple as clicking a link. The design center of a dozen users, so hard to serve in the past, may become normal practice.

What Next?

So what happens next? If what I'm seeing is not transitory or limited to a narrow set of situations, then we'll see a rise in these small form-fit applications. This will carry some obvious downsides, including tying the developers of such applications to community support roles, and shortening the useful lifespan of the software made in this way.

Expectations of longevity, though, are the temporal version of scale -- we assume applications should work for long periods in part because it costs so much to create them. Once it's cheap and easy to throw together an application, though, that rationale weakens. Businesses routinely ask teams of well-paid people to put hundreds of hours of work creating a single PowerPoint deck that will be looked at in a single meeting. The idea that software should be built for many users, or last for many years, are cultural assumptions not required by the software itself.

Indeed, as a matter of effect, most software built for large numbers of users or designed to last indefinitely fails at both goals anyway. Situated software is a way of saying "Most software gets only a few users for a short period; why not take advantage of designing with that in mind?"

This, strangely, is a kind of progress, not because situated software will replace other kinds of applications, but because it mostly won't. For all the value we get out of the current software ecosystem, it doesn't include getting an application built for a handful of users to use for a few months. Now, though, I think we're starting to see a new software niche, where communities get form-fit tools for very particular needs, tools that fail most previous test of design quality or success, but which nevertheless function well, because they are so well situated in the community that uses them.

Thanks to Shawn Van Every for invaluable comments on an earlier draft of this piece.

First published March 30, 2004 on the "Networks, Economics, and Culture" mailing list

Metropolis by Pat Helland

A metaphor for the evolution of Information Technology into the world of service-oriented architectures.

Explores the idea that Information Technology is evolving in a fashion similar to how American cities have evolved over the last two centuries. The opportunities and pressures of the technological revolution have driven our metropolises to adopt new frameworks, models, and patterns for commerce and communication. Recent developments in IT are analogous. What can we learn about the present and future directions of IT by studying the recent history of our urban centers?

Introduction

In this paper, we are going to explore how there are similarities between the evolution of cities in the 19th and 20th centuries and the development of IT shops. In both cases, we saw gradual evolution of environments that developed in isolation. This independent development resulted in many differences of culture and how things were done.

In the middle of the 19th century, the railroads connected the majority of the cities in the United States. This resulted in people and stuff moving around in a fashion not previously possible. Moving people and stuff provided the impetus for ensuring the stuff worked together and met standards of compatibility. The changes in expectations and capabilities fueled an explosion in retailing, manufacturing, and led to the urbanization of American life.

For many years, IT shops have developed in isolation with independently developed applications and little overlap in how things were done. Since the applications weren't connected, this seemed of little consequence. Recently, it has become very practical to interconnect both the applications inside an IT shop and multiple IT shops spread around the world. People can now easily browse and visit distant applications. Chunks of data are easily transmitted to remote applications. What is still difficult is to make the data work across different applications.

Metropolis is an examination of this analogy in an attempt to both explain what is happening in Information Technology today and to show us what we can expect to happen in the future. There are eight facets to this analogy that we explore:

- *Cities* map to *IT shops*—these are systems of systems, isolated from each, trying to cope with the arrival of the railroad.

- *Factories or Buildings* map to *Applications*—the broad-stroke componentization of the isolated systems.

- *Transportation* maps to *Communication*—the impact of the railroad being analogous to the impact of the Internet.

- *Manufactured Goods* map to *Structured Data*—each changing with the arrival of standards that are so disruptive to the existing custom wares.

- *Manufactured Assemblies* map to *Virtual Enterprises*—as bicycles became assemblies of best-of-breed components, so business processes will become pipelines of best-of-breed service providers.

- *Retail and Distribution* maps to *Business Process*—interoperable metadata, such as standard sizes and ingredients lists, permit transformations and compositions.

- *Urban Infrastructure* maps to *IT Infrastructure*—as the city grows, economic pressure mounts to develop common services, such as water, sewer, and road maintenance.

- *City Government* maps to *IT Governance*—both experience the pressure to balance investment in functional growth with investment in infrastructure. Our cities transformed themselves from isolated, quirky heterogeneous systems to highly inter-operable systems in less than a century. Let us see what we can learn from their experience on our own path to streamlined interoperability!

Cities—IT Shops

Cities gradually evolved as sites to gather for both commerce and manufacturing. Inside the cities there were independent buildings with little or no connection between them. You might consider placement with respect to the road, but that was about the extent of the relationship to other buildings in the city.

Most of us forget today that it was a hard day's ride on horseback to go 100 kilometers. Only the most hardy and adventurous would travel that far in their lifetime. Cities had only limited exposure to each other and developed their own culture, style, and way of doing things.

Similarly, IT shops gradually evolved as new applications were built and then extended and evolved. Each application stood apart and independent of its neighbors in the same IT shop. Each IT shop had its own culture, style and way of doing things. Only the most hardy and adventurous traveler would visit multiple IT shops.

Economic pressures changed our cities. Certainly the best intentions of city planners eased the transitions—and saved some historic monuments—but economic opportunity is what really drove cities to modernize, to share services, and to devise creative means to achieve efficiencies. Economic pressures are changing our IT shops, with or without master planning. As you build new applications and 'renovate' old ones, you must consider how to link them to the shared infrastructure. How will they be connected? How can they leverage common information architecture? How will they be factored to maximize reusability? These are the challenges and trade-offs we all need to consider.

Factories and Buildings—Applications

In the early part of the nineteenth century, manufacturing was typically simple and independent. The goods that were produced were limited by both the appetites of the local market and the sophistication of the manufacturing process. Factories were largely vertically integrated, producing all of the parts of the final assembly, assembling them, and even selling them. If you wanted boots you might go to the tannery. This was not the most efficient approach to the creation of goods and the manufactured items were expensive and usually not of the highest quality.

Most of our applications today are like those tanneries of the early 1800s.They produce processed data independent of each other, and deliver into limited 'markets'. They are vertically integrated and don't very often accept the work of other applications as input.

The railroad profoundly altered manufacturing. By driving down the cost of transporting manufactured parts, transportation permitted local manufacturers to produce higher quality, more sophisticated goods. Now the boots from the tannery had steel eyelets to keep the boots from tearing at the laces, and woven laces that held up better than leather thongs. Componentization allowed artisans to focus on their core competencies, rather than have to understand the diverse processes necessary to produce all of a sophisticated assembly.

Moreover, transportation made new markets available to businesses, allowing them to grow and specialize. A talented potter might come to dominate a regional market by shipping her wares up and down the rail line. ISVs—independent stuff vendors—proliferated.

For both factories and applications, independence is essential. You simply can't get any work done if you need to get everything to work together perfectly. It is only by decoupling the evolution of these pieces that you can achieve change. Yet there are inescapable advantages to interconnection. You can leverage the work of others (factories or applications) to accomplish your work. The demand of others for your work provides the economic stimulus that gives you a reason for existing.

Transportation—Communication

In the middle of the 19th century, the railroad arrived! Tremendous amounts of money were made moving people, coal, and wheat. It was the delivery of people and the basic (non-manufactured) goods that drove the creation of the rails. Incredible booms and busts occurred in the 1840s and 1850s as speculators built short lines connecting a couple of cities. Eventually, these were consolidated and standards were established to allow nationwide connection by rail.

The movement of people by rail stimulated tremendous changes. People traveled to strange and wondrous places! In addition to the sweeping cultural changes brought about by travel, retail began to expand dramatically as people hopped the train to go buy stuff from other cities. Retailers were now able to gather goods into stores to offer it for sale in new ways. The movement of stuff also caused change as there were new expectations that things would work together. Before railroads it simply didn't matter if one manufacturer's goods were incompatible with another manufacturer's goods.

At the end of the 20th century, the Internet arrived! Tremendous amounts of money were made in browsing, email, jpegs, mp3s, and chat. The wires were laid to provide browsing and the movement of the simplest forms of data. The .COM boom and bust are now legendary.

People browsing changed things. The browser allowed a person to be transported to directly interact with a distant application. This direct access has driven demand for sophisticated business processing as people question why automated interaction can't replace their direct interaction via browsers. The changes from the movement of data are just beginning, though. Data still does not work together well and automated business process is still very limited.

Both transportation and communication started by moving people and the basic commodities (either commodity goods or data with simple structures). These new connections drove new changes in the standardization of stuff and data. They drove changes in retail and (soon) in business process.

Manufactured Goods—Structured Data

In the early 1800s, goods were hand-crafted. Assemblies were created with 'trim and shim'; if the bolt of a lock didn't quite fit the slide, you trimmed a bit off with a file; if the bolt rattled in the catch, you shimmed the catch to get a tighter fit.

Pioneers like Honore LeBlanc and Eli Whitney introduced the idea of standardized parts into the manufacturing process. By establishing tight controls over the specification and production of component parts, Whitney was able to produce 12,000 muskets for the US military, effectively freeing the United States of its dependence on overseas craftsmen for its military weapons. But this was still 'in house' standardization: all of the parts were produced in one place, under one roof, and with one set of controls.

By the late 1800s, the idea had expanded across manufacturers, and de facto standards had emerged for common parts. There were sizes for nuts and bolts and cylinders, with the expectation that the ones produced by one factory would be interchangeable and interoperable with similar and complementary components produced by another. Companies that produced parts with a high degree of precision thrived; those with less consistent processes failed.

Today we still have mostly non-standard data structures. Every application models information its own way, and we depend on human operators to 'trim and shim' to integrate the applications. We see the beginnings of this movement in the XML and Web services specifications. We now have language syntax and some rudimentary rules for exchanging structured data.

Moving forward, we need to add semantics to our cross-application understanding. This will occur both in horizontal and vertical sectors. Just as the marketplace demanded interchangeability of goods in the late 1800s, it will demand the interchangeability of data in the near future.

This interchangeability will be at the level of the semantics for real business-level interaction. This means standardizing the functionality of business concepts such as customer and purchase order. Data items that will be shared across applications need standardization.

Applications must retool or perish. Organizations that fail to realize the efficiencies of integration by-design will lose in the long run to those who pursue them. The efficiencies resulting from these changes will be an economic windfall to the companies that survive the transition! Just as manufacturing standards have dramatically improved our lives, the effective use of business-level standards for data will dramatically improve our lives.

Manufactured Assemblies—Virtual Enterprises

Most bicycle manufacturers do not produce tires, just as dressmakers do not manufacture their own eyelets. By creating assemblies out of best-of-breed components, individual bike makers can produce higher quality, more sophisticated products. Competition among the component manufacturers drives efficiencies and quality improvements. Bikes just keep getting better.

To do this, they need detailed specifications for the component parts. You have to match the width of the tire with the wheel with the fork with the brakes with the axle bolt. You have to consider the context in which the part will be used. Is weight or ruggedness the principle concern?

Manufacturing became a value chain driven by information, reputation, and trust. Companies partnered to change the process of bringing goods to market.

Today, companies are 'creating assemblies' of their business functionality. Rather than create a distribution and shipping department, the work is outsourced. Rather than actually building the product owned by the company, its creation is outsourced to a company that specializes in low cost, high quality manufacturing. The engineering, marketing, and ownership of the product may remain in-house (or may not remain in-house). The definition of a 'company' is evolving as surely as the definition of an assembly did in the last century.

High-speed communications and structured information offer the same promise for many other business functions, giving rise to the 'virtualization' of our organizations. A business component model can be created by clearly defining the semantics and operational requirements of our business capabilities. With clear interface definitions, we can encapsulate the details of how these capabilities are implemented. Business process becomes a traversal of these component capabilities, so each component can be orchestrated as a member of any number of processes, and may be transparently relocated inside or outside of the organization.

Value chains can be created and recreated using best-of-breed business capability providers. The 'owner' of a business process might do little more than orchestrate it. Marketing, sales, manufacturing, distribution, legal services, and human resources support might all come from specialized business service providers. The best result is agility and competitive flexibility. If distribution is backed up you just engage additional logistics providers; if your accounting service is unresponsive you replace them.

To do this, you need detailed specifications for the component capabilities. You have to match the volume of goods shipped with the countries into which you sell with the delivery guarantees consistent with the service levels your customers demand. You have to consider the context in which the capability will be used: is security or transparency the principle concern?

Standards allow the composition of stuff. Better stuff is created, because component providers can leverage the cost of optimization across a broader market. Competition drives increased efficiencies, as does a sharper focus on the unique competencies of each provider in the value chain. Business process will just keep getting better.

Retail and Distribution—Business Process

By the late 19th century, urban centers had developed significant retail districts. Goods had gotten more sophisticated and consumer choice had improved, but shopping was still quite an expedition. Shopping day might include taking a train into town, and then going from butcher to baker to greengrocer to dressmaker to milliner to cobbler to jeweler in search of everything you needed that week.

Stores were often still the front rooms of the factory. Visiting the shoe store might receive a request to return in hour because your shoes were not quite ready. Much of what was purchased was still custom made, and therefore quite expensive.

The new distribution capabilities enabled new approaches to retail. The standardization of sizes significantly reduced the cost of many goods by permitting mass production (while at the same time encouraging people to wear ill-fitting clothes - Most of us forget that standardized clothing was a prerequisite for daily bathing. Few could afford more than one custom-made suit and it didn't make sense to bath if your clothes were going to stink, anyway!). And the ability to transport goods to central locations for sale gave rise to the department store and the supermarket.

And then along came Wal-Mart! Wal-Mart achieved new efficiencies by wielding the power of retail over the manufacturers. Wal-Mart set the standards, not the manufacturers; manufacturers complied or Wal-Mart did not carry their goods. The effectiveness with which Wal-Mart delivered pleasant, low-cost, one-stop shopping made the store a destination for many shoppers; the power had effectively shifted to the retailer.

Now let's examine the state of the art for business process. A major innovation is swivel chair integration. Today's leading form of B2B computing is known as fax-and-pray integration. An important technique for reducing integration errors is called ALT-TAB integration which allows the use of the clipboard to copy data between applications.

If we are to do better, we need interchangeability of our data and operations. Standardized and interchangeable clothing allowed for inexpensive production of the clothes. Furthermore, this approach allowed the separation of retail and distribution from the creation of the goods. For us to make major inroads in business process we need standardized and interchangeable data and operations to allow for better composition. Then we can create computing resources and pre-allocate them for later use. This technique allows the manipulation of the resources to be handled separately from the creation of the resources. This is an essential requirement to the creation of a separate mechanism specifically for business process.

We have seen an amazing transformation in retail. People cheerfully accept standard stuff and customization is rare and expensive. But business process is still largely hand-crafted. There are poor standards. It involves a lot of 'trim-and-shim'. We have very poor 'interchangeability'.

Finally, it is clear that business process will grow to be the driving force that dictates the shape and form of applications. The work is done via business process. This will become more malleable and separate from the resources being managed. As business process becomes the economic driver, it will dictate the shape, form, and standards of applications as surely as Wal-Mart drives the standards for many, many manufactured goods!

Urban Infrastructure—IT Infrastructure

By the late nineteenth century, the cities had grown and lots of people were living in them. Pretty soon ... it smelled bad. Urban density drove urban infrastructure. Common services such as water, sewer, gas, electricity, and telephony were built or licensed by city governments to achieve efficiencies, realize opportunities, and make the city a more livable place. These efforts required metropolitan services like dams, power plants, and sewage treatment plants (or perhaps just sewage pipes run into the bay). In addition to the metropolitan services for the infrastructure, you also needed to hook the services up to every building in the city. Running the services to the buildings was the first problem; connecting to legacy buildings was frequently a nightmare.

Many buildings were retrofitted. The Cathedral Notre Dame de Paris has flush toilets and electric lights. They were not installed when the structure was first built. The pace of change in building technologies over the last fifty years has taught us a lesson: now we put conduits from the street to the building to anticipate evolving cabling requirements.

Building and connecting to infrastructure services that are shared is usually a mix of public and private funding. Huge infrastructure projects are usually funded by the city, but individual connections are usually paid for by the businesses and homeowners. Major new private developments may not be approved unless they commit to paying for infrastructure improvements. For example, a new shopping center might have to pay for road improvements in front of the complex.

IT shops have grown and lots of applications are living in them. Some IT shops ... smell bad. Business process owners need to re-authenticate application to application. Process ownership roles are hard to map to application-specific authorization schemes. Dozens of applications produce dozens of logs in dozens of formats. Exceptions can be hard to route, parse, or use to take action. Process data is dispersed across many application-specific databases, inhibiting transparency and data mining.

Common services, such as authentication, authorization, logging, naming, and directories need to be commissioned by organizational governments, and applications need to be built or retrofitted to use them. This may require metropolitan support: without funding and a mandate from senior management, the investment is likely to be beyond what an individual process owner can afford.

Once the mandate and common services are in place, operational compliance will be required and paid for by every new application. Ease of operational integration will become a key criterion in the selection of packaged applications.

Crowded environments need well-designed infrastructure services to function smoothly. The cost can appear daunting in the short term, but the long-term cost of not doing it may drive you out of business. Just as with metropolitan infrastructure, there is competition for funding between the goals for new business functionality and the infrastructure needed to make the whole mess work well.

City Government—IT Governance

Cities have different visions for their shape and form. To realize their visions, governments engage in city planning. Seattle envisioned itself as a world-class city, and so engaged in bold reinventions of itself, from flattening Denny Hill, to linking the lakes to the sea, to building the space needle for the 1962 World's Fair, to spanning Lake Washington with bridges that usually float. Other cities take the opposite approach, using city planning to limit growth in order to protect livability.

To implement their vision, cities typically enlist the cooperation of both business and government. Usually, businesses are the drivers of the growth and municipalities constrain and direct the growth to match their vision.

Different visions lead to different infrastructure goals. To encourage growth, cities need to overbuild infrastructure capacity. Care must be taken to balance infrastructure investments! If a city actively pursues growth but fails to anticipate the impact on transportation, for example, congestion and inefficiency will result (come visit Seattle if you have any doubts).

Zoning, available infrastructure, and business incentives drive investment in private industry. Trade-offs are made in public/private funding according to the perceived value to the community. An easy way to start a civic debate is to propose a new sports stadium be built using public funds.

So city governments must allocate resources across an array of competing priorities, taking care to protect the sacred—such as education—and balancing the short-term, long-term, and speculative. Private industry makes decisions about what buildings to erect; constrained and controlled by planning rules.

IT governance is not so mature. Who makes the tough choices in IT? Is it the CEO, the CIO, the business unit leaders, techies, or perhaps committees? Are priorities established based on cost, flexibility, or asset utilization? What is success, and how is it measured? Are we seeking cost reductions, business process transparency, or competitive advantage?

Enterprises might learn a lot by looking at how cities manage the difficult process of resource allocation. What proposals are projected to pay for themselves? What is the timeframe and risk analysis around those projections? What in your organization is sacred? What resources remain after funding those efforts? What balance of short term, long-term, and speculative investments are right within the specific corporate culture? These problems are common for metropolitan and IT environments.

It is interesting to note that most American cities allocate resources in a way that is optimized for growth. The decision to build is usually in the hands of the business and this optimizes for growth over cost management.

Looking to the Future

So where do we sit in this timeline when we compare urban development with IT shop development?

We've seen the usage of sophisticated data structures that interchange within a single application. This is analogous to single-factory interchangeability. We've seen the Internet connect IT shops and the applications within those shops similar to the railroad's growth. It is commonplace to browse a strange and distant application just as our grandparents hopped the train for a shopping excursion and visited many different stores in a distant city. Virtual enterprises (analogous to manufactured assemblies) have barely begun. We are at the cusp of succeeding in simple business process (analogous to department stores). We are at approximately the early 1880's in urban development in our parallel IT shop's growth!

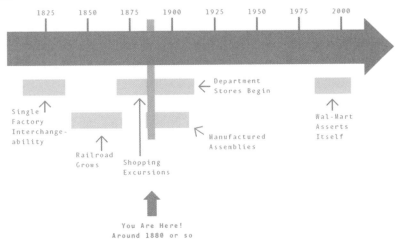

Figure 1. Development Timeline

We can see from this the innovations ahead lie in the creation of standards and interchangeability. These will allow the interconnection of interoperable pieces of computing that can move into these different roles. This will allow tremendous growth in business process and, as that business process spans companies, the increasing growth of virtual enterprises.

It is this need for independent, and yet interoperable, pieces that leads us to the Service Oriented Architecture and the changes we see beginning in application architecture. This is not to suggest that it will take 100 more years to see a Wal-Mart equivalent, but we will the economic forces driving us to the dominance of business process over application and service standards.

Conclusion

We have a fun time ahead of us. We are building boomtowns with no end in sight. Sure, it won't take a hundred years for us to get there, but we won't be done tomorrow, either. The same forces that drove the maturation and sophistication of cities, civic infrastructure, and business models are driving IT today.

What do we have to look out for? How do we prepare for this adventure?

Remember that heterogeneity happens. Unless you have a very simple application portfolio, shared services will not be achieved by trying to put all of your applications on one version of one platform. Even if you could, the next merger would change that! Rather, you have to design for interoperability and integration across platforms. This is the force that is driving the industry wide work in service-oriented architectures.

IT investment is a balance of funding the sacred, protecting historic monuments, and allocating spending between infrastructure and business opportunity. Striking this balance is a key facet in effective governance, and in realizing the potential of IT in your organization.

Our standards efforts are just beginning. Most integration today is done by people. It is expensive and has high rates of error. Information integration should be a focal point for IT, since it offers such tremendous opportunity for returns on investment. Benefits will be realized through cost reduction, error elimination, more effective customer interactions, and generally better business intelligence.

Business process modeling and orchestration, too, is nascent, but will grow to become a dominant force in how applications are designed and integrated. Most understanding of organizational business processes is in the heads of the process owners. Tools and techniques for capturing and refining these processes will greatly enhance the productivity of those process owners.

You have to maintain a light hand. It is counterproductive to try to dictate what happens in every structure in town, what color shirts are made, and how much is charged for soap. You have to embrace the semi-autonomous approach to governance that is characteristic of our cities, and allow the process owners to optimize and achieve efficiencies with as few constraints as possible.

Enterprise application portfolios will undergo a significant refactoring process to embrace a model that allows more autonomous control of business capabilities.

Effective modeling and a light hand on the tiller will permit dynamic, distributed organizations to create and deliver more value than ever before. In ten years time, IT shops will evolve from looking like the cities of he 1880s, to looking much more like the cities of today. Just remember to invest in the transportation systems!

Portals: Business on the Network Edge
by Barry Morris

In the next few years, commercial Websites, as we know them, will vanish. As organizations increasingly move to do business on the Internet, their Websites will evolve into enterprise portals. Ultimately, all organizations will use an enterprise portal to establish their Internet presence. They'll discover that stand-alone application and integration servers cannot sustain an enterprise portal strategy, and will have to exploit service-based application architectures and deploy portal servers.

Some fundamental aspects of enterprise computing will change completely. You'll see no more:

Websites, applications, application servers, and operating systems as you know them today

Status quo — in a business world surviving on the network edge.

No More Websites

Websites — even straight-ahead, high volume e-commerce sites — don't represent an effective, credible e-business strategy. The reason behind the demise of the Website lies at the network edge. Organizations have spent years evolving their information systems infrastructure, which are typically one or more operating platforms with some combination of mainframe, Unix, and Windows environments. The infrastructure also typically includes various applications designed to automate business processes. Depending on an organization's sophistication and technical prescience, these applications interoperate to some degree. Finally, the infrastructure contains content, comprising both structured application data and unstructured text, Hypertext Markup Language (HTML) pages, and other material.

Meanwhile, the evolution of access technologies continues. Broadband technologies provide an ever-growing pipe to end users, which spurs their appetite for access, which drives the growth in pipe capacity, and so on. A growing variety of appliances, some user-driven and some automated, place ever-greater demands on organizations to furnish information in multiple formats simultaneously. The growth in wireless access technology in particular means that appliances and users can demand information wherever they are, whenever they want.

Infrastructure and access meet at the network edge, where organizations are increasingly driven to deliver pervasive, personalized content and commerce. Outside the network edge are billions of Internet devices. Inside the network edge is the enterprise's competitive machinery. Whatever organizations erect at the network edge must be highly scalable, reliable, available, and secure all the time.

We're not describing a Website. Instead, we're describing a new use of the Internet — an enterprise portal — designed to meet unique demands placed on an organization at the network edge. An enterprise portal is an Internet site owned and operated by an organization to support its operations. The enterprise portal is a single point of contact and community between the enterprise and all its stakeholders and prospects. Like the popular consumer portals, an enterprise portal organizes various information using indexes and visual presentation.

A company's Web presence is as important to its brand identity, customer perception, and overall performance as its storefronts, selling process, and channels. Most enterprise Websites now contain huge amounts of information, managed by dozens of servers. Enterprise portals will help companies better organize all this information, partly by letting stakeholders create custom views of it.

In addition to information, an enterprise portal also organizes tools, applications, and transactions the enterprise provides to employees, customers, and other stakeholders. Enterprise portals support customized views of these applications, data, and transactions, as well as access to those resources and external resources such as news and procurement sites.

Enterprise portals are also the platform for active delivery of information and commercial transactions. A customer's view of the portal will contain resources and data different from an employee's view, but a common architecture will provide both.

Access, delivery, and personalization are the architectural bedrock. However, enterprise portals will also support linkage between and integration of information and processes — both online and offline — and the provision of new services and products.

Linkage is the interconnection of different applications, data, and transactions to support a user action. For example, linking ordering, inventory status, and credit checking into a single user action may require coordination of three different systems. To accomplish this linkage, the enterprise portal must be able to maintain the user's context, including security, transmit the right instructions and values to each system, and ensure that each operation occurs in the proper sequence.

Integration requires that the portal be able to integrate data from different places and make it work together. For example, a customer-care application may pull information from multiple sources, filter that information, and then present it in a single customer screen.

Properly designed enterprise portals create enormous opportunities for organizational effectiveness and agility. They make it possible for companies to explore new business models, products, and ways of connecting with important entities. However, poor design, disjointed processes, system outages, and botched interactions can destroy these benefits. So, enterprise portals will either distinguish their owners from the mass of Internet commerce sites or damage franchises and brand names built up for years. Success will require careful design, robust infrastructure, and an architecture that can sustain value through rapid changes to portal content and organization.

As enterprise portals become the new standard definition of e-business, organizations will need to provide this level of service and connectivity to stakeholders, or risk damaging their competitive posture.

No More Application Servers

How will these portals be built and supported? Application servers, the application platform of choice today, are insufficient as a portal platform. Instead, organizations will adopt what Gartner Group calls portal servers.

Application servers were to late 1990s computing what database servers were to the early 1990s. Just as database servers liberated developers from many of the programmatic responsibilities associated with data storage and management, so application servers make it easier to programmatically isolate business logic into a separate application tier. Application servers, components, and the Java programming language are highly complementary, and each has contributed to the others' popularity. Application servers are useful for function- rich Websites, and even for low-end consumer portals, because they provide a rich container for new application logic. However, enterprise portals are far more demanding than this.

For example, enterprise portals require extensive integration of enterprise applications on various platforms. This integration needs to be ©intrusive, standards-based, both synchronous and asynchronous in nature, and driven by a flexible process modeling and workflow mechanism. Additionally, enterprise portals require extremely feature- rich, Web-facing capabilities. Portal implementers will need features such as personalization, access control and management, and content management. They'll want to be able to expose portal content to various client devices.

Application servers are good at supporting business logic, but not at application integration, content management, or any of several other important enterprise portal functions.

As more organizations realize the importance of back-end integration to their portal strategies, application server vendors have begun to bolt integration capabilities onto their standard application server offerings. This is a misguided approach to portal construction that ultimately won't let developers keep pace with the nature of Internet application development. The approach ignores the fundamental imminent change in application architecture — that application servers will become portal servers.

Portal servers provide organizations with all the development, deployment, and management functions they need to build effective enterprise portals. They offer an application platform, integration platform, and Web-facing platform. They provide the combined functionality organizations need to build and deploy enterprise portals.

Portal servers are more than a loose collection of application server, integration server, and Web development technologies. They're designed from scratch to supply what Gartner Group calls "front-end to back-end integration via composite- applications-oriented solutions."

No More Applications

Applications today, whether they're intended for mainframes or Java 2 Platform, Enterprise Edition (J2EE) application servers, tend to be built as distinct, single systems. These applications may be designed to interact with other systems and may even support standard distributed application architectures, but they're islands nonetheless. Integrating the islands is a difficult, expensive task.

For an e-business to succeed, its applications must readily integrate and interoperate with other applications on other platforms and other environments. They must become what GartnerGroup calls composite applications. This is the definition of e-business computing. Today's application architectures don't easily meet these criteria. We must begin to build applications in an entirely different way to leverage the benefits of enterprise portals and the Internet.

The next generation of applications will be designed from the ground up to interact and collaborate with other systems. A new approach to application development — one that relies on a services- based application architecture — will make this possible. More than ever, we'll build applications using components. These components will present themselves as a collection of services, operating in a context in which discovering and invoking services occurs in a standard manner.

These services will be entirely independent of underlying Application Program Interfaces (APIs) and component models. The services will also be location, language, and platform independent. They'll reside and interconnect on the Internet-standard transport, Hypertext Transfer Protocol (HTTP). They'll communicate using the Simple Object Access Protocol (SOAP), which works similarly to Remote Procedure Call (RPC) technology.

Services-based architectures are familiar to organizations that employ Common Object Request Broker Architecture (CORBA), the Object Management Group's standard for platform- and language-independent application interoperability. However, the typical CORBA developer is a software engineer writing C++ applications. For mainstream application developers, services-based architectures represent a different approach to application design and implementation.

Microsoft, with its .NET strategy, is promoting services-based application architectures to application developers. These architectures are at the heart of Microsoft's strategy. That strategy envisions "constellations of computers, devices, and services that work together to deliver broader, richer solutions where computers, devices, and services will be able to collaborate directly with each other. Businesses will be able to offer their products and services in a way that lets customers embed them in their own electronic fabric."

Applications built around what Gartner Group calls e-services and Microsoft calls Web services will feature:

- Business services that involve both new functionality and recapture existing application functionality

- Front-end services providing portal access to various users at various clients.

Expect that these applications will involve an enormous variety of data. Today's application developers are often concerned with database-centric transactions. Many application server vendors respond by focusing on their Online Transaction Processing (OLTP) capabilities. But enterprise portal users will need access to more than database data. With exposing the entire enterprise to a heterogeneous audience as a design goal, enterprise portals will support applications concerned with mixed and often unstructured data. Accordingly, developers of services-based applications will focus primarily on interactions. Certainly, these interactions may subsume traditional transactions, but they'll also involve unstructured data and business logic.

You can expect that:

- These applications and their services will involve transactions and interactions that transcend machine, application space, and even enterprise boundaries.

- SOAP will provide the communications protocol for these services and Internet-wide computing generally.

- These services-based applications will have to accommodate various client devices and, on each device, various customized and personalized interfaces.

- Users will expect each application's front-end services to accommodate their unique needs.

- One or more standard e-business platforms will provide a vast collection of standardized services.

No More Operating Systems

These new services-based applications will require an underlying e-business infrastructure designed to support such applications and the enterprise portals that contain them. Whereas once the terms infrastructure and operating system were largely synonymous, the coming e-business infrastructure is entirely operating system independent. In fact, operating systems have already become less important, and as enterprise portals increasingly drive end-users' computing experiences, operating systems will become entirely irrelevant.

The Internet represents the triumph of computing standards. The e-business platform will be entirely standards-based, with support for:

- eXtensible Markup Language (XML), the well-known language that's both human- and machine-readable — with support for content modeling, content management, and application data storage and manipulation — and that easily interoperates with existing Internet technologies

- SOAP, authored by Microsoft, IBM, and others, which provides an open network protocol supporting invocation of application functionality across the Internet. SOAP opens the door to the device-, platform-, and language-neutral, service-based application architectures that will change the way applications are designed and deployed.

- Universal Description, Discovery, and Integration (UDDI) proposed by IBM, Microsoft, and Ariba begins to solve the problems inherent in bringing together e-businesses — each with its unique processes, collection of automation technology, and services — made available to customers and prospects. UDDI provides a universally available, standard means for unique entities to describe and promote themselves on various dimensions.

- J2EE, Sun Microsystems' specification for large-scale distributed Java systems, which is intended to provide a standardized, services-rich platform for building enterprise Java applications.

- .NET, Microsoft's vision for the future of the Internet, which provides a device- and platform-neutral architecture on which you can build and deploy application services across the Internet and make them available to various clients.

Because Internet applications demand it, the e-business platform will be tremendously scalable. It must be constructed on technology that can scale quickly, both in volume and function. It cannot be device dependent, nor can it deliver poor performance to scale.

Given that it must support composite applications, with their substantial back-end services and concomitant application integration, the e-business platform must provide support for synchronous and asynchronous transactional event/message paradigms.

With composite applications running on top of it, the e-business platform must provide a service-based, location-transparent architecture for systems and application components. Developers from several backgrounds and disciplines, using several programming languages, will rely on the e-business platform to solve various challenges. This means the platform must provide programming personalities for native XML, Enterprise JavaBeans (EJB), J2EE, mainframe programs such as Customer Information Control System (CICS), Information Management System (IMS), COBOL, and PL/1, CORBA and Component Object Model/Distributed Component Object Model (COM/DCOM).

Enterprise portal applications will present a dizzying variety of services and functionality to a diverse population of end users. Developers will need some application features and services and not others. The e-business platform must allow for this and provide options for service, including security, distributed transactions, management, load balancing, and fault tolerance.

Application developers using XML and Java, who have no particular .NET or CORBA-like experience, will particularly appreciate the e-business platform. With its ability to expose existing back-end applications and other enterprise resources as services, it will ease the transition into services-based architectures and portals.

No More Status Quo

The Internet changes everything. Organizations are rapidly gravitating to enterprise portals that become the vehicle by which they expose enterprise processes to customers and partners at the network edge. Enterprise portals will be built and deployed in a new kind of container, a portal server. Portal servers will provide developers with business logic, application integration, and portal access in a controlled development and deployment environment.

Executing in these environments will be composite applications that conform to a services-based architecture. In these applications, both new components and existing applications will present themselves according to the services they can provide. Developers will work to assemble the services they require to meet a particular composite application need. Finally, underlying all this will be an XML-native e-business platform, providing a standards-based infrastructure and a set of enterprise services for all the layers and devices above it.

Barry Morris is President and CEO of StreamBase Systems (http://www. streambase.com), Formerly CEO of IONA Technologies (http://www.iona. com). This article first appeared in Business Integration Journal (formerly EAI Journal).

Endnotes

1 *The American Heritage® Dictionary of the English Language*, Fourth Edition. Boston: Houghton Mifflin, 2000.

2 Pat Helland. "Metropolis." *Microsoft Architect's Journal*, April 2004. http://msdn. microsoft.com/architecture/journal/default.aspx?pull=/library/en-us/dnmaj/html/ aj2metrop.asp.

3 Ibid.

4 Jason Bloomberg (Zap Think). "SOA Governance: IT Governance in the Context of Service Orientation." October 2004.

5 IBM Corporation. "Avis Futures Drives Customer Service Innovation to Grow Avis Brand." *IBM Corporation*, August 2004. http://www-306.ibm.com/software/success/ cssdb.nsf/cs/schs-63klw7?opendocument.

6 Microsoft Corporation. "Smart Client Definition." http://msdn.microsoft.com/ smartclient/understanding/definition/default.aspx (accessed June 6, 2005).

7 E-Health Insider. "Digital Pen Makes Light Work of Filling Out Care Forms." *E-Health Insider*, December 7, 2004. http://www.e-health-insider.com/news/item.cfm?ID=957.

8 Denis Howe (Ed.). "The Free On-line Dictionary of Computing." http://www.foldoc. org/ (accessed June 6, 2005).

9 This phrase is a trademark of Sun Microsystems: http://www.sun.com.

10 Ivar Jacobson, Magnus Christerson, Patril Jonsson and Gunnar Overgaard. *Object-Oriented Software Engineering: A Use Case Driven Approach*. Upper Saddle River, NJ: Addison Wesley, 1992.

11 Gregor Hohpe, Bobby Woolf, Bobby Woolf. *Enterprise Integration Patterns: Designing, Building, and Deploying Messaging Solutions*. Upper Saddle River, NJ: Addison Wesley, 2004.

12 Evans Data Corporation. "Web Services To Dominate Enterprise Application Integration, New Evans Data Survey." http://www.evansdata.com/n2/pr/releases/EDCWS04_02.shtml (accessed June 6, 2005).

13 Technically this may not always be completely true. A server with additional memory leverages it in the system cache. So if the application is running on the system, and/or reading files from the system, more of this information would be stored in memory which would result in a performance increase for the application. In other words, additional memory can be leveraged by the OS to increase application performance even when the application wasn't designed for the additional memory.

14 Microsoft Corporation. *Microsoft Dynamic Systems Initiative Overview*. Redmond, WA: Microsoft Corporation, March 2004.

15 Jim Collins. *"*Good to Great: Why Some Companies Make the Leap... and Others Don't.*" Fast Company*, October 2001.

16 Ibid.

17 Robert McDowell and William L. Simon. *In Search of Business Value*. New York: SelectBooks, 2004.

18 Contract first service development should be viewed differently from the older contract driven design. Although they are related, contract first service development is a more specific instance of the general concept of contract driven design, and applies specifically to SOA. Briefly, contract first service development refers to the practice of designing a service interface before creating the implementation of the service, as opposed to letting the interface develop as a side-effect of the implementation.

Index